# Global Change, Civil Society and the Northern Ireland Peace Process

*New Security Challenges Series*

General Editor: **Stuart Croft**, Professor in the Department of Political Science and International Studies at the University of Birmingham, UK

The last decade demonstrated that threats to security vary greatly in their causes and manifestations, and that they invite interest and demand responses from the social sciences, civil society and a very broad policy community. In the past, the avoidance of war was the primary objective, but with the end of the Cold War the retention of military defence as the centrepiece of international security agenda became untenable. There has been, therefore, a significant shift in emphasis away from traditional approaches to security to a new agenda that talks of the softer side of security, in terms of human security, economic security and environmental security. The topical *New Security Challenges series* reflects this pressing political and research agenda.

*Titles include:*

Christopher Farrington *(editor)*
GLOBAL CHANGE, CIVIL SOCIETY AND THE NORTHERN IRELAND PEACE PROCESS
Implementing the Political Settlement

Andrew Hoskins and Ben O'Loughlin
TELEVISION AND TERROR
Conflicting Times and the Crisis of News Discourse

Brian Rappert
BIOTECHNOLOGY, SECURITY AND THE SEARCH FOR LIMITS
An Inquiry into Research and Methods

Brian Rappert *(editor)*
TECHNOLOGY AND SECURITY
Governing Threats in the New Millennium

New Security Challenges Series
Series Standing Order ISBN 0–230–00216–1 (hardback) and
ISBN–0–230–00217–X (paperback)

You can receive future titles in this series as they are published by placing a standing order. Please contact your bookseller or, in case of difficulty, write to us at the address below with your name and address, the title of the series and the ISBN quoted above.

Customer Services Department, Macmillan Distribution Ltd, Houndmills, Basingstoke, Hampshire RG21 6XS, England

# Global Change, Civil Society and the Northern Ireland Peace Process

## Implementing the Political Settlement

Edited by

Christopher Farrington

*School of Politics and International Relations*
*University College Dublin, Ireland*

First published 2008 by
PALGRAVE MACMILLAN
Houndmills, Basingstoke, Hampshire RG21 6XS and
175 Fifth Avenue, New York, N.Y. 10010
Companies and representatives throughout the world

PALGRAVE MACMILLAN is the global academic imprint of the Palgrave
Macmillan division of St. Martin's Press, LLC and of Palgrave Macmillan Ltd.
Macmillan® is a registered trademark in the United States, United Kingdom
and other countries. Palgrave is a registered trademark in the European
Union and other countries.

ISBN-13: 978–0–230–01995–9 hardback
ISBN-10: 0–230–01995–1 hardback

This book is printed on paper suitable for recycling and made from fully
managed and sustained forest sources. Logging, pulping and manufacturing
processes are expected to conform to the environmental regulations of the
country of origin.

A catalogue record for this book is available from the British Library.

A catalog record for this book is available from the Library of Congress.

10  9  8  7  6  5  4  3  2  1
17  16  15  14  13  12  11  10  09  08

Printed and bound in Great Britain by
CPI Antony Rowe, Chippenham and Eastbourne

# Contents

## PART III  Consociationalism and Civil Society

# Acknowledgements

This book emerged from an ESRC project entitled 'Interpreting Ongoing Crises in the Northern Ireland Peace Process: International and Civil Society Dimensions' (RES-223-25-0045) conducted in the School of Politics, International Studies and Philosophy at Queen's University Belfast. The editor would like to thank the ESRC for their research funding.

# Notes on Contributors

**Christopher Farrington** is a Research Fellow in the Institute of British–Irish Studies, University College Dublin. He is the author of numerous articles in journals such as *Irish Political Studies, Political Studies, British Journal of Politics and International Relations* and *Contemporary European History*. He is the author of *Ulster Unionism and the Peace Process in Northern Ireland* (2006).

**Gladys Ganiel** is a lecturer in reconciliation studies in the Irish School of Ecumenics, Trinity College Dublin. She has written extensively on the role of religion in politics, in particular focusing on Northern Ireland, South Africa and Zimbabwe. She has published in *Irish Political Studies, Nationalism and Ethnic Politics* and *Sociology of Religion*. Her book, *Evangelicalism and Conflict in Northern Ireland*, will be published by Palgrave Macmillan USA in 2008.

**Adrian Guelke** is Professor of Comparative Politics and Director of the Centre for the Study of Ethnic Conflict at the Queen's University Belfast. He is the author of *Northern Ireland: The International Perspective* (1988), *The Age of Terrorism and the International Political System* (1998), *Rethinking the Rise and Fall of Apartheid* (2004) and is co-editor of *A Farewell to Arms? Beyond the Good Friday Agreement* (2006).

**Elizabeth Meehan** is Professor Emeritus in the School of Law, Queen's University Belfast. She was previously Director of the Institute of Governance, Public Policy and Social Research at Queen's University Belfast. Her best-known books are *Equality, Politics and Gender* (1991) and *Citizenship and the European Community* (1993).

**Michael Potter** is a Policy and Research Officer with Training for Women Network, a non-profit organisation which is Northern Ireland's leading network for the promotion of women's training and development, through policy, training, networking and education.

**David Russell** is Policy Analyst at the Northern Ireland Council for Integrated Education and a Visiting Research Fellow at the School of Education, Queen's University Belfast. He is also a Research Associate of the Belfast-based think tank Democratic Dialogue. Previously, he was employed as Policy Officer at the Northern Ireland Community Relations Council and was a Research Associate of The Centre for Lebanese Studies, University of Oxford. He holds a BA and MA from Queen's University Belfast and a PhD in politics from the University of York. His most recent publications include (with Ian O'Flynn, eds) *Power-Sharing: New Challenges for Divided Societies* (London, New York: Pluto Press, 2005).

**David E. Schmitt** is the Edward W. Brooke Professor of Political Science, Northeastern University, Boston, Massachusetts. His research interests include the Republic of Ireland, Northern Ireland, Canada, ethnic conflict and US national security policy. He is author of *The Irony of Irish Democracy* (1973) and co-editor of *Ireland and the Politics of Change* (1998) and *Ireland on the World Stage* (2002). His other published work covers a broad range of topics including third world politics, public administration, Canada and ethnic conflict theory.

**Rupert Taylor** is Associate Professor of Politics at the University of Witwatersrand, Johannesburg, South Africa. He has written extensively on civil society, South African politics and the Northern Ireland conflict. He is currently the editor of *Voluntas: International Journal of Voluntary and Nonprofit Organizations*.

**Robin Wilson** is a former Director of the Belfast-based think tank Democratic Dialogue. He is an Honorary Senior Research Fellow at the Constitution Unit, University College London.

# Introduction: Political Change in a Divided Society – The Implementation of the Belfast Agreement

*Christopher Farrington*

Political change is typically seen as hard to come by in ethnic conflicts. Ethnic conflicts are characterised by security dilemmas and a rhetoric of total war (Stedman, 1996). They, therefore, tend to be highly resistant to change and persist over very long periods of time. This has led Ruane and Todd to suggest that ethnic conflicts display path dependent characteristics, with positive feedback mechanisms, which explains why changes in the patterns of the conflict happen rarely (Ruane and Todd, 2004). Thus, the negotiation of a successful peace agreement must be seen as a highly significant stage in the development of divided societies in that they represent an attempt to break the path dependency of the conflictual relationships between groups.

The Belfast Agreement of Good Friday Agreement 1998[1] was thus an important juncture in attempting to resolve the conflict between Protestants and Catholics. The Agreement established an institutional infrastructure which was designed to address the patterns of relationships which constituted the conflict. The Northern Ireland Assembly was designed to protect each community's interests while also providing for a method of getting the two communities to work together. The North–South bodies were designed to provide a meaningful recognition of Nationalists' Irish identity, while the East–West bodies were similarly designed to reflect the British identity of Unionists. The Agreement also included a range of additional bodies and changes to the legal and institutional structure of Northern Ireland, which were designed to fundamentally alter the political framework in Northern Ireland (see O'Leary, 1999).

However, the question as to whether the Agreement could resolve the security dilemmas, the security issues and change the rhetoric of the parties to the conflict was not clear. The expectation was that the system of consociationalism would be a first step in that process and that the resolution of other issues would follow from that. Consociationalism in a devolved framework emerged as a consensus from an extensive debate occurring over the course of the Troubles (Horowitz, 2002). There is a strong case for seeing consociationalism as a long-term policy goal of the British Government (Dixon, 2001). Consociationalism, or power-sharing as it is colloquially known, was seen as a way of restoring the governmental arrangements that existed prior to direct rule but reforming them in such a way as to make them acceptable to the nationalist community.

However, the extent to which an institutional framework, of whatever shape, by itself would be able to bring about an end to the conflict in Northern Ireland needs to be questioned. It is significant that a negotiated institutional solution was not successfully institutionalised until after a security solution was found to the organised political violence which characterised Northern Ireland from 1969 to 1994. This is despite the fact that the process emerged because of changing approaches of both the British Government and the Republican movement away from a security approach to a political approach. The ceasefires of 1994, in particular, turned out to be just ceasefires rather than permanent security solutions. This was obvious almost as soon as the IRA ceasefire was announced insofar as it prompted much discussion as to its permanency, as the ceasefire statement only announced a 'complete cessation of military operations'.[2] Although it may have been a self-fulfilling prophecy, Unionist suspicions over the permanency of the Irish Republican Army (IRA) ceasefire were vindicated when the IRA ended the ceasefire in February 1996. The subsequent history of the Agreement and its implementation was characterised by debates over security issues, whether they were the continuation of paramilitary activity, reform of the police service or the demilitarisation of Northern Ireland.

This book is about how some of those security issues were overcome. How did the IRA move from a position where it retained the option of armed struggle to a position where it had put all its weapons 'beyond use' and moved to exclusively peaceful means? How has Northern Ireland dealt with the residual aspects of paramilitarism, particularly the long-term legacy which such a conflict leaves? How does a society deal with changing long-term processes of hardened political attitudes and relations so that peace means more than merely the absence of violence? However, these security issues have been set in a complicated institutional, legal and political context and unravelling how that context helped resolve the issues is the theme running through all the contributions to this book. This brief introduction sets out the main issues and difficulties of the implementation process and sets the contributors into this framework. In particular, we want to analyse how political actors and events outside the more recognisable avenues of political activity in Northern Ireland affect the political process. We have seen most of the attention focused on the political parties and the two governments. These are obviously the most important political actors in the process but they are not the only political actors and understanding the alternative points of pressure is crucial in tracing the process from the successful referendum on the Agreement in May 1998, through the periods of stalled implementation and post-Agreement agreements, to the point where Sinn Féin and the Democratic Unionist Party (DUP) have agreed to share power in a devolved Northern Ireland Assembly. This introduction will briefly trace events and developments in Northern Ireland since the Belfast Agreement of 1998 before placing the contribution of the book into the context of these developments.

## Implementing the agreement

### The Northern Ireland institutions

After the Good Friday Agreement was concluded, there was still a significant amount of work to do in terms of drafting legislation, establishing institutions and building relationships between political parties. Much of the legislative and institutional work had to be done by the British Government. However, it became clear over the course of time that simply giving effect to the institutions and legislation that was agreed in the Agreement would be insufficient in order to provide a lasting, stable government for Northern Ireland which would fundamentally alter the antagonistic relationships between Unionists and Nationalists. To give an indication of how quickly most of the institutional and legal framework was established post-Agreement and to show where the problems arose we can look at the 'to do lists' for all of the major parties on 11 April 1998. These lists give some indication as to where difficulties in the implementation process lie. The British Government may have had the most extensive list but those tasks were administrative and legal and were relatively easy to implement. The difficulties for the British Government occurred when their 'to do list' involved co-operation or action from parties in Northern Ireland. It is here where we find the difficult issues and the stumbling blocks to full implementation. The two governments had actually done all that they had to do to implement the agreement by the time the British Government devolved power on 1 December 1999. The only remaining issue was the reform of policing (see Tables 1, 2, 3 and 4).

*Table 1*   The implementation 'to do list' for the British Government

| The implementation 'to do list' for the British Government | |
| --- | --- |
| Organise and hold referendum on the Agreement and elections to the Assembly | 22 May 1998 and 25 June 1998 |
| Draft and introduce legislation giving effect to the Agreement | 15 July 1998 (became law 19 November 1998) |
| Establish the Assembly in shadow form, elect First and Deputy First Ministers, establish shadow executive | 1 July 1998 (shadow executive not established until 29 November 1999) |
| Obtain agreement on number and form of departments | 18 December 1998 |
| Establish Northern Ireland Human Rights Commission | 1 March 1999 |
| Establish Northern Ireland Equality Commission | Assumed functions 1 October 1999 |
| Establish North/Bodies | Agreement on number 18 December 1998; Treaty on establishment signed 8 March 1999 |
| Establish North/South Ministerial Council | Treaty on establishment signed 8 March 1999 |
| Establish British Irish Council | Treaty on establishment signed 8 March 1999 |
| Establish the Independent Commission on Police Reform and implement its conclusions | Established 3 June 1998; report published 9 September 1999; implementation plan published 17 August 2001; PSNI comes into being 4 November 2001. |
| Establish mechanisms for early release of prisoners | 5 June 1998 (became law 28 July 1998). First prisoners released 11 September 1998 |
| Establish mechanisms for decommissioning | 29 June 1998 |
| Begin demilitarisation of Northern Ireland | Started 30 September 1998 |
| Devolve powers to the Northern Ireland Assembly and run D'Hondt, thereby establishing an Executive | 1st attempt: 15 July 1999; 1st successful attempt 1 December 1999. |

*Table 2* The implementation 'to do list' for the Irish Government

| The implementation 'to do list' for the Irish Government | |
|---|---|
| Hold referendum on Good Friday Agreement | 22 May 1998 |
| Establish North/South Bodies | Agreement on number 18 December 1998; Treaty on establishment signed 8 March 1999 |
| Establish North/South Ministerial Council | Treaty on establishment signed 8 March 1999 |

*Table 3* The implementation 'to do list' for pro-Agreement Unionists and pro-Agreement Nationalists

| The implementation 'to do list' for pro-Agreement Unionists and pro-Agreement Nationalists | |
|---|---|
| Campaign for a 'yes' vote in referendum | 22 May 1998 |
| Campaign in elections | 25 June 1998 |
| Nominate First Minister/Deputy First Minister | 1st attempt: 15 July 1999; 1st successful attempt 1 December 1999. |
| Nominate ministers | 1st attempt: 15 July 1999; 1st successful attempt 1 December 1999. |

*Table 4* The implementation 'to do list' for Republicans and Loyalists

| The implementation 'to do list' for Republicans and Loyalists | |
|---|---|
| Campaign for a 'yes' vote in referendum | 22 May 1998 |
| Campaign in elections | 25 June 1998 |
| Nominate ministers (if appropriate) | 1st attempt: 15 July 1999; 1st successful attempt 1 December 1999. |
| Secure decommissioning | Republican decommissioning: summer 2007 <br> Loyalist decommissioning: to be completed |

The subsequent difficulties with implementation derived from the unwillingness of the British Government to allow the institutions (particularly the Executive) to function in the absence of Unionist participation. Thus, the Secretary of State replaced an existing Standing Order of the Assembly to the effect that the Executive needed to have at least three designated Unionists and three designated Nationalists,[3] when it was

*Table 5*   Dates of suspension

| | |
|---|---|
| 11 February 2000–30 May 2000 | IICD reports that it received no information from IRA on commencement of decommissioning. Devolution resumed following IRA statement and commitment that it would allow its arms dumps to be inspected |
| 10 August 2001–11 August 2001 | Trimble's resignation on 1 July 1999 as First Minister prompted a political crisis. The one-day suspension was necessary to allow a further six-week period for re-election |
| 21 September 2001–22 September 2001 | The one-day suspension was necessary to allow a further six-week period for re-election |
| 14 October 2002–26 November 2003 | The Assembly is suspended after the PSNI raid Sinn Féin offices in Stormont. The suspension lasts until the next Assembly elections |
| 26 November 2003–15 May 2006 | The Assembly was not recalled after the 2003 Assembly election until May 2006 but failed to elect a First and Deputy First Minister or select an Executive. |

clear that Unionists were not going to nominate ministers on 15 July 1999 when D'Hondt was going to be run for the first time. It was not necessary for the Assembly to have representation from both Unionists and Nationalists under the terms of the Agreement and therefore an all Nationalist Executive would have been legally formed. The result of this was that the British Government continually suspended the Assembly on the threat of resignation by Trimble as First Minister or other Unionist ministers until the crisis issue was resolved. These crises issues invariably revolved around the decommissioning issue, as Table 5 outlining the dates of suspension and the reasons for these suspensions demonstrates.

## The North–South dimension

The North/South Ministerial Council (NSMC) was established on 8 March 1999 and held its first plenary meeting on 13 December 1999. It is supported by a joint secretariat, which is based in Armagh. The NSMC meets in various formats. The plenary format is tasked with overseeing North–South co-operation and institutions and is attended by delegations from Northern Ireland and the Republic of Ireland led by the First Minister and Deputy First Minister and the Taoiseach and Tánaiste, respectively. It also meets in sectoral format to oversee co-operation in the agreed 12 areas, where the two governments are represented by their respective ministers. The final type of meeting which the NSMC holds is an institutional meeting, with Northern Ireland represented by the First Minister and Deputy First Minister and the Irish Government represented by the Minister of Foreign Affairs. In this format, the NSMC considers institutional and cross-sectoral issues. In addition to the NSMC, the Agreement provided for implementation bodies. The bodies which were agreed upon were: Waterways Ireland; Food Safety Promotion Board; Trade and Business Development Body (InterTradeIreland); Special European Union Programmes Body; The Language Body/An Foras Teanga/North-South Body o Leid (consisting of two agencies i.e. Foras na Gaeilge and Tha Boord o Ulster-Scotch); and Foyle, Carlingford and Irish Lights Commission (consisting of two Agencies i.e. The Loughs Agency and Lights Agency). In addition to these implementation bodies, it was agreed that there would be six areas where common policies and approaches would be agreed in the NSMC but implemented separately in each jurisdiction. These six areas are: agriculture, education, environment, health, tourism (including Tourism Ireland Ltd) and transport.[4]

There has been a significant amount of North–South activity since 1998. Indeed, this has prompted David Ford of the Alliance Party to argue that the North–South dimension has been the quiet success story of the Belfast Agreement (Ford, 2004). However, as a consequence of the difficulties since 2002, there have been no inter-governmental meetings. Instead, the NSMC and the North–South implementation bodies have been governed under 'care and maintenance' legislation. Under this legislation, the two governments agreed to allow the North–South bodies to function but without any expansion of their functions. In reality, the 'care and maintenance' legislation gave the North–South bodies a degree of flexibility, which led to the Ulster Unionist Party (UUP) launching a 'North South Watch' on the basis that:

> We [the UUP] are greatly concerned that North South Bodies have gone into mission creep. Internal and external issues were supposed to exist as mutually dependent entities. If the Assembly falls, the North South element should also fall. But regrettably this has not been the case.[5]

The North–South dimension was a significant part of Plan B, which was threatened by the British and the Irish Governments in the event that the Assembly would not be re-established. As Peter Hain explained in April 2006:

> The two Governments would then continue their commitment to developing North-South cooperation and structures as set out in the Good Friday Agreement. In this scenario, the Agreement would remain very much alive.[6]

This was reiterated in the St Andrews Agreement, which stated: 'Failure to agree to establish the Executive will lead to immediate dissolution of the Assembly, as will failure to agree at any stage, and the Governments will take forward new partnership arrangements on the basis previously announced'.[7]

### The British–Irish dimension

The East–West strand of the Agreement was less extensive than the North–South or Northern Ireland strands. The East–West strand consisted of two bodies: the British-Irish Council (BIC) and the British-Irish Intergovernmental Conference (BIIC). The Intergovernmental Conference was to replace the Anglo-Irish Intergovernmental Conference which was established as part of the Anglo-Irish Agreement. The BIC, however, was a new body which includes representation from the UK Central Government, Ireland, devolved assemblies in Scotland, Wales and Northern Ireland, the Isle of Man and the Channel Islands. Like the NSMC, the Council meets in summit and sectoral formats. The Council has eight agreed work sectors: Misuse of Drugs, Environment, Social Inclusion, Transport, Knowledge Economy, Tourism, Telemedicine, Minority and Lesser-Used Languages. The BIC continued to meet during the suspension of the Assembly but the British Government represented Northern Ireland. Under the St Andrews Agreement, it was proposed that the BIC would get a standing secretariat like the NSMC.

## The difficulties of implementation

Ultimately, the most important issue in the implementation process was the one which was at the heart of the peace process itself: how does Northern Ireland bring about the end of organised violence and fundamentally change the patterns of conflict which permeate almost all levels of society? It is acknowledged that the second part of the question has no easy fix or answer and much of this book addresses this explicitly. However, we must acknowledge the difficulties which the failure to fully resolve the first question in the Belfast Agreement had on the implementation process. All of the suspensions of the Assembly were connected with the inability of Unionists to fully trust Republican's stated commitment to peaceful means.

The importance of the decommissioning issue has been subject to many different interpretations. Republicans and Nationalists argued that Unionists used the issue to cover their objections to other aspects of the Agreement, such as power-sharing; they further argued that decommissioning was not an issue because the guns were silent and, after all, what is more important, the guns or the willingness to use them? Other sources argued that decommissioning was a non-issue because even if guns were decommissioned, it would still be possible to buy more. None of these arguments persuaded Unionists, who saw the decommissioning issue as something much more fundamental to a process of change: it was the process of putting the arms beyond use by which Unionists judged Republican willingness to use them. It is clear that the IRA's decision to decommission fully in the summer of 2005 and the subsequent reduction in its other activities fundamentally changed the context for breaking out of the stalemate caused by suspension of the Assembly and IRA activity.

The decommissioning issue was perhaps responsible for the biggest obstacle which faced the British and Irish Governments during the implementation phase, which was the changing preferences of the Northern Irish electorate. The pattern of Nationalist representation was beginning to change prior to 1998, although the Social Democratic and Labour Party (SDLP) obtained its best electoral result at the 1998 Assembly elections. Electoral preferences within Unionism, on the other hand, had appeared stable since 1982. The UUP dominated Unionist politics, with the DUP a significant minor party. However, there were signs of electoral changes within Unionist politics in the period 1996–98. The 1996 election to a Northern Ireland Forum saw a number of independents and minor political parties win a significant section of the Unionist vote. This performance was almost replicated in the 1998 elections. This initially leakage of support from the UUP did not result in a growth for the DUP until the 2003 elections (Farrington, 2006, 162–9). It was the 2003 election which changed many of the parameters which the two governments had been working with. This change in the preferences of voters posed important new challenges for the British and Irish Governments, which developed a joint relationship in order to try and resolve the issues which stalled the process towards full implementation. Until 2003, the two governments had been working with the UUP and Sinn Féin to find a political 'fix' to the implementation problems. When the 2003 election results were finalised, it became clear that a significant shift within Unionism had occurred and an Executive could not be formed without the active and willing participation of the DUP. At this stage, it seemed that the process and the Agreement were beholden to its fundamental flaw: it could not work if public opinion and political representatives did not want it to work. The 2003 elections were followed by a period of political stalemate, punctured by attempts by the two governments to broker an agreement between Unionism and Nationalism. This was now made more difficult by the fact that the two blocs were represented by the DUP and Sinn Féin.

It was reasonably obvious that, regardless of how monumental the Belfast Agreement was, it was premised on a certain level of ambiguity and promises and it is unsurprising that these caused difficulties in the implementation phase. When these intersected with changing patterns of political representation, the British and the Irish Governments attempted to produce supplementary agreements to break the deadlock (for an outline of these various attempts, see Table 6). It should be noted that none of these were agreements which the parties signed up to and instead represented the view of the British and Irish Governments on the political way forward. Each addresses the three issues which frustrated implementation: decommissioning, power-sharing and policing.

The Mitchell Review of 1999 concerned the dual issues of decommissioning and executive formation. Mitchell obtained agreement that decommissioning would occur through the Independent International Commission on Decommissioning (IICD), it was a voluntary act and that devolution and power-sharing would be established. This was enough to establish the institutions, run D'Hondt and select an Executive (*Irish Times*, 29 November 1999) but when IRA decommissioning was not forthcoming, the Secretary of State suspended in the Assembly in order to avoid David Trimble resigning as First Minister. This impasse was overcome when the IRA agreed to 'initiate a process that will completely and verifiably put IRA arms beyond use. We will do it in such a way as to avoid risk to the public and misappropriation by others and ensure maximum public confidence'.[8] This process included the inspection of arms dumps by former Finnish President Martti Ahtisaari and ex-African National Congress (ANC) secretary-general Cyril Ramaphosa (*Irish Times*, 8 May 2000). As a result, David Trimble persuaded the Ulster Unionist Council (UUC) to re-enter an Executive without prior IRA decommissioning (*Irish Times*, 29 May 2000).

*Table 6*  Significant attempts to break the political deadlock

| Date | Subject |
| --- | --- |
| 8 March 1999 | Agreement on NSMC, BIC and BIIC |
| 2 July 1999 | Joint statement from British and Irish Governments on decommissioning and devolution |
| 9 September 1999 | Publication of Patten Report on Policing |
| October–November 1999 | Review of the peace process chaired by George Mitchell |
| 5 May 2000 | British and Irish plan to restore devolution |
| 9 July 2000–1 August 2000 | Weston Park discussions followed by implementation plan |
| April 2003 | Joint Declaration by the British and Irish Governments |
| 15 September 2003 | Establishment of the Independent Monitoring Commission |
| 21–22 October 2003 | Series of political moves to secure devolution after November 2003 election |
| February 2004 | Review of the Good Friday Agreement |
| 25 June 2004 | Talks at Lancaster House |
| 16–18 September 2004 | Talks at Leeds Castle |
| 8 December 2004 | Proposals for a Comprehensive Agreement |
| 28 July 2005 | IRA statement on ending its armed campaign |
| 26 September 2005 | IRA decommissioning |
| 11–13 October 2006 | Talks at St Andrews, Scotland, which resulted in the Agreement at St Andrews. |

*Source: Irish Political Studies*, 22:2.

Despite three inspections of arms dumps by Ahtisaari and Ramaphosa, there was still no decommissioning by the summer of 2001. This prompted Trimble to resign and nominate his deputy leader Reg Empey as caretaker First Minister, thus giving six weeks to resolve the impasse under legislation which stated that the Assembly had to elect a First Minister within six weeks or there would be an election (*Irish Times*, 2 July 2001). The attempt to resolve these difficulties occurred at Weston Park in July and August 2001. Here, the British and the Irish Governments published proposals for the full implementation. They stated that:

> The outstanding issues relate to policing, the stability of the institutions, security normalisation and decommissioning. While each of these issues is best addressed in its own terms, rather than being seen

as a precondition for progress on any other, the Agreement can only succeed if all parts of it are implemented together.[9]

This, again, failed to resolve the deadlock and the Secretary of State suspended the Assembly again. While the prospects for the restoration of the Assembly and the resolution of the various issues seemed bleak at this stage, there was a clear example of how events could change the political situation more quickly and more fundamentally than the careful choreography of the British and Irish Governments. On 13 August, three suspected members of the IRA were caught training Fuerzas Armadas Revolucionarias de Colombia (FARC) rebels in Colombia (*Irish Times*, 14 August 2001). This clearly gave an indication that the IRA was not winding down but was instead still involved in transnational networks and the Colombian connection had particular relevance for American foreign policy interests. The Colombia Three saga was closely followed by the attacks on the Twin Towers on September 11. An act of IRA decommissioning followed soon after (see the discussions in Chapters 2 and 3) and the Executive was re-established. The Executive then functioned continuously until October 2002, when an alleged spy-ring in Stormont by Republicans led to a collapse of trust in Republican involvement in the system and the suspension of the institutions. It should, however, be noted that there was an impending crisis before the spy-ring incident, as David Trimble was threatening that the UUP would resign from the Executive on 18 January if Republicans had not demonstrated that they had moved away from violence for good. Indeed, throughout the period of the first Assembly from 1998 to 2003, much of the political debate centred on the question of trust between the various political protagonists. This indicates that we must see the implementation process as a one which means more than simply establishing political institutions. Tony Blair, at the launch of yet another initiative on 6 April 2006, identified this as the primary difficulty of the Agreement:

What has happened subsequently [to the GFA] is an object lesson in all conflict resolution. The problem is that agreements such as the GFA can provide procedures, mechanisms and laws. What they can't do is enforce a belief in the other's good faith. That can't be forced. It can only come through genuine conviction. Essentially, in the eight years since the GFA, that has been the issue. Of course it has manifested itself in endless wrangles over the procedures, mechanisms and laws. But the true problem has been that each side has believed in its own good faith but doubted that of the other. Naturally, most of the time, everyone has doubted the good faith of the Governments! So unionism has often thought that republicanism was adopting a series of tactics in the name of peace; but its strategy was in reality still one of physical violence to circumvent the principle of consent. Republicanism believed it was making the most mighty moves to set aside the past and that unionism was only interested in peace not equality, and without equality there could be no proper peace.[10]

The October 2002 suspension turned out to be the longest and most enduring suspension. Elections to the Assembly were due in May 2003 but these were postponed in the absence of any realistic expectation that there would be a functioning Assembly and Executive afterwards. The elections were eventually held in November 2003 but the attempted choreography of IRA statements, IICD statements and UUP statements failed to satisfy the UUP and so it was unlikely, even in the event of a UUP victory, that there would be an Assembly post-election (see Farrington, 2004). In the event, the DUP became the largest Unionist party and the short-term prospects for a restoration of power-sharing looked slim. After the failure of these attempts to break the deadlock and the political changes in Northern Ireland, the British and the Irish Governments could no longer get the political parties to negotiate among themselves and instead had to present proposals which they considered to be a compromise position between the two sides. There were two attempts to do this. The first was the Comprehensive Agreement of December 2004 and the second was the St Andrews Agreement of October 2006.[11] Both documents were aimed at resolving the issues of paramilitary activity, policing and ensuring the stability of the political institutions. The two documents are almost identical in their provisions for changing the way in which the institutions operate. They both proposed a statutory ministerial Code, which would ensure that all sections could participate and be protected. The Code also introduced a mechanism whereby three members of the Executive could require a decision of the Executive to be taken on a cross-community basis. The Code also had implications for Strand Two and Three issues. The Code would require that NSMC and BIC papers would be circulated to Executive members in advance and contained provisions in the event that a Minister would not be attending a NSMC or BIC meeting. The two Agreements also provided a procedure whereby the Assembly could refer decisions back to the Executive. They proposed a change to the Pledge of Office, which would now include a requirement that 'Ministers would participate fully in the Executive and NSMC/BIC, and would observe the joint nature of the office of First Minister and Deputy First Minister'.[12] There were various review mechanisms put in place and the British Government pledged to repeal the Northern Ireland Act 2000, which provided for suspension and a stipulation that an MLA could not alter designation for the whole of the Assembly term unless they changed political party. There were some minor changes proposed to the North–South and East–West dimensions. There will be new mechanisms for looking at the accountability of the North–South bodies; proposals for North–South and East–West Parliamentary Forums, as well as a North–South consultative Forum which would be representative of civil society.

The major difference between the Comprehensive and St Andrews' Agreements is to the method of selecting an Executive. In the Good Friday Agreement, the First and Deputy First Ministers were elected by a cross-community vote in the Assembly and the Executive would be selected by D'Hondt. Under the Comprehensive Agreement, this was to change so that the leader of the largest party in the largest designation would nominate the First Minister and the leader of the largest party in the second designation would nominate the Deputy First Minister. This would be followed by running D'Hondt for the rest of the Executive and then the whole Executive would face a ratification vote in the Assembly. Any member of the Executive who did not vote for the Executive in such a vote would not be allowed to remain a member of the Executive. The St Andrews' Agreement dropped the requirement for the Executive to be ratified in the Assembly.

The Comprehensive Agreement ostensibly failed because the IRA refused to provide photographs of decommissioning and Ian Paisley's demand that the IRA wear 'sackcloth and ashes'. However, the Comprehensive Agreement suffered from the same flaws as many of its predecessors insofar as it consisted of a choreographed series of statements and events rather than a fundamental resolution of the issues which remained problematic: decommissioning and policing. Its failure, however, provided the context for yet another example of how events can change political contexts absolutely. The Comprehensive Agreement was published on 8 December 2004. On 20 December 2004, the Northern Bank in Belfast was robbed of over £26 million (*Irish Times*, 22 December 2004) and security sources in Northern Ireland and Ireland pointed the finger at the IRA (*Irish Times*, 8 January 2005). This led to widespread condemnation of the IRA and increased pressure from governmental and public sources for unconditional decommissioning and an end to criminal activities. The Northern Bank robbery was then followed on 30 January 2005 by the murder of Robert McCartney. Robert McCartney was killed after an apparent argument with an IRA member (*Irish Times*, 2 February 2005). The IRA subsequently hindered the police investigation and the family found it impossible to get witnesses to come forward. The media and public reaction was one of widespread and hostile condemnation of the murder and towards Sinn Féin. The governments refused to talk to Sinn Féin and the American Government applied pressure.

The reaction to these two events, and the McCartney murder in particular, can be seen as the catalyst for the full decommissioning of the IRA, which occurred in the summer of 2005, and Sinn Féin signing up to support the Police Service of Northern Ireland (PSNI), which occurred on 28 January 2007. There was widespread public criticism and the Sinn Féin leadership was clearly taken aback by the strength of this criticism. Why these two events in particular should have sparked such a reaction and been such a catalyst for change, given that there had been numerous previous other robberies and murders, is slightly puzzling. However, the reaction to these events was framed by the way the issues had been discussed in the previous seven or eight years. The end of paramilitary activity had been on the agenda as something that should happen and much of the debate was over the timing and the sequencing for the end of such activity. The public reaction to these events effectively said that the time had come and there were few excuses or reasons left not to make these final changes.

It was this changed context which allowed the British and the Irish Governments to overcome the changing preferences of the electorate. Sinn Féin transformed itself from a 'slightly constitutional party' into a constitutional party and in the process changed how Unionists interpreted Sinn Féin's goals and intentions. Despite all the choreography, agreements and sequencing, it was the resolution of the issues which were at the core of the relationship between the two communities which really set the context for the full implementation of the Agreement.

## Alternative peace-making strategies in Northern Ireland

While a peace agreement may be a significant document on the road from political change to conflict resolution, we also know from comparative data that negotiated settlements to ethnic conflicts are not usually successful. In 1995, Roy Licklider found that 'negotiated settlements of identity civil wars are less likely to be stable than military victories' (Licklider, 1995: 686). This has prompted a literature advocating partition and/or military victories as the most realistic method of bringing stability to such conflicts (see, for example, Downs, 2004). Northern Ireland is thus an interesting case. It cannot be said that Northern Ireland is an unambiguous success story, as the institutions of the Agreement have not operated for longer than they have operated and Northern Ireland is a society which is still characterised by segregation and sectarianism. However, Northern Ireland has not seen a return to violence by the major protagonists and has witnessed relative economic prosperity. Moreover, one of the important debates within Northern Ireland, and particularly Northern Irish civil society, is whether there should be an integrated 'shared future' or a separate future for the two communities (OFMDFM, 2005). The subsidiary question is: how do you bring about such a 'shared future'?

The institutional route (described above) was only one avenue of conflict resolution adopted by the British Government, although it is the avenue which has understandably dominated public and political attention. It is particularly unclear whether such a consociational system is likely to bring about long-term change in party structures and the patterns of conflict (Ruane and Todd, 2007). However, there have simultaneously been efforts to address the micro-security issues such as interface violence, ethnic riots, issues of identity, attitudinal and ideology change through civil society actors on the ground. If we examine the changing patterns of paramilitary activity in Figure 1, we can see that although the number of paramilitary killings has declined, the number of paramilitary assaults and shootings has increased. This is a very crude indicator of how paramilitaries continue to operate in Northern Ireland. We must also note that, although it was IRA activities and motivations which were the major stumbling blocks to full implementation, it was Loyalists who were most active in the period after 1998. Loyalists breached their ceasefires more regularly and systematically than Republicans, prompting the Secretary of State to declare their ceasefires over on occasions. However, there was a notable change in the type of activity in which paramilitary organisations engaged in post-Good Friday Agreement. As the defensive rationale for organised paramilitary groups diminished or disappeared with the progression of time and the lack of activity from Republican organisations, attention turned inwards and loyalists have been more active at internal feuds and general criminal activity.

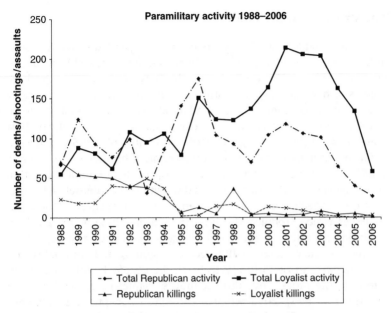

*Figure 1* Patterns of paramilitary activity since the Agreement
*Source*: http://www.psni.police.uk/index/statistics_branch/pg_security_stats.htm.
'Killings' refers to deaths due to the security situation, whereas 'activity' refers
to the combined number of assaults and shootings perpetrated by paramilitary
groups.

These kinds of problems necessitated alternative ways of dealing with
these security issues. In particular, there has been an emphasis on
community and economic development of areas worst affected by the
Troubles and on attitudinal change. This agenda has been developed by
the European Union and funded through its Peace and Reconciliation
fund and has been delivered primarily by civil society organisations or
semi-state bodies such as the Community Relations Council. The contribution of these organisations and this agenda is discussed in more
detail in the second section of this book. Such organisations have a different conception of how politics operates and how conflict resolution
occurs. Typically speaking, they stress a participative and dialogic model
of conflict resolution rather than an elite and institutional one. The contributors to this book have different perspectives on these models but one
of the purposes of this book is to start a discussion on the relationship
between the two approaches.

## The structure of the book

The book is divided into three parts, each dealing with distinctive aspects of the problems which the Belfast Agreement encountered in its implementation phase. However, the emphasis is not solely on the high politics of negotiations and institutions. Instead, as our first focus, we wish to know how events, people and trends outside of this narrow focus can affect conflict resolution. Our second focus is more explicitly on how these outside influences regulate the high politics of agreement negotiation and implementation. In the first section, Schmitt, Guelke, Meehan and Farrington deal with international aspects to the implementation of the Agreement. The four chapters deal with three inter-related issues. First, the connection between the international dimension and the security issues which troubled the implementation phase is discussed. In particular, Schmitt and Farrington are concerned with how September 11 changed the context for IRA decommissioning and criminality and thus provided an opportunity to break the deadlock which was characterising the process by 2001. Schmitt's chapter examines this from the American perspective, whereas Farrington's chapter uses interview material from political actors in Northern Ireland. Secondly, Guelke looks at issues surrounding truth and reconciliation in Northern Ireland. These debates were framed in conscious imitation of the South African experience of this process. Guelke shows how, first, this imitation occurred within contested patterns of the South African comparison and then shows how Northern Ireland's peace process does not have the trajectory which might allow it to follow the South African model. Thirdly, Meehan examines the European dimension. Unlike the 'war on terrorism', the American dimension, or the South African comparison, the European dimension is not as tied up in issues of legitimacy of any of the competing ideologies in Northern Ireland. Meehan shows that Europe plays an important role in the politics and society of Northern Ireland, whether or not institutions are functioning or there are ongoing security issues.

The second part of the book deals with civil society in Northern Ireland. Potter, Ganiel and Farrington are primarily interested in organised associational life in Northern Ireland and how that affects ongoing security and implementation problems. Farrington's chapter sets out a framework for understanding how civil society operates in Northern Ireland, which builds on general discourses about civil society in the wider comparative literature. He argues that civil society's role in the politics of post-Agreement Northern Ireland is shaped by its relationship with the state. The radical changes to the nature of the state in terms of consultation, devolution and governance posed new challenges for civil society. The corollary of this is that civil society retreated from engaging with the political difficulties of implementation. This was despite the fact that one of its roles has been to address some of the most acute security issues in Northern Ireland: interface disputes and trust between working class communities most affected by the Troubles. Potter picks up on these issues and looks specifically at the role of women in promoting peace. He analyses how the European funding for peace and reconciliation has promoted the role of women in post-conflict Northern Ireland in an attempt to build social capital which would make a resumption of low-level hostilities less likely and promote real reconciliation in the longer term. The women's sector in Northern Ireland has always been seen as a promoter of peace and we need look no further than the Peace People to see that that depiction has some historical justification. Ganiel, however, looks at a sector which has traditionally had a bad press in terms of promoting reconciliation: evangelical Protestants. Ganiel shows this is undeserved, as religion can also bring about identity and attitudinal changes which reduce conflict. She shows how there have been competing tendencies within evangelicals but that among those who have been at the forefront of promoting peace, their efforts and ideas are understood through their religion. If civil society is understood as the range of associational life between the state and the family, then understanding and appreciating how religion and religious groups react to conflict and to peace is crucial to understanding how civil society can make a resumption of conflict less likely.

The final section of this book picks up on the theme implicit in the first two sections. Namely, how do the processes of conflict resolution outlined connect with each other? How do elites respond to these processes and how do they shape them? Taylor, Wilson and Russell are all slightly pessimistic in their analysis. They all see the consociational system of government in Northern Ireland as flawed insofar as it builds on existing ethnic divisions rather than: attempting to promote a dialogue with engaged citizens (Taylor); allowing for a real input from non-ethnic non-party political actors into the political and policy process (Wilson); or encouraging political actors to think in terms of civic responsibility to all citizens of Northern Ireland regardless of the ethnic background of the politician or the citizen (Russell). The evidence from the five years of political stalemate in Northern Ireland lends credence to the idea that political developments stymied the development of democratically engaged citizens and non-ethnically engaged politicians.

# Notes

1. The terminology is deliberately cumbersome and reflects in part the fact that the 1998 Agreement is one of only a number of agreements in Northern Ireland. Its official name is 'The Agreement reached in the multi-party talks' but this has understandably not gained popular currency. Throughout this book, the titles Belfast Agreement and Good Friday Agreement are used as the names of the 1998 Agreement and are used interchangeably.
2. IRA ceasefire statement, 31 August 1994. Available at: http://cain.ulst.ac.uk/events/peace/docs/ira31894.htm.
3. Official Report, 15 July 1999. Available at: http://www.niassembly.gov.uk/record/reports/990715.htm.
4. See the website of the North/South Ministerial Council, http://www.northsouthministerialcouncil.org/.
5. http://www.uup.org/welcome_northsouthwatch.htm. Accessed 1 April 2007. Launched 28 September 2006. http://uuptoday.org/newsroom/2006/09/28/uup-shines-a-light-into-mission-creep-of-northsouth-bodies/.
6. Statement by Peter Hain in the House of Commons, 18 April 2006. Available at: http://www.nio.gov.uk/statement-made-by-the-secretary-of-state-in-the-house-of-commons-on-tuesday-18-april-2006/media-detail.htm?newsID=12974. Accessed 1 April 2007.
7. St Andrews Agreement, Annex D. Available at: http://www.nio.gov.uk/st_andrews_agreement.pdf.
8. IRA statement of 6 May 2000. Available at: http://cain.ulst.ac.uk/events/peace/docs/ira060500.htm.
9. Implementation Plan issued by the British and Irish Governments on 1 August 2001.
10. Statement by Tony Blair on 6 April 2006, http://www.pm.gov.uk/output/Page9289.asp. Accessed 1 April 2007.
11. The Comprehensive Agreement can be found at http://www.nio.gov.uk/proposals_by_the_british_and_irish_governments_for_a_comprehensive_agreements.pdf and the St Andrews Agreement can be found at: http://www.nio.gov.uk/st_andrews _agreement.pdf.
12. St Andrews Agreement Annex A. Available at: http://www.nio.gov.uk/st_andrews_agreement.pdf.

# References

Dixon, P. (2001) *Northern Ireland: The Politics of War and Peace.* Basingstoke: Palgrave Macmillan.

Downs, A. (2004) 'The Problem with Negotiated Settlements to Ethnic Civil Wars', *Security Studies*, 13:4, 230–79.

Farrington, C. (2004) 'The Northern Ireland Assembly Election 2003', *Irish Political Studies*, 19:1, 74–86.

Farrington, C. (2006) *Ulster Unionism and the Peace Process in Northern Ireland.* Basingstoke: Palgrave Macmillan.

Ford, D. (2004) 'Alliance Annual Conference: Leader's Speech'. Available at http://www.allianceparty.org/news/000301.html.

Horowitz, D.L. (2002) 'Explaining the Northern Ireland Agreement: The Sources of an Unlikely Constitutional Consensus', *British Journal of Political Science*, 32, 193–220.

Licklider, R. (1995) 'The Consequences of Negotiated Settlements in Civil Wars, 1945–1993', *American Political Science Review*, 89:3, 681–90.

OFMDFM (2005) *A Shared Future Policy and Strategic Framework for Good Relations in Northern Ireland*. Belfast: OFMDFM.

O'Leary, B. (1999) 'The Nature of the Agreement', *Fordham Journal of International Law*, 22:4, 1628–67.

Ruane, J. and J. Todd (2004) 'The Roots of Intense Ethnic Conflict May Not Themselves Be Ethnic: Categories, Communities and Path Dependence', *Archives Européennes de Sociologie*, 45:2, 209–32.

Ruane, J. and J. Todd (2007) 'Path Dependence in Settlement Processes: Explaining Settlement in Northern Ireland', *Political Studies*, 55:2, 442–58.

Stedman, S. (1996) 'Negotiation and Mediation in Internal Conflict', in M.E. Brown (ed.), *The International Dimensions of Internal Conflict*. Massachusettts: MIT Press.

# Part I

# Global Change and the International Dimension

# 1

## 'We're Not Quite as Interesting as We Used to Be': Interpreting the International Dimension*

*Christopher Farrington*

There is no real consensus as to the precise importance or influence of the international dimension to the Northern Ireland conflict and, while globalisation has the potential, if not the actuality, to change the political, economic, social and cultural context in which politics is practiced (Meehan, 2000; Ruane and Todd, 2002), most analysts have tended to remain focused on the relationship between high politics and the international dimension. One of the major criticisms of those who have stressed the international dimension as a key aspect in changing politics in Northern Ireland is that the types of changes they have attempted to explain can be more easily explained by internal factors. This debate has sometimes led a mischaracterisation of the arguments of people such as Cox and Guelke, who have been more sensitive to the limits of their causal statements than is frequently acknowledged (Guelke, 2005). A mediating position was suggested by Darby and MacGinty, who argued that external actors 'contributed to the gradual spread of new ideas and approaches... although intangible and impossible to track from source to outcome, much of the peace process was informed by outside forces' (2002, 122). However, this position is particularly unsatisfactory: if we cannot trace the influence of external actors, how can we possibly assert with any confidence that they had an effect? This methodological problem is echoed by many political actors in Northern Ireland who are unable to make a strong empirical case for international influence. However, we do not have to be as cautious as Darby and MacGinty. By

* This article was written with funding from the Economic and Social Research Council (ESRC), grant number: RES-223-25-0045. I would also like to thank Adrian Guelke and Colin Irwin for their help on this project.

identifying areas where the international dimension operates, we can find empirical evidence for its effects.

I argue in this chapter that there are three main areas of international activity that are pertinent to this discussion: international opinion, the international political system and international connections between political parties and movements in Northern Ireland and other parties and movements elsewhere. By drawing on interviews with a number of politicians, I will seek to establish the existence and importance of each area. However, we need to be able to go further and establish how each of these methods of influence affected politics in Northern Ireland. In other words, how do we seek to go beyond the current debate and establish some causal significance for the international dimension? I suggest three possible measures of influence: policy, political decisions and political ideas. Finally, my intention is to try and trace changes in how these dimensions operate to establish their influence on the implementation process of the Belfast Agreement.

## International opinion

I use the term international opinion to refer to prevailing norms within the international community, which in turn can shape political developments in Northern Ireland. Writing in 1988, in the first major study of the international aspects to the Northern Ireland conflict, Adrian Guelke identified international opinion as the most significant aspect of the international dimension. He claimed that international opinion is a powerful influence shaping the policy options of political actors (Guelke, 1988). The question then becomes: how does it influence policy? Guelke argued that international opinion provided certain norms which affected the legitimacy or otherwise of the political positions of key political actors in the conflict (Guelke, 1988). It specifically affected the legitimacy of partition (Guelke, 1985) and thus the British Government and Republicans were particularly susceptible to its use and abuse (Guelke, 1988); we can see this more recently in the way Loyalists have begun to use international examples to defend partition (Ulster Volunteer Force, 2002, 29–31). The differentials in international support for political positions has affected how different parties reacted to and engaged with the international dimension. This has been implicit in the work of Cox and Guelke, who have noted the important role internationalisation plays in Republican ideology. However, as Guelke has noted, the lack of external support for Loyalists was as important as the wealth of external support for Republicans (Guelke, 1988). Guelke has also argued that the international legitimacy of the Belfast Agreement is affected by international norms on the partition of islands and therefore the North–South aspects are critical to ensuring international acceptance of the accord (Guelke, 2001). However, the evidence presented here from post-Belfast Agreement Northern Ireland indicates that political actors found their awareness of international opinion in the context of the peace process rather than as another aspect of the legitimisation or delegitimisation of political ideologies.

If we want to trace the impact of the 'international' on policy-making, then we first have to acknowledge the constraints on the ability of international opinion to make an impact. An Alliance interviewee noted:

> Certainly amongst Unionism in particular it wouldn't matter what any other person on planet earth thought, it's what sounds right standing beside the Orange Arch in Ahoghill that makes all the difference. . . . There is always a level of impact but this society is so introspective at times that it's maybe not that much.
>
> (Interview with APNI politician, 22 January 2004)

These observations raise important questions about the ability of international norms to influence policy decisions of political actors. If politicians are ignoring international norms because maintaining political credibility and support with their own constituency is more important, then this fundamentally constricts the ability of international opinion to play a significant role in changing the patterns of conflict. However, other politicians were not quite so pessimistic. As a Unionist interviewee observed:

> I think there is a suggestion in my mind that divided and parochial societies take hitherto unknown sense of responsibility when the world watches. I know that there will always be those who, in the glare of the limelight and publicity, will behave badly but in the main people do act more responsibly when the world watches. In Northern Ireland, in its parochial backwater mindset, heed was taken, whether they were always impressed favourably or not by international opinion is not the point, but they acknowledged and accepted that international opinion was playing a role in their lives.
>
> (Interview with Unionist politician, 13 January 2004)

This interpretation of international opinion was fairly common and might be described as international opinion functioning as 'watching and observing'. A UUP interviewee explained how international attention was focused:

> Effectively it's a lobby group that kind of says 'look you make comparisons with the Middle East peace process and compare that to Northern Ireland'...and others will point out and say 'well don't make the mistakes they made' and 'keep the pressure on' and 'keep the political institutions alive' or 'get them up and going' or 'give a bit more and we can have more peace'. So all of those are pressure points really and are used as pressure points to the political parties, particularly I suppose, Unionism.
>
> (Interview with UUP politician, 9 February 2004)

Similarly, as an SDLP interviewee argued:

> I think certainly leading up to the agreement and so forth it did have some bearing on the way certainly politicians were looking at themselves and looking at the overall problem. They knew that they were in the international spotlight, they knew that people like the Americans and members of the European Union were very involved and very interested in what was going on here and they knew generally that people throughout the world were watching to see just how this whole thing was going to pan out.
>
> (Interview with SDLP politician, 14 January 2004)

This is obviously a very limited form of influence and one could legitimately query whether that kind of pressure would have any bearing at all on the decisions of political leaders; without the threat of any kind of consequences (negative or positive), why would politicians risk credibility among their own supporters in order to conclude a peace settlement?

Nevertheless, if political actors identify a 'watching and observing' role, how do they respond to the 'glare of limelight and publicity'? If a leader makes a political decision based, if only partly, on their assessment of the opinions of actors outside Northern Ireland, then we have a direct link between 'the international' and political change in Northern Ireland. This allows us to trace the effects of 'the international' on policymaking. We can see Trimble's policy towards the peace process as being decided at least partly because of the influence of American policy preferences, whereas Paisley's policy was not. We can see this through debates within the UUP in the 1990s about the role and significance of the international dimension and support among those we would now consider anti-Agreement. In 1995, for instance, Jeffrey Donaldson wrote of the importance of a public relations campaign in America (Donaldson, 1995) and David Burnside is on record as stating that an achievement of Trimble's has been the increased and improved profile that Unionists have enjoyed in the United States and elsewhere (see Wilson, 2000). One UUP interviewee argued:

> Unionists generally didn't want outsiders meddling in their affairs and what they considered was their own business and therefore had to be resolved by themselves. It quickly became clear, thankfully, that this was an issue which could not really be resolved alone, that we needed the help of outsiders and in that regard of course we got a huge help from the Clinton Administration and then eventually the Bush Administration and we got help too from those who had experienced similar problems from ourselves i.e. the South Africans who allowed the parties here the use of their facilities ... where all parties attended meetings in South Africa to bang a few heads together, to concentrate their minds on the issues confronting them and methods of peace and reconciliation.
>
> (Interview with UUP politician, 2 February 2004)

This is even clear with the SDLP, unsurprisingly given John Hume's efforts on the world stage: 'I suppose on the nationalist side it was not only welcome but had been sought' (Interview with SDLP politician, 26 January 2004). Another stated:

> I don't think we would have had the Agreement at all but for the fact that we internationalised the problem. We found out after so many years that we couldn't sort it out on our own here ... It was mainly John Hume walking around the world, literally, talking to people about the problem here in the States, with people like Tip O'Neill, and indeed in the European Parliament. I think it was when it was internationalised and we had people from outside looking in giving advice and helping and I think also having the eyes the world on us [helped] to some extent.
>
> (Interview with SDLP politician, 29 January 2004)

Nevertheless, there was not the sense that this was necessarily for the SDLP's benefit: 'In a sense my analysis of the interest which the wider world takes in Northern Ireland is that it is curiously altruistic' (Interview with SDLP politician, 26 January 2004).

However, this 'watching and observing' role had declined since the Agreement and the international community was less interested in Northern Ireland. The consensus was that the Agreement changed the nature of international interest because, in the context of the peace process, the interest was centred on the quest for a political solution. A UUP interviewee: 'I think basically the Americans see the agreement as being the settlement and they have gone off to do other things and are not persuaded to come back and sort everything out' (Interview with UUP politician, 9 February 2004). An SDLP interviewee:

> We've had a lot of focus here, a lot of money, a lot of attention but I think the focus has moved now there are so many big problems in other parts of the world and really at this stage we have identified the problem. We have the solution in the agreement.
>
> (Interview with SDLP politician, 29 January 2004)

Describing the 'boredom' of the international community, an SDLP interviewee argued:

> I think first of all world opinion has become less obviously interested in what's going on here. I think also probably people in the rest of the world are becoming increasingly disinterested in the interminable quarrels that have followed the Good Friday Agreement and certainly the big players like the United States and the Europeans have become less and less directly involved in our politics.
>
> (Interview with SDLP politician, 14 January 2004)

Boredom was a recurrent observation of the interest in Northern Ireland:

> You had . . . a lot of international interest and excitement at the cease-fires in the run-up to and probably just after the Belfast Agreement; there perhaps just isn't that same level of interest, just the way things have developed I think people have probably become bored of the story.
>
> (Interview with DUP politician, 15 January 2004)

The limits of the effects of international opinion became obvious when the Assembly was established and the onus was once again on internal actors. Many interviewees stressed that the problems of the implementation of the Agreement were primarily internal difficulties and the ambivalent attitudes of some political actors and parties towards certain elements of what they had agreed. As an Alliance interviewee argued:

> I'm not sure how much the international dimension has helped; it depends upon how much you think the international dimension really helped things. If it was some sort of part of the final jolly along process, Bill Clinton ringing up people and coming and slapping them on the back and saying how great fellas they were, that's fair enough but I don't know it was that much more than that because I think even those that use international rhetoric tend to be much more concerned about what's happening on this island than they really are about the international scene.
>
> (Interview with APNI politician, 22 January 2004)

It is useful to think in terms of phases of the peace process in order to appreciate the changes in how the international dimension functions in Northern Ireland. During the conflict, the international dimension was merely another arena of the conflict. When the peace process began with the ceasefires of 1994, there was a shift. International actors began to use their influence to push the process along or change the context (O'Clery, 1996; O'Dowd, 2002). Many still interpreted this within the framework of the conflict, particularly the Unionist analysis of the Americans, but in retrospect there was an important change. The international dimension appears to have shifted again in this latter phase of the peace process in the context of the conclusion of the Agreement. Northern Ireland is a less-contested space because Republicans and Nationalists have accepted the legitimacy of the status quo through the Agreement and therefore there are fewer legitimacy issues. International opinion has regarded the Agreement as the solution to the conflict and the culmination of the process started with the ceasefires and therefore interest has waned in the implementation phase. However, there is also a case for arguing that it is the type of assistance that has changed and that it now operates at a different level in tandem with changes in the peace process. There are now many international observers and monitors for a range of issues related to implementation, such as decommissioning, policing and collusion. The difficulty for the macro-political process is that this international assistance is not creating the opportunities for political change that it did in the 1990s.

## International political climate

In 1997, Michael Cox argued that scholarship on Northern Ireland paid too little attention to the changing international environment and, in particular, the important repercussions of the end of the Cold War for the Republican struggle. Cox's central argument was: 'that by altering completely the global framework within which the IRA campaign had...been conducted, the end of the Cold War made it far more difficult for the organisation to legitimise a strategy which by the end of the 1980s had already reached a dead end' (Cox, 1997, 677). Since 1998, we have seen the major shifts in the international political climate that were precipitated by 9/11. We can trace the impact of 9/11 in two ways. First, did 9/11 have any direct impact on the policy of any of the political actors in Northern Ireland? Secondly, did 9/11 and the subsequent discourse on terrorism constrain the political or military options of any of the political actors?

9/11 was cited by several of my interviewees without prompting as an important external event impacting upon Northern Ireland. This was in the context of America's experience of 9/11 and the implication was that this would be interpreted in the same manner as Unionists interpreted the IRA campaign. A DUP interviewee argued:

> I think that can be quite a variable thing and clearly it could have some degree of impact and you can look at specific examples. I think that the most recent example is the events of...9/11. I think that applied a degree of international pressure to the Provos to make some kind of shift in terms of decommissioning. I think in that sense you can have some international events that can have a fair degree of impact some others less so.
>
> (Interview with DUP politician, 15 January 2004)

The media certainly reported a great deal of international pressure, American (*Irish Independent*, 5 October 2001) and South African (*Irish Times*, 8 October 2001), on Republicans between September 11 and 23 October 2001, when the IRA decommissioned some weapons. Therefore, 9/11 has been seen as a direct causal factor in the IRA's decision to decommission some of its weapons for the first time in October 2001 (see Schmitt in Chapter 2).

However, there is a strong counter argument from political actors outside the immediate dispute between Unionists and Republicans which stresses the internal dimensions.[1] When asked if there was a linkage between 9/11 and decommissioning, an Alliance interviewee remarked:

> I just don't know. I mean clearly there was an atmosphere around 9/11, whether that directly or indirectly attributed to the decision on decommissioning I don't know. I'm not sure whether the first act of decommissioning was related more to the context of being seen to get activity back into the assembly... There was obviously a degree of an atmosphere around the place but I'm not sure because the first act of decommissioning had to persuade Trimble, it wasn't actually done for the benefit of the rest the world. Some of the subsequent acts, which were not accepted by Unionism but were accepted by the rest the world, would be more, in some sense, more logically linked to the 9/11 aftermath than the one that happened two months later, which is a slightly cock-eyed way of looking at it but I don't see the international issue really featuring at that point. I suppose part of it is because I know the lengths to which republicans went to persuade people that the first act of decommissioning was serious and genuine and I mean people in Northern Ireland. I'd presume I was not the only member of the Assembly who got a personal phone call from a high level to tell me that they understood that something was going to happen and they understood it was for real... there was a concerted effort by Sinn Féin to sell the first act of decommissioning in Northern Ireland. I never had a phone call about any other actions so therefore I don't see it being particularly linked to 9/11, though it didn't do any harm.
> (Interview with APNI politician, 22 January 2004)

An SDLP interview similarly remarked: 'that one act immediately after may give a false impression; most of the moves had taken place as a result of internal pressure here' (Interview with SDLP politician, 26 January 2004).

The change in the international discourse on terrorism would have important repercussions in the domestic sphere for both Unionists and Republicans. One of Unionists' main objections to the presence of Sinn Féin was that they were still 'inextricably linked' to terrorism and were still willing to use violence. Therefore, the recognition that the international situation makes a return to violence politically inopportune and unlikely, undoubtedly impacts upon the Unionist analysis of Republican strategic options. It is therefore feasible to argue that, while the ending of the Cold War facilitated the IRA ceasefire, 9/11 again changed the context and has made it possible for Unionists who were sceptical of Republican motivations to accept that violence is not part of the Republican agenda. As one interviewee pointed out:

> Well I suppose the thing that impacted the most was 9/11 because the threat of terrorism that had been used throughout the process up until that point decreased significantly as a result of that... certainly in America it's not going to be tolerated any more and, if the United Kingdom decides to stand up to the threat of terrorism, they're not going to come under pressure from America to cave-in because of the politics that there is back home... Republicans have achieved a lot from being involved in politics and using the threat of terrorism rather terrorism itself... I think it's got to the stage where the international aspect has created the situation where they can't actually use the threat any more. They could go back to terrorism but they're going to be international pariahs... and I don't think that's a situation where Republicans want to be to be seen as international pariahs, to be held in the same in esteem as Osama Bin Laden. I don't think that's the route that they would want to go. So the international aspect has speeded up what might have happened in a much slower way.
>
> (Interview with DUP politician, 19 January 2004)

A theme that ran through Unionist reactions to 9/11 was that IRA violence was connected to the attack on the twin towers by association. In other words, the IRA were terrorists, Al Qaeda are terrorists, and therefore Al Qaeda and the IRA are connected by their terrorism. Ian Paisley stated in the debate in the Assembly offering condolences to the victims of the attacks:

> I must point out that there are those in the House whose organisation is part of the international organisation that brought about those awful crimes. There is a time to speak and a time to take action. The only action that those who believe as I do can take is to withdraw from the House while the spokesperson of that organisation, which is allied with international terrorism, makes his remarks.[2]

This, in turn, gave Republicans an incentive to decommission weapons because Americans also made this linkage:

It gave the Americans a whole new perspective on terrorism and the effects of terrorism and I think too it had an effect on particularly the republican element and very quickly after the September the 11th we had an act of decommissioning here.

(Interview with UUP politician, 2 February 2004)

This was clear in the political aftermath of 9/11 when a number of issues collided to make Sinn Féin's position over decommissioning difficult. In particular, September 11 occurred in the context of reports of IRA connections with FARC guerrillas in Colombia and an impending Trimble-imposed deadline over the decommissioning of IRA weapons. Indeed, Richard Hass was in Dublin on 9/11, after spending the previous day in London talking to the Irish and British Governments about the peace process and with intentions to talk to Sinn Féin about the Colombia issue (*Irish Times*, 10 September 2001, 11 September 2001). A Unionist interviewee argued:

At one point people believed the process of peace in Northern Ireland or process of politics in Northern Ireland let's separate them . . . if it crumbled, wouldn't displease the Provos that much. At one point in this process that seemed to change and certainly vigorously changed after September 11th where the fall of the process was potentially a forerunner to one kind of violence or another. Whoever was going to be pre-eminent in that violence depends upon why that situation would break down, but it almost became a Solomonesque situation where a short time before September 11th, if Unionism walked away from the process, it was seen that the Provos wouldn't be too displeased; not long after September 11th, if Unionists had walked away from the process the Provos weren't very happy about it because essentially it had become a Solomonesque situation, that they were also losers because the option of violence, whether it was pre-eminent from Loyalism and then reacted to by Republicanism was still one and the same, it was a pollutant and a cloud against which Republican ideology or changing ideology could not be easily identified from far away. It was like myopia because violence is all the same.

(Interview with Unionist politician, 13 January 2004)

Sinn Féin was obviously influenced by this 'guilt by association' thesis and the reaction by key members at the time illustrates the difficult ambiguity they took towards the motives and actions of Al Qaeda. For example, Jim Gibney said: 'Those who carried out the attack, whatever the conditions of their lives, and the lives of the people on whose behalf they acted, have acted outside a moral frame for resistance movements' (*An Phoblacht/Republican News*, 20 September 2001). Even retrospectively, Sinn Féin sought to minimise the perception of the effects of this thesis:

> There was certainly a strong attempt to, at least in the public mind, link of the activities of Al Qaeda with the IRA by Unionists and by some others of the British establishment as well but we didn't notice any change of approach with the American administration towards Ireland.
>
> (Interview with Sinn Féin politician, 10 February 2004)

This assessment may well be sound but it does not necessarily detract from the arguments of Unionists; America may have kept continuity in their policy but only on the condition that Republicans made some movement on weapons (Smyth, 2001). Moreover, Republican expertise in the politics of the international dimension may have limited some of the damage that could have been done:

> There is no doubt that all actors have attempted to use all areas of influence to pressure other actors to get them to do things that they wouldn't otherwise want to do first of all and one of the big battles is decommissioning and the attempt to mobilise the American government...I was in the States five days after September 11th, it's a small anecdotal thing but it will give you a very micro kind of version of it, and it was a six Party delegation; all the main parties including the DUP, all people my age group newly elected political representatives and we were meeting very high powered people in the States [such as Henry Hyde]...and we were sitting in these meetings and the DUP and the Ulster Unionists would list off this catalogue they would say: 'Colombia, Florida and you know blah, blah, blah, blah' and this is a week after September 11th and they said 'would you allow Osama Bin Laden to run your education system because that's what we're being asked to do?' Now that's a tiny example. What they're trying to do is convince these Americans that what the Americans would never conceive of doing at that moment at that time is something that the Americans were asking people here to do and they were trying to find ways of demonstrating how unacceptable that was to them. I think that stuff has failed; it's poor, it's bad argument, it's a different historical context, it's a different reality and in that regard I think a lot of those arguments have been seen as very negative.
>
> (Interview with Sinn Féin politician, 5 February 2004)

They have some support in making this distinction and it would seem that the American press and public did not conflate the international terrorism such as Al Qaeda and Nationalist terrorism of ETA or the IRA (Traugott and Brader, 2003). Nevertheless, even if 9/11 did not change the American analysis of IRA terrorism, it made Sinn Féin more sensitive to the discourse on terrorism.

Perhaps the most interesting question is why 9/11 should have had an impact. After all, even if the IRA was to continue a campaign of violence, it would seem highly improbable that Northern Ireland would become a strategic issue for American foreign policy, or the IRA would be part of the 'axis of evil'. Indeed, at various points in the process since 9/11 Tony Blair has been at pains to make an analytical distinction between IRA violence and Al Qaeda violence.[3] The answer to this question lies in the change which 9/11 effected in the relationship between the British and American Governments. The timeline is significant here; the relationship did not change with the investiture of George W. Bush but rather with the different American policy priorities after 9/11. One journalist suggested that this had occurred when the allegations about Republican involvement in Colombia emerged, as he was told by a senior Congressional aide that Northern Ireland had impinged upon the vital strategic interests of the United States for the first time (Smyth, 2001). The Clinton presidency was crucial in altering the American relationship with Northern Ireland.[4] America was cited as the most influential political actor outside of the British Isles by almost all of the interviewees. Clinton was important because he moved Northern Ireland from an ethnic issue amongst Irish-Americans to a governmental issue and, moreover, because he combined this with a policy that was independent of the British Government (MacGinty, 1997; O'Clery, 1996; Wilson, 2003). The most important repercussion of this was Clinton's ability to pursue policy options which advanced the process in significant ways in which neither the British nor Irish Governments were able. The implementation of the Agreement could, therefore, have been made more difficult if the American connection was constrained. However, the change in the White House in 2001 was interpreted in two ways: First, as not significant or, second, marking a decline in US involvement.

There were two main reasons cited for the argument that there was no significance of the change of Presidency. First, the SDLP, in particular, argued that there was not the internal space for the Americans to make a telling contribution:

> Well even if Clinton had been back for a third, let's say he could have, I don't think he would have sustained his [interest]. Well what was

there to do except maybe to keep pressure on the IRA? But the people that Bush has sent have done exactly that, they have maintained pressure on the IRA and the IRA haven't responded any more readily to them. I don't know if Clinton was there they would have responded more readily to him or his representatives.

(Interview with SDLP politician, 26 January 2004)

Similarly, another argued:

Well I think that you're talking about a post Good Friday Agreement situation so I don't think it mattered particularly who was in the White House at that point in time because the ball was now very firmly in the court of the local politicians and it was up to them to act either positively or negatively and I think they've acted quite negatively.

(Interview with SDLP politician, 14 January 2004)

Secondly, there were those who argued that the role and strategies that Bush and Haas pursued were not significantly different from those of Clinton and Mitchell. A UUP interviewee argued:

There was a huge concern, particularly in the Unionist community, that Northern Ireland would no longer figure in the thinking of the US administration, as you quite rightly said, Clinton had a hands on approach to Northern Ireland and helped greatly in pushing the whole agreement forward. Our fear was that once Bush came into [power] international issues would certainly disappear from his agenda and certainly Northern Ireland, being such a small part of this globe, would disappear entirely and we were proved wrong in our assessment; although he hadn't the hands on approach that his predecessor had, his appointment of Richard Haas underlined to everyone that America still had an interest in what was happening here and it was in their interest as well as in the interest of the whole global aspect that the peace which was negotiated in 1998 should continue and it should be held up to the world as a way of resolving centuries old problems.

(Interview with UUP politician, 2 February 2004)

A Sinn Féin interviewee argued that this was due to the success and durability of the Clinton policy:

I think what that [Clinton's policy] did was that it set a standard which Bush hasn't been able to move substantially away from, which meant that the relationship between America and Britain over Ireland changed and it was seen to be a good thing to do with experience because the peace process by and large has worked and certainly substantially scaled down the conflict, so therefore it seems a success story, so there is no excuse for Bush to revisit America's approach and Richard Haas, in fairness to him, and we were wary of his appointment at the start, adopted the same sort of line as George Mitchell had done and tried to be very firmly neutral in his approach, neither into the pro-British approach or a pro-unionist approach . . . we know that the administration's line hasn't substantially changed under Bush and I think that's because it was seen to be a success, that approach was seen to be a success under Clinton so therefore there's no reason to substantially alter that.

(Interview with Sinn Féin politician, 5 February 2004)

Those who detected a decline in American interest advanced explanations which varied from a decline in the influence of the Irish American lobby because Clinton depended on Irish American votes while Bush's depended on Hispanic votes (Interview with DUP politician, 19 January 2004) to a more general isolationist foreign policy by Bush followed by more important international concerns (Interview with DUP politician, 15 January 2004).[5] Others recognised a decline in interest but tempered with the appointment of Haas, a high profile figure (Interview with Sinn Féin politician, 5 February 2004). However, there was an observation of a substantial qualitative drop in American interest:

I don't think Bush is seen as anything like as involved, anything like as interested. He still played some role in April last year coming round Hillsborough but there was really no great substance to it. Whereas, I suspect that had Clinton still been in office in April last year there would be one or two private meetings with a few people that the rest of us wouldn't have known the detail as to what was said inside the room. With Bush there really wasn't really anything of any substance there; it was really 'here's the US president to tell you guys all to behave yourselves' and, not regarding the Alliance Party as one of the major intransigents nor one of the major problems at that stage, our 10 minute chat with the Prime Minister, the President and the Taoiseach was a *ten-minute chat*, nothing else to it.

(Interview with APNI politician, 22 January 2004)

In many respects, the Clinton Administration's interest and involvement in Northern Ireland should be seen as an exception. Clinton effected a 'qualitative change' in White House attitudes towards Northern Ireland that was facilitated by the combination of the end of the Cold War, his domestic concerns (Dumbrell, 1995, 124) and his foreign policy priorities (Briand, 2002, 172). Bush's foreign policy appears to have changed that balance again and moved the locus of America's policy decisions back to the State Department, which has been more concerned with the relationship with the United Kingdom, and thus altered the position of the British Government. As a DUP interviewee observed:

> We found that Haas really took the Blair line. Whatever Blair told the Americans to take in Northern Ireland, the Americans accepted that. I think basically the Americans' point of view was 'if we can be useful to the UK and to a lesser extent the Irish government in Northern Ireland then we'll do that'... But with Clinton it was much more hands-on and this guy was in there and keeping Clinton fully briefed on a regular basis and Clinton was involved himself in what, in world terms of things, in what is a small dispute realistically.
>
> (Interview with DUP politician, 19 January 2004)

The impact of the change in the international political climate has to be understood in the context of the various types of political conflicts in which Northern Irish politicians were engaged. The end of the Cold War was significant because it altered global politics in a way that usefully tied in with moving Republicans away from the armed struggle. September 11 had a similar effect in that it coincided with the security issues which were creating political difficulties in the peace process. Republicans have been highly effective in understanding and changing the various political discourses in Northern Ireland (Shirlow and McGovern, 1998) and their ability to utilise that discourse insulated them from damaging criticism, but the discourse of terrorism made it more difficult for Sinn Féin to stress the reticence of the IRA to decommission weapons, despite the ideological reasons for that reticence remaining unchanged.

## International connections

The third aspect of the international dimension to Northern Ireland has been contacts, connections and dialogue with other areas of the world. MacGinty and Darby suggest that there was an 'exemplar effect' of peace processes on each other and that those in South Africa and the Middle East 'had an inspirational effect on Northern Ireland' (MacGinty and Darby, 2002, 118). In Chapter 3, Guelke shows how the South African model continues to have an important role in political debate in Northern Ireland. There are several types of international connections and parties engage with these on several different levels. For most of the parties, these are restricted to two avenues: governmental connections and track two diplomacy. The influence of external governments on the peace process is limited beyond the American Government but informal diplomacy has been important in assisting the process at key stages (Arthur, 1999). There were three distinct areas of the importance of these connections: general climate, dialogue and political links.

The comparative study of peace processes in the 1990s has examined three main cases: Northern Ireland, the Middle East and South Africa (Arthur, 1995; Gidron, Katz and Hasenfeld, 2002; Giliomee and Gagiano, 1990) and the connections between the three have been significant in the development of the peace process in Northern Ireland. One SDLP interviewee said:

> Well you're right, you're setting the Northern Ireland peace process in the context of the South African process and in the context of some of the Middle Eastern peace process and of course many parallels have been drawn as amongst and between the different peace processes.
>
> (Interview with SDLP politician, 14 January 2004)

Some interviewees suggested that there was even a causal connection, mirroring what Guelke has termed 'the zeitgeist of peace processes' (Guelke, 2000a, 227–8; 1996): 'I think it is infectious' (Interview with Unionist politician, 13 January 2004); 'If there is an atmosphere that there is change in a number of areas, then those kinds of things are mildly infectious' (Interview with APNI politician, 22 January 2004). Another metaphor which was used was 'mood music':

> Sometimes international events can create a mood...if we are in the middle of a conflict and there's conflict resolution processes being successful in other areas, for instance, the Middle East and South Africa are always cited around the time that our own peace process started to develop.
>
> (Interview with Sinn Féin politician, 10 February 2004)

The metaphors in themselves are interesting. Whereas with the international opinion and international events we could trace their impact upon policy, the metaphors of 'infection' and 'mood music' imply something much more passive.

Of course, given the nature of these metaphors, there was also some scepticism about the usefulness of these parallels, while recognising that they existed:

> These things, while they did run in parallel, I suppose they were more coincidental because certain things happened in each of them at the same time, not necessarily planned, that they happened at the same time but they happen and therefore they tended to move in parallel; the pace that they moved was very different and the difficulties that they experienced was very different. So I wouldn't say there is any kind of 'oh they are doing it therefore we must do it', we're doing it and somebody says 'the Irish are at it therefore we must be at', they just happen and people say 'there's peace breaking out all over' for a while.
>
> (Interview with SDLP politician, 26 January 2004)

The interviewee further suggested that the importance of the context of these peace processes was determined by their position in the conflict:

> Maybe those who felt that they were the ones who had to take the biggest steps in order to make peace that they might not have wanted to let the opportunities pass them by in Northern Ireland and to appear as if it was out of step with the rest of the world in terms of peacemaking.
>
> (Interview with SDLP politician, 26 January 2004)

A DUP interviewee concurred: 'I don't feel see an awful lot of parallels. There were three peace processes going on at different times' (Interview with DUP politician, 19 January 2004).

However, we can identify some stronger links between peace processes in various parts of the world and that of Northern Ireland as dialogue between peace processes has also been an important part of the international dimension to the peace process. Some of the benefits for advancing the process of such low key conversations and meetings have been discussed elsewhere (Arthur, 1999). However, the analysis of the nature of these contacts and discussions reveals much about how the various parties see the political development of the process. None of the parties, other than Sinn Féin, saw much direct political impact from these discussions and it is an indicator of how unthreatening these contacts were that, despite traditional support for Republicans from the African National Congress (ANC), Nelson Mandela and the South African press (Guelke, 1996, 141–2, 144), one UUP interviewee was still able to claim that this was not an issue (Interview with UUP politician, 2 February 2004). An SDLP interviewee argued

> I think if you haven't got those programmes you still have the same situation here, you still have the same progress and the same lack of progress. I don't think they make any serious difference, they might make some difference to some individuals and . . . I've been on Justice in Times of Transition . . . and it was good, it was interesting and all the rest but at the end the day I don't think it makes any difference, I really don't.
> (Interview with SDLP politician, 14 January 2004)[6]

Another SDLP politician argued:

> Well I certainly wouldn't exaggerate the claim that it's of huge import- ance; the Northern Ireland process was going to go ahead whether or not we went to South Africa. I don't think any of us who went to the South Africa meetings would say that those were the meetings that enabled us to break the logjam, such as they existed at that time.
> (Interview with SDLP politician, 26 January 2004)

A DUP politician argued:

> I don't think you can particularly point to where something has par- ticularly changed as a result of either some piece of advice that has come from somebody from South Africa, a talk that has been given, I don't see as having a particularly transforming influence in Northern Ireland.
> (Interview with DUP politician, 15 January 2004)

Those who measured the impacts in terms of political breakthroughs also seemed sympathetic to the idea that such contacts could have personal effects, which could be significant. However, there were interviewees who did argue that the context was as important as the detail:

> I think probably rather than the actual content I think the almost subconscious comparison between apartheid and sectarianism . . . was

always useful to try and concentrate minds over here. I'm not sure that there's any detailed negotiation that led to something really but it was useful to see at first hand what apartheid had done or created in South Africa against sectarianism in Northern Ireland.

(Interview with UUP politician, 9 February 2004)

Similarly, an Alliance interviewee argued:

It is part of the psychology build up ... I don't know whether there has been very much in way of detailed issues of negotiation, strategies or detailed issues of policies, detailed issues of structural proposals ... but it's all been part of the building up the psychology.

(Interview with APNI politician, 22 January 2004)

Nevertheless, the range of opinion also included those who explicitly rejected the importance of this dialogue: 'It makes people feel good who are in some way involved in the situations but, in essence, there are three completely different situations' (Interview with DUP politician, 19 January 2004).

However, Sinn Féin has a different type of engagement with international actors than other political parties involved in the peace process (Frampton, 2004). One of Cox's central arguments was that the end of the Cold War altered the ability of the Republican movement to effectively appeal to struggles of national liberation because the connections that they had made were made in a Cold War context (Cox, 1997, 678–82). However, Republicans have international connections that have been made and maintained in a post-Cold War context and they have a different type of engagement with these contacts than the engagement of other parties and this is illustrated by the South African connection. Other parties stressed the minimal importance of South Africa:

I think on a scale ... if the Americans are at number 7 or 8 I think South Africa is well down between 1 and 2. Some of the personalities have expressed an interest and maybe visited and there have been counter visits and things like that but I'm not sure that it's been all that significant.

(Interview with UUP politician, 9 February 2004)

However, the South African dimension has a qualitatively different importance for Sinn Féin than it does for other political actors. Guelke has argued: 'In many ways the South African relationship has been as

important to the Republican movement as the American connection'
(Guelke, 2000b, 138). Adams has also lent credence to this view:

> The South African involvement may have been overshadowed on
> the world stage by the US endeavours but those who have atten-
> ded Sinn Féin Ard Fheiseanna and listened to the ANC contribution
> will know how much they want this to work. Both Nelson Man-
> dela and President Mbeki have made wonderful contributions to this
> process.
>
> *(An Phoblacht/Republican News*, 8 July 1999)

Moreover, Guelke has argued that there was some basis for concluding
that Republicans had 'internalised the comparison [with South Africa] to
the point where it has had an impact on their decision making' (Guelke,
1997, 40) but there seems a level beyond this, for example, an anecdote
from a Sinn Féin interviewee illustrates the point:

> The Parades Commission organised a trip to Africa this time last
> year [February]...of people involved in parading disputes in Bel-
> fast...we met with all sorts of people and met with ANC gov-
> ernment ministers...and there was a Unionist on the delegation
> who...came up to me at the end of the trip and said 'I noticed
> something throughout this trip and through the course of all these
> meetings: you guys speak the same language as the ANC and we
> are talking to each other and there is a level of engagement that
> you're having with these people that the rest of us aren't having'.
> And I hadn't noticed but it's my personal answer to your ques-
> tion which is why South Africa and Ireland are a hugely different
> context...Republicans are not even suggesting that these things are
> comparable in a detailed sense the...type of ideological approach
> that Sinn Féin as a party takes to things in general is really similar to
> the ANC right down to the very language that we used, the types of
> vocabulary, particularly our internal vocabulary which you wouldn't
> necessarily hear a lot of publicly but how we talk outside of the public
> arena.
>
> (Interview with Sinn Féin politician, 5 February 2004)

Republicans have had a much more concrete dialogue with the ANC
than other parties, as one interviewee argued: 'What the other parties
are talking about is when they were invited to South Africa after the
Ceasefires; what I'm talking about is the political relationship between

Sinn Féin and the ANC which dates back much, much earlier' (Interview with Sinn Féin politician, 5 February 2004). Another stated:

> Certainly at the start of this peace process we would have had had quite an interaction with the South Africans and the ANC in particular. We would have had ANC people over talking to us, we would have been over talking to them and we would have learnt quite a bit from their approach to negotiation and to conflict resolution... One of the first lessons that I always quote to people that I think we learned off them was that the most important negotiation that you undertake is with your own people and they paid a particular degree of attention because negotiation inevitably means compromises and particularly on the back of conflict in which most people have been very hardened by their experience and it makes it very difficult just to readily move into an negotiation/compromising phase. So I think it was not just a matter of learning from their peace process and negotiation. I think when ANC people came over here to talk to republicans... they carried a certain amount of validity with them; it wasn't that we needed to invite them over to tell our people what we were going to do but people were interested, people respected them, people felt they had a validity for what they had achieved in their own country and therefore they were able to explain to people in perhaps in a way we couldn't have about how these processes work and about how a revolutionary movement could enter into a negotiation process without abandoning its principles.
>
> (Interview with Sinn Féin politician, 10 February 2004)

According to my Sinn Féin interviewees, the reasons for this affinity included the solidarity between revolutionary groups, which was the self-image of both the Republican movement and the ANC and shared experiences of, for example, repressive legislation, imprisonment and the emergence of a political party from the resistance to the existing regime, combined with a broadly leftist ideology (Interview with Sinn Féin politician, 10 February 2004).

In conjunction with the South African dimension, Republicans also have access to the Irish Diaspora constituency, which other parties are either unwilling to engage with or do not see any particular usefulness in spending the resources to develop those links. Most Unionists, for instance, argued that the importance of selling their case in America was because of the influence that Irish America had on the American Government which in turn had influence on the British Government. In comparison, Republicans have spent resources courting the Irish Diaspora. Adams even spent the first week of the 2003 Assembly election campaign addressing Irish Americans in New Orleans (*Tulane Hullabaloo*, 31 October 2003, *http://hullabaloo.tulane.org/ story.php?sid=2132&section=news&date=20031031*). Moreover, they have been active in extending the areas of the world where they have a presence. In 1999, for instance, Sinn Féin opened an office in Australia and embarked on a strategy to improve the party's profile there (*An Phoblacht/Republican News*, 25 February 1999). It is perhaps unsurprising that Adams is most vocal about the importance of the international dimension in international contexts but at a keynote address to the University of New South Wales in Sydney he outlined his interpretation of the international dimension:

> Sinn Féin long ago recognised the importance of the international community in conflict resolution processes. This is especially important because Ireland is so much smaller than our off-shore neighbour Britain and is consequently at a great disadvantage. The international dimension can make a difference. Just look at South Africa! And there was never a time more than now when that vast lobby is needed. We are swiftly advancing towards the first anniversary of the Good Friday Agreement and the talk is of postponement, missed deadlines, parking the peace process.
>
> (*An Phoblacht/Republican News*, 4 March 1999)

It is difficult to see the exact impact that the Irish-Australian Diaspora could have on the peace process, given the well-defined international avenues of political influence already in existence. It seems that Adams, in this case, is looking for legitimacy for the Republican position rather than lobbyists.

The international dimension can be used as a barometer of the changes within Sinn Féin's political programme. English has noted that, during the conflict, interest in international conflicts and parallels was most pronounced in the thinking of Republican prisoners but that this was not mirrored by Republican activists outside the Maze (English, 2003, 231–7). However, there has certainly not been a decrease in the interest Republicans have shown towards other areas of the world; to give two examples, Martin McGuinness has taken an interest in Native Americans (*An Phoblacht/Republican News*, 16 August 2001) and Martin Ferris wrote to the then Irish Foreign Minister Brian Cowen asking the Irish Government 'to state publicly its support for self-determination for the people of West Papua' (*An Phoblacht/Republican News*, 20 December 2001). One caustic Loyalist observer noted: 'Today . . . *An Phoblacht* would appear to be more concerned with the events pertaining to obscure extremist Marxist groups on hunger strike in Turkey than the age old "war against the Brits" ' (*Combat*, Issue 5, April 2002). Solidarity with national liberation movements is still a common feature in *An Phoblacht/Republican News'* International News section but the shift in the international agenda away from territorial notions of self-determination (Guelke, 1998a, 208; 1998b) and an increase in interest in human rights norms has been mirrored by a shift in Sinn Féin's discourse (McLaughlin, 2002; Todd, 1999), which has increasingly sought to attach its ideas of equality and human rights in Ireland to issues of persecution and repression in the wider world[7] and radical leftist and anti-globalisation groups.[8] This was demonstrated by Adams in Australia when he effortlessly combined many elements of Republican political discourse and international agenda by calling himself a 'native aboriginal person from Belfast' (*An Phoblacht/Republican News*, 25 February 1999). This has reflected the move Sinn Féin made in signing up to the Belfast Agreement, which thereby recognised the problems with a territorial definition of the nation and changed the major policy issue for the party to one of equality and human rights. This has mirrored more general changes in the attitudes of Northern Ireland Catholics (Mitchell, 2003). Thus, the party's campaign slogan's for the last number of years have been 'Building an Ireland of Equals' and 'Time for Change: Vótáil Sinn Féin'.[9] The international dimension is crucial for the construction and affirmation of these two slogans and this is most clearly demonstrated by the types of murals which have appeared in Republican areas since the Agreement, visually reaffirming similarities between Republicans and other areas that would not previously have been part of the Republican canon. As one interviewee explained:

> I think that's one of the ideological strands of Republicanism . . . [that] differentiates us from most of the other political parties. Most of the other political parties are, rightly or wrongly, are interested primarily in gaining institutional power in Ireland or in that section of Ireland which is important to them. Sinn Féin has a much broader ideological project . . . it's not about membership of a party, it's about commitment to a struggle, it's not about personal advancement, it's about dedication of your life to a political process of change. There's a whole range of things in there and in addition to that both of our movements

are greatly influenced by the proliferation of the New Left politics from the Sixties onwards...black liberation movements and gender politics and green politics and all those things in the mix and the same with the ANC. And the other thing of course is their extra-parliamentary activity, whether it's non-violent campaigning street politics, [which is] crucial to both movements or a belief that at certain moments in history that armed struggle is a necessary to the advancement of certain objectives so I think all of those things created a bond or a context or a relationship between us and the ANC that from the outside you don't see or you can't grasp unless you know these things well.

(Interview with Sinn Féin politician, 5 February 2004)

## Conclusion

There is no doubt that the contribution of the international dimension is as complex as much of the conflict and a proper understanding of its role in Northern Ireland is contingent upon understanding how political actors within Northern Ireland understand and interact with its various dimensions. Throughout the peace process, there is clear evidence that every political party was affected to some degree by involvement of people from outside the United Kingdom and Ireland. However, since the conclusion of the Agreement, there has been a decline in how most parties perceive the effects of the 'international'. This is for a number of reasons: first, there is less space in which it can make a telling contribution; secondly, the international perception of the Agreement was that it was the solution and has moved its interest to an advisory capacity in areas of implementation; thirdly, there is the argument that the international dimension was effective during the peace process because it created new spaces and types of political pressure but that similar pressure after the Agreement will not have the same effects because, like certain bacterial infections, political actors in Northern Ireland have become resistant to that kind of pressure. This was most forcefully put by an Alliance interviewee:

Somebody talked to me recently about getting a big international speaker to come to an Alliance event and I said 'like who? Hello President W. Hello Bill.' Who is there? There's no corner of Western Europe where society is so small and has had so many of the big names in the world. De Klerk? Been there done that. Mandela? 'Hi Nelson'. It really is quite ridiculous, in some instances, the level of international flattery, which has now devalued the currency of all international flattery because there is nobody much left to come and flatter us all. In that sense, it certainly has had an impact in the past but I think the international spectre really is fairly shadowy now and I think the effect international figures have on intransigent politicians in Northern Ireland is pretty minimal... There is a real danger in effect that people have been rewarded for their intransigence by getting to meet all kinds of influential and important people on the world stage and they've had a grossly inflated idea of the importance of a small corner of the offshore island of the offshore island of Western Europe.

(Interview with APNI politician, 22 January 2004)

However, there is still evidence that where the international dimension was first noticed, within Republicanism, it still has the potential to offer avenues out of political deadlock. This was most clearly the case with the impasse of 2001 but what this most clearly illustrates is how Republicans engage with these factors at a different and more complex level than other political parties. Moreover, the international links and interests that Sinn Féin has developed since the peace process have grown out of a political agenda in Northern Ireland which stresses human rights, equality and radical political change. There has been an increased courtship of the Irish Diaspora outside America and it appears that, in the context of the Agreement, the international dimension has resumed its status as part of the conflict in tandem with new roles less obviously associated with high politics.

## Notes

1. This has always been a criticism of this approach, see Dixon (2002) and English (2003); see also the response of Guelke (2002) to critics more generally.
2. http://www.niassembly.gov.uk/record/reports/010913.htm.
3. See his comments during the press conference transcribed at: http://www.number-10.gov.uk/output/Page7999.asp.
4. For the best assessments of the American relationship with Ireland, see Wilson (1995) and Holland (1987).
5. These are common perceptions of Clinton's (self-) interests in Northern Ireland but for a measured assessment of these issues, see Dumbrell (2000, 218–21).
6. Justice in Times of Transition is a project conducted by Harvard University which has organised conferences and seminars for politicians and members of civil society in Northern Ireland; see their website: http://www.ksg.harvard.edu/justiceproject/.
7. See, for example, some of the Republican involvement with the hunger strikes in Turkish jails in 2001, *An Phoblacht/Republican News*, 12 July 2001 or Republican involvement in Palestinian Solidarity campaigns, *An Phoblacht/Republican News*, 22 May 2003.

8. See the accounts of Irish and Sinn Féin involvement in the anti-globalisation movement in *An Phoblacht/Republican News*, 12 July 2001.
9. See its 2004 European election manifesto for the clearest exposition of the 'equality' and 'change' discourses (Sinn Féin, 2004).

## Bibliography

Arthur, P. (1995) 'Some Thoughts on Transition: A Comparative View of the Peace Processes in South Africa and Northern Ireland', *Government and Opposition*, 30:1, 48–59.

Arthur, P. (1999) '"Quiet Diplomacy and Personal Conversation": Track Two Diplomacy and the Search for a Settlement in Northern Ireland', in J. Ruane and J. Todd (eds), *After the Good Friday Agreement: Analysing Political Change in Northern Ireland*. Dublin: UCD Press.

Briand, R.J. (2002) 'Bush, Clinton, Irish America and the Irish Peace Process', *The Political Quarterly*, 73:4, 172–80.

Cox, M. (1997) 'Bringing in the "International": The IRA Ceasefire and the End of the Cold War', *International Affairs*, 73:4, 671–93.

Cox, M. (1998) 'Thinking "globally" about Peace in Northern Ireland', *Politics*, 18:1, 57–63.

Darby, J. and R. MacGinty (2002) *Guns and Government: The Management of the Northern Ireland Peace Process*. Basingstoke: Palgrave Macmillan.

Dixon, P. (2002) 'Northern Ireland and the International Dimension: The End of the Cold War, the USA and European Integration', *Irish Studies in International Affairs*, 13, 105–20.

Donaldson, J. (1995) 'The U.S.A. Effect', in A. Aughey, D. Burnside, J. Donaldson, E. Harris and G. Adams (eds), *Selling Unionism: Home and Away*. Belfast: Ulster Young Unionist Council.

Dumbrell, J. (1995) 'The United States and the Northern Irish Conflict 1969–1994: From Indifference to Intervention', *Irish Studies in International Affairs*, 6, 107–25.

Dumbrell, J. (2000) 'Hope and History: The US and Peace in Northern Ireland', in M. Cox, A. Guelke and F. Stephen (eds), *A Farewell to Arms? From 'Long War' to Long Peace in Northern Ireland*. Manchester: Manchester University Press.

English, R. (2003) *Armed Struggle: A History of the IRA*. Basingstoke: Pan Macmillan.

Frampton, M. (2004) '"Squaring the circle": The Foreign Policy of Sinn Féin, 1983–1989', *Irish Political Studies*, 19:2, 43–63.

Gidron, B., S.N. Katz and Y. Hasenfeld (eds) (2002) *Mobilizing for Peace: Conflict Resolution in Northern Ireland, Israel/Palestine and South Africa*. Oxford: Oxford University Press.

Giliomee, H. and J. Gagiano (eds) (1990) *The Elusive Search for Peace: South Africa, Israel, Northern Ireland*. Oxford: Oxford University Press.

Guelke, A. (1985) 'International Legitimacy, Self-Determination and Northern Ireland', *Review of International Studies*, 11, 37–52.

Guelke, A. (1988) *Northern Ireland: The International Perspective*. Dublin: Gill & Macmillan.

Guelke, A. (1996) 'The Influence of the South African Transition on the Northern Ireland Peace Process', *South African Journal of International Affairs*, 3:2, 32–48.

Guelke, A. (1997) 'Comparatively peaceful: The Role of Analogy in Northern Ireland's Peace Process', *Cambridge Review of International Affairs*, XI:1, 28–45.

Guelke, A. (1998a) 'Northern Ireland and North/South Issues', in W. Crotty and D.E. Schmitt (eds), *Ireland and the Politics of Change*. London: Longman.

Guelke, A. (1998b) 'Northern Ireland and the International System', in W. Crotty and D.E. Schmitt (eds), *Ireland on the World Stage*. London: Longman.

Guelke, A. (2000a) '"Comparatively peaceful": South Africa, the Middle East and Northern Ireland', in M. Cox, A. Guelke and F. Stephen (eds), *A Farewell to Arms? From 'Long War' to Long Peace in Northern Ireland*. Manchester: Manchester University Press.

Guelke, A. (2000b) 'Ireland and South Africa: A Very Special Relationship', *Irish Studies in International Affairs*, 11, 137–46.

Guelke, A. (2001) 'Northern Ireland and Island Status', in J. McGarry (ed.), *Northern Ireland and the Divided World: Post-Agreement Northern Ireland in Comparative Perspective*. Oxford: Oxford University Press.

Guelke, A. (2002) 'The International System and the Northern Irish Peace Process', IBIS Working Paper No. 21. Dublin: Institute for British-Irish Studies, University College.

Guelke, A. (2005) 'The Global Context: The International System and the Northern Ireland Peace Process', in J. Coakley, B. Laffan and J. Todd (eds), *Renovation or Revolution? New Territorial Politics in Ireland and the United Kingdom*. Dublin: UCD Press.

Holland, J. (1987). *The American Connection: US Guns, Money and Influence in Northern Ireland*. Boulder: Roberts Rinehart.

MacGinty, R. (1997) 'American Influences on the Northern Ireland Peace Process', *Journal of Conflict Studies*, XVII: 2, 31–50.

MacGinty, R. and J. Darby (2002) *Guns and Government: The Management of the Northern Ireland Peace Process*. Basingstoke: Palgrave Macmillan.

McLaughlin, M. (2002) 'Redefining Republicanism', in J. Coakley (ed.), *Changing Shades of Orange and Green: Redefining the Union and the Nation in Contemporary Ireland*. Dublin: UCD Press.

Meehan, E. (2000) 'Europe and the Europeanisation of the Irish Question', in M. Cox, A. Guelke and F. Stephen (eds), *A Farewell to Arms? From 'Long War' to Long Peace in Northern Ireland*. Manchester: Manchester University Press.

Mitchell, C. (2003) 'From Victims to Equals? Catholic Responses to Political Change in Northern Ireland', *Irish Political Studies*, 18:1, 51–71.

O'Clery, C. (1996) *The Greening of the White House: The Inside Story on How America Tried to Bring Peace to Ireland*. Dublin: Gill and Macmillan.

O'Dowd, N. (2002) 'The Awakening: Irish America's Key Role in the Irish Peace Process', in M. Elliott (ed.), *The Long Road to Peace in Northern Ireland: Peace Lectures from the Institute of Irish Studies at Liverpool*. Liverpool: Liverpool University Press.

Ruane, J. and J. Todd (2002) 'The Northern Ireland Conflict and the Impact of Globalisation', in W. Crotty and D.E. Schmitt (eds), *Ireland on the World Stage*. London: Longman.

Shirlow, P. and M. McGovern (1998) 'Language, Discourse and Dialogue: Sinn Féin and the Irish Peace Process', *Political Geography*, 17:2, 171–86.

Sinn Féin (2004). *An Ireland of Equals in a Europe of Equals: Sinn Féin EU Election Manifesto 2004*.

Smyth, P. (2001) 'US Always believed in SF's Contribution to Process', *Irish Times*, 24 October 2001.

Todd, J. (1999) 'Nationalism, Republicanism and the Good Friday Agreement', in J. Ruane and J. Todd (eds), *After the Good Friday Agreement: Analysing Political Change in Northern Ireland*. Dublin: UCD Press.

Traugott, M. W. and T. Brader (2003) 'Explaining 9/11', in P. Norris, M. Kern and M. Just (eds), *Framing Terrorism: The News Media, the Government and the Public*. London: Routledge.

Ulster Volunteer Force (2002) *The Principles of Loyalism: An Internal Discussion Paper*. n.p.

Wilson, A. (1995) *Irish America and the Ulster Conflict 1968–1995*. Belfast: Blackstaff Press.

Wilson, A. (2000) 'The Ulster Unionist Party and the U.S. Role in the Northern Ireland Peace Process, 1994–2000', *Policy Studies Journal*, 28: 4, 858–74.

Wilson, A. (2003) '"Doing the Business": Aspects of the Clinton Administration's Economic Policy for the Northern Ireland Peace Process, 1994–2000, *Journal of Conflict Studies*, 23:1, 155–76.

# 2
# The US War on Terrorism and its Impact on the Politics of Accommodation in Northern Ireland

*David E. Schmitt*

This chapter will build on the analysis of Farrington's previous chapter by focusing on the impact of the American War on Terrorism from the time of the 11 September 2001 attack on the United States through the US-led attack on Iraq in 2003 and subsequent developments through the summer of 2006.[1] Of particular concern will be the impact of these events on the IRA and Sinn Féin, the impact on American–British relations, the impact on Unionists within Northern Ireland and the overall consequences for the ongoing efforts to find enduring accommodations. The term 'War on Terrorism' refers to the overall plans, strategies and policies of the Bush Administration, including the attack on Iraq, to combat the threat of violence from the Al Qaeda ideological movement, a loosely affiliated or Al Qaeda-inspired group of organisations that seek through violent terrorist attacks to force the United States and Western powers out of Muslim politics and society. The Al Qaeda movement and organisations, of course, have many subgoals, including the establishment of fundamentalist Islamic republics. It should be emphasised that the Muslim religion itself stresses values radically different from terrorism. It should also be noted that many question the legal and ethical basis of specific components of the Bush administration's policies as well as their effectiveness. Most importantly, there is substantial disagreement both within the United States and abroad about the wisdom of the decision to attack Iraq.

Almost any crisis has some positive consequences, however tragic the results in human terms. Had the initial attacks of September 11 occurred at a much later date, for example, it is possible that members of the

Al Qaeda movement might have by then acquired weapons of mass destruction (WMDs). Of particular relevance for the Northern Ireland conflict is that September 11 and subsequent terrorist attacks elsewhere created a level of revulsion against terrorist violence in the United States and the democratic world that made all but the most ardent supporters of the Republican movement (referring mainly to Sinn Féin and the IRA) likely to view future IRA bombings and terrorist attacks as unacceptable. Large-scale terrorist attacks, such as the October 2002 bombing in Bali, the March 2004 bombing of trains in Spain, and the July 2005 bombings in London, reinforce the unacceptability of terrorist methods.

First, a brief discussion of the strategic circumstances of the United States will be undertaken, in order to set in context both the political and psychological imperatives operating on the American Government and public. Next, an analysis of the consequences of the War on Terrorism for Sinn Féin and the IRA will be undertaken. Following will be a consideration of the changes in British–American relations after September 11. The chapter will then analyse consequences of the War on Terrorism for politics within Northern Ireland and the United Kingdom that bear upon the future direction of the peace process. Finally, further aspects of American influence will be noted.

## The decline of American influence and military/diplomatic capacity

Much of the controversy surrounding the policies of the Bush administration in its War on Terrorism is the result of structural imperatives, aggressive military actions as well as style. The United States is commonly referred to as a hegemon, a country with predominant power in the military, diplomatic and economic spheres. From a positive perspective, supporters of US policy argue that as the world's only superpower, the United States has an obligation to provide strong leadership in the major security problems facing modern states and the world in general. From this perspective, the overwhelming military advantages produced by technological superiority and budgetary commitment put the US armed forces in a class by themselves, so that the United States has an obligation to act as the lead guardian of the international community. Conversely, the same military capacity can be viewed as means of coercing others to serve the perceived self-interest of the American state. In any case, from the predominant power's position, it may feel compelled to act because no one else can or will.

Of course, the policies of pre-emptive force and the commitment to retain unchallenged military capability in the world appear excessively aggressive to many in the world community as well as within the United States (White House, 2002). Moreover, the style of President Bush and key government officials such as Vice President Cheney and former Secretary of Defence Rumsfeld sometimes have appeared to have an arrogant and imperious tone, although by 2006 US foreign policy was officially a bit less aggressive and President Bush's tone had softened somewhat. (Gordon, 2006; White House, 2006) Indeed, the United States may have squandered the high level of international sympathy and support it acquired after September 11. Yet it can be argued that any Democratic or Republican president could be forced by circumstances to take an independent stand that went against the wishes of major allies (Naím, 2004). The bottom line from the standpoint of British–American relations is that the United States is likely to continue to benefit from the strong support of the United Kingdom, whoever the US president may be. Despite its clearly superior military power, the experience of the United States to date in Iraq demonstrates, as did September 11, that there are profound limits to the power and capacity of a supposed hegemon. Indeed, from the standpoints of manpower, budgetary constraints and public support, the ability of the United States to undertake military action elsewhere has been greatly reduced. Furthermore, resentment by allies against perceived American hubris has weakened the diplomatic ability of the United States to garner international support, particularly from its European allies.

## New constraints on the IRA and Sinn Féin

The attacks of September 11 on New York and Washington, DC radically altered the playing field for the IRA. Bombing had been one of the IRA's main strategies during the conflict, with many attacks on civilian and security-force targets, particularly during the 1970s. In addition to numerous explosions within Northern Ireland, the IRA also carried out bombings outside Northern Ireland, especially in England. Among the more recent instances were the bombings at Canary Wharf in London and in Manchester in 1996, with two deaths and over three hundred people wounded in these attacks (English, 2003; Maloney, 2002).

September 11 and the subsequent War on Terrorism have left vivid images in the minds of American citizens. From the sight of the twin towers collapsing in New York to footage of the damage caused by attacks in Madrid, Bali and London, Americans as well as most citizens of the modern democracies now have an internalised view of terrorists as direct personal threats to their way of life. If the IRA were to launch another war or even engage in a few demonstration bombings, its actions would be roundly condemned. Even if the Republican movement were provoked by Loyalist violence to retaliate militarily, a terrorist campaign would alienate its international support base. Sinn Féin and the IRA would be dramatically weakened in their ability to raise funds and in their capacity to generate political pressure from international sources on behalf of their goals or complaints against the British. The United States imposed a ban on Sinn Féin fundraising in 2005 over its continuing link to crime in Northern Ireland. Even though that ban has now been lifted (*Irish News*, 8 November 2006), it would probably be reinstituted with the support of the British and Irish Governments should the IRA return to violence and crime recur. Of course, there is a possibility that some international funding of the Republican movement could occur illegally. If a low-intensity war were to re-emerge, such funding would be crucial. Moreover, assassination of British officials, security force personnel and others connected with the Northern Ireland administration would similarly be viewed by all but the most extreme American supporters as illegitimate. The pronounced growth in sympathy and support for Sinn Féin since it entered the peace process would quickly erode. After the attack on Iraq and the subsequent effort to pacify the country, the United Kingdom is perceived as America's most loyal ally when many others have withheld support. An attack on Britain would be regarded as an attack on the War on Terrorism by government officials of any US administration as well as the American public.

One of the major obstacles to successful implementation of the 1998 Agreement, which led to a power-sharing regional assembly, was the delay by the IRA in completing decommissioning. From the standpoint of Sinn Féin and the IRA, too rapid movement on decommissioning might have created a threat of defections by more militant members into offshoot groups such as the Real IRA, which has continued the armed struggle. The Republican leadership may have believed that an excessively rapid accommodation could even have motivated dissidents to take over the IRA, perhaps sparking an internal war and threatening the lives of IRA and Sinn Féin leaders.

On the other hand, the war on terrorism has enabled moderate Republican leaders such as Gerry Adams to exert additional pressure on militarists within the IRA, because they could point out that the ability of the IRA to engage in violence was radically constrained by

September 11. Also, Republican leaders undoubtedly saw the retention of weapons as a bargaining chip. Indeed, prior to September 11, there had been no decommissioning of weapons by the IRA. September 11 put great pressure on the IRA to begin the process of decommissioning. In October, in the presence of international inspectors, the IRA decommissioned some of its weapons, and additional decommissionings took place in April 2002 and October 2003. The final placing of weapons beyond use was certified by the Independent International Commission on Decommissioning in September 2005, although the IRA has undoubtedly retained some small arms for self-defence (Independent International Commission on Decommissioning, 2005).

In sum, the events of September 11 have placed serious constraints on IRA military operations and have made a major return to violence by the IRA improbable. Should an unlikely major excess by British or Northern Irish security forces occur against members of the Catholic community, it is possible that the number of Irish-Americans who would support such measures might increase. Nevertheless, in the environment of the War on Terrorism, the majority of Irish-Americans would condemn such measures. Also, given the likelihood that negotiations would at some point continue, Sinn Féin and the IRA would need the goodwill of the Irish and American Governments. Leaders in Washington are unlikely to be as tolerant towards Sinn Féin and the IRA while waging the War on Terrorism as was the Clinton administration. A resumption of a full-fledged terrorist campaign of the IRA would virtually assure that President George W. Bush or any future president would follow the wishes of the British Government concerning any contacts with the Republican movement. Should further attacks on the United States occur, the ability of the IRA to attack targets in Britain would be still more constrained. Nevertheless, it is remotely possible that dissidents could take over the IRA or defect in significant numbers to paramilitary organisations such as the Real IRA. If the IRA were to return to a violent campaign, Loyalist paramilitary organisations would undoubtedly expand their operations, with the major efforts directed at targets identified as Republican. Mounting violence could bring the return of larger-scale attacks on Catholic citizens. At this juncture, however, such a scenario appears highly unlikely, and, in any event, the limitations created by September 11 would still hold.

It should be acknowledged that other forces also dramatically reduce the desire and ability of mainstream Republicans to return to a campaign of violence. It is clear that the Republican movement's leaders view as impossible the goal of militarily forcing the British out of Ireland, and

Sinn Féin's electoral gains in Northern Ireland and in the Republic also preclude a full-fledged campaign of violence (Huggler, 2006). Support from voters would surely fall-off dramatically were violence to re-emerge.

## Changing patterns of British–American relations

The British Government has considered its 'special relationship' with the United States as a centre pin of its foreign policy, although it should be added that the major basis for this relationship has been national interest. (Arthur, 2000; Drumbell, 2001). In return, the United States has regarded the United Kingdom as it's most loyal and important ally from the standpoint of consistent support on a range of international issues around the world. As one illustration, during the Reagan administration the British allowed American attack aircraft to be launched from the British mainland in 1986 for a counter-terrorist attack against the Khadafi government of Libya. The importance of this support from a political as well as military perspective is indicated by the fact that the French Government would not allow these aircraft to fly over French territory, necessitating an inefficient circuitous route to the target (Shultz, 1993). British support for the American position in international politics, especially on military and national security matters, has been of enormous benefit to several American presidents. During the Cold War, the United States could ordinarily depend on British support and assistance from a variety of perspectives. Despite the loss of empire and its declining status as a world power, British diplomatic, military and intelligence resources were of excellent quality, and in many ways provided support for US efforts vis-à-vis the Soviet Union and its allies. The US Department of State maintained a particularly close relationship with its British counterparts, and the British Government could ordinarily depend on the support of the United States in its anti-terrorist campaign against the IRA.

Of course, throughout the Troubles and peace process, American support for the British Government was neither cohesive nor consistent. The US Congress, for example, has had radical as well as moderate pro-Irish factions. The 'four horsemen' (Speaker of the House Thomas P. O'Neill, Senators Ted Kennedy and Patrick Moynihan along with Governor Hugh Cary of New York) were an especially effective team in arguing for the rights of the Catholic minority of Northern Ireland from the standpoint of a constitutional and non-violent perspective. Private Irish-American organisations such as NORAID (Irish Northern Aid) raised money for the Republican cause. Other Irish-American organisations and individuals backed democratic reform and a fair system of government for the North. Overall, American financial assistance for economic development and other projects in Northern Ireland has been significant (Finnegan, 2002).

There was a subtle but fundamental shift in British–American relations after the end of the Cold War (Cox, 2000, 249–62). The British Government appears to have lost substantial influence over the United States regarding its handling of the Northern Ireland problem, because the United States need for British backing was now much less intense. It is unlikely that President Clinton would have allowed Gerry Adams into the United States over the vociferous objections of the British Government had he needed British support in his management of the Cold War. Adams' visit to the United States and his meetings with President Clinton and other officials established important links that contributed to the signing of the Agreement. It should be noted that Clinton and other government officials also met with David Trimble as well as other politicians from Northern Ireland.

The intensity of the US Government's resolve on security issues results from its belief that terrorism is a threat to the survival of the American way of life. The symbolic impact of September 11 was far greater than the considerable harm caused by the attacks themselves. The collapse of the World Trade Center towers, the assault on the Pentagon and the crash of the hijacked airplane in Pennsylvania disrupted business, especially in New York, cost the lives of approximately 3000 people, set back economic recovery from a recession, and seriously damaged specific economic sectors such as tourism. Tragic as the human consequences were, the much greater impact of these attacks was the transformation of the American view that wars happen elsewhere to the realisation that this time the war was being brought to US soil. Indeed the main target of Al Qaeda and similar organisations is the United States, although it may find it tactically easier to mount more frequent attacks in Europe.

Furthermore, there was an immediate validation of the view of many public officials and scholars that the United States was vulnerable to attack by WMDs, including chemical, biological and nuclear devices (U.S. Commission on National Security/21st Century [Hart-Rudman Commission], 1999, 2000, 2001). The problem of Russia's control over thousands of nuclear weapons, the existence of poorly guarded weapons-grade materials around the world, and the relative ease of manufacturing some biological and chemical warfare agents all create a realistic fear of a cataclysmic attack on the United States.

It is not that the United States is going to be taken over by a foreign power or that a huge percentage of the population is going to be killed. The threat of takeover does not exist, and the country is too large in physical size as well as population for such a catastrophic loss of population to be possible in all but the most extreme scenarios. But the potential for the loss of hundreds of thousands if not millions of lives is real, and the US and world economies could be crippled for decades. Despite Russian assurances, it is quite possible that some nuclear weapons and weapons-grade materials may have been stolen and that terrorists will acquire nuclear devices. It is even more possible that terrorist organisations may possess or obtain chemical, biological or nuclear-contamination weapons.

After September 11, then, the United States found itself in a quite vulnerable situation. It was suddenly in a new and unique war in which its traditional military assets were of limited value in protecting the American homeland. Although there had been earlier terrorist attacks in the United States, these were of relatively limited consequence. The United States itself had now become a significant battleground, and the main target of the enemy. The US Government needed every available resource in its fight against terrorism. As of this writing, British support for US policy has been consistently strong since September 11, and Britain appears to have acquired its former influence with the US Government. The extent of British support is indicated in a variety of ways, most notably in its backing of President George W. Bush's attempt in 2002 to build support for the US attack on Iraq and its subsequent participation in the invasion and occupation of Iraq.

During the Cold War, Americans recognised the threat posed by the Soviet Union and its allies, but the conflict remained abstract and distant. The Berlin and Cuban missile crises never resulted in open warfare, and the fighting in places such as Korea and Vietnam were far away conflicts that did not threaten the American homeland. The threat of a nuclear holocaust was real, as indicated by the Cuban missile crisis of 1962, when the Soviet Union and the United States almost went to war (Allison and Zelikow, 1999). But for the most part this threat was so apocalyptic that it seemed rather remote.

In contrast, the United States homeland was directly attacked in 2001 in a brutal and highly symbolic way. The World Trade Center towers and the Pentagon were core symbols of the economic and military power of the United States. There is a general recognition by the American citizenry that the United States will almost certainly be hit again, probably repeatedly. The enemy is illusive and widespread around the world; it may have the tacit and possibly direct support of a few national leaders, not to mention many citizens of some Arab and Muslim countries. Moreover, there are many serious gaps in security arrangements within the United States (O'Hanlon *et al.*, 2002).

As Adrian Guelke has pointed out, there are, of course, limits to British influence over the United States. Each country has its own economic agenda and political realities to confront. In particular, membership in the European Union means that many of Britain's basic economic interests are linked to those of the EU (Guelke, 2002). On the other hand, by maintaining its influence on the United States, Britain can try to position itself as an intermediary between the European Union and the United States, thus further enhancing its influence on both the United States and the EU. Of course, many other factors are central to the issue of British relations with and influence upon the EU, not the least of which is the extent to which Britain is willing to subscribe to new directions and policies of the EU.

If the War on Terrorism has drastically reduced the options of the Republican movement, it has also significantly impeded the ability of the British Government to combat any renewed insurgency by the IRA. The military resources consumed by the Northern Ireland conflict prior to September 11 had already limited the ability of the British Government to conduct military operations abroad. The demands of the War on Terrorism, especially the commitment of troops to Iraq, limit the ability of the British to wage low-intensity warfare in Northern Ireland. As a target for the Al Qaeda movement itself, the British Government needs the flexibility to conduct any necessary operations abroad. Whatever the merits of the Iraq campaign, situations such as the former Taliban regime's support for Al Qaeda in Afghanistan suggests the potential for future similar scenarios that could require a significant military response. It is probable that there will be a much more multilateral approach in the future, especially since there is a strong likelihood of further successful military attacks in Europe. Indeed, scenarios such as a dirty bomb attack or even a small nuclear bomb attack on, for example, NATO headquarters could produce total chaos and political breakdown or, more probably, a joint international response to the threat to Western civilisation. In sum, increasing clout with the United States resulting from its support for the American War on Terrorism has helped enable the British Government to manage the peace process more effectively, in part because it has acquired additional influence with the United States and can be relatively confident of its support in exerting pressure on the Republican movement to refrain from violence and to reduce criminal activities.

## Consequences within Northern Ireland

While the War on Terrorism gave the British Government greater influence with the United States, it also created difficulties for Prime Minister Blair in his dealings with the Unionist community. The fact that Blair was strongly condemning international terrorism and insisting on harsh measures against Al Qaeda and its supporters meant that the Unionist community of Northern Ireland could charge him with hypocrisy when he appeared to take an insufficiently strong stand against the Republican movement in Northern Ireland. Blair faced a dilemma. He had to be accommodating to Sinn Féin and the IRA to enable the Agreement to be achieved in the first place, but this required private assurances to the Unionists that he would insist on decommissioning (Hennessey, 2000). Blair also recognised the problem for Sinn Féin and the more moderate IRA leadership that a too compliant approach to decommissioning by the IRA leadership ran the risk of major defections. But the British Government also has faced the wrath of the Unionists who saw a double standard in Blair's tough line taken against international terrorism and an accomodationist approach to the IRA and Sinn Féin.

Because of IRA foot dragging on decommissioning, undemocratic behaviour by Republicans, as well as anger as over the transformation of the RUC to the Police Service of Northern Ireland and other changes, the majority of the Unionist community had turned against the Agreement. Owing primarily to these problems, the Assembly has been suspended four times. The 2002–7 suspension was sparked by events surrounding an alleged Republican theft of sensitive information from the Northern Ireland Office, although the British Government chose not to submit evidence at the trial of the accused, which resulted in acquittals. The continuing support of David Trimble and the Unionist Party for the Agreement led to the November 2003 assembly elections producing a crucial change, with the Democratic Unionist Party (DUP) replacing the UUP and Sinn Féin replacing the Social Democratic and Labour Party (SDLP) as the leading parties in their respective communities.

A number of important incidents have contributed to increasing hostility to the Agreement from the Unionist community. The credibility of Sinn Féin and the IRA were undermined by the capture of two IRA and one Sinn Féin member by the Government of Colombia in

August 2001. These individuals were charged with providing training to FARC terrorists. Naturally, reaction among Unionists and moderate Nationalists in Northern Ireland was highly negative. The hostile attitude of American politicians towards international terrorist activity by the Irish Republican movement is suggested by a majority staff report on the investigation into this incident by the Committee on International Relations of the US House of Representatives, which pointed out that American personnel in Columbia would be endangered by such training. (Majority Staff, Committee on International Relations, 2002). The Colombian Court in April 2004 found the accused guilty of travelling under false passports, rather than teaching bomb making and other terrorist techniques. It is probable that many American politicians and other government elites concerned with Northern Ireland believe the verdict to have been politically motivated. At this writing, the prosecution has appealed the decision. The conviction of three men in Florida in 2000 of illegally exporting arms, probably to the IRA, suggests that the IRA may also have been attempting to rearm while making limited concessions on decommissioning. A major bank robbery in Belfast in December 2004, allegedly committed by mainline Republicans, and the murder of Robert McCartney in January 2005 further alienated the Unionist as well as much of the Nationalist community, and, of course, officials and supporters in the United States.

Furthermore, the IRA continued its pattern of vigilante justice, although by 2002 the number of such cases appeared to have begun to decline (*Irish Times*, 18 July 2002). Rather than relying on the criminal justice system to punish wrongdoers, paramilitaries employed beatings, exiling and other punishments against alleged offenders (Independent Monitoring Commission, 2004, 2005; Knox and Monaghan, 2002). This fundamentally undemocratic behaviour and violation of the rights of the accused to an orderly and fair legal process offended democratic politicians throughout Northern Ireland and the Republic, not to mention the United States. It seems apparent, however, that by 2006 efforts by Sinn Féin and the IRA to reign in criminality and vigilantism have made some progress (Independent Monitoring Commission, 2006).

Largely because of the Republican movement's involvement with criminality, violence and vigilantism as well as the IRA's reluctance to implement decommissioning, the leaders of the principal political parties in the Republic of Ireland stated they would not serve in a coalition government with Sinn Féin candidates elected in the Republic's national elections held in May 2002. Their decision made David

Trimble's position all the more difficult in confronting dissidents in his own party. How could he justify continuing to serve in the Executive with Sinn Féin politicians when even the Republic of Ireland's leaders would not form a government with Sinn Féin? More broadly, Sinn Féin and the IRA had committed themselves to a democratic solution to the conflict, and Sinn Féin held important leadership roles in the Northern Ireland Government.

In October 2002, the IRA and Sinn Féin were alleged by the government to have carried out a spying operation within the Northern Ireland Office of the British Government. This body has been intimately involved in security measures during the existence of the assembly and during periods of direct rule. Especially ominous was the taking of data on security guards and other officials, who could some day be considered as targets for the IRA in the event of renewed hostilities. However, the individuals arrested in this case were acquitted when prosecutors declined to produce evidence, citing national security considerations. With David Trimble planning to resign from the Executive in the aftermath of the spying incident, the British Government had no alternative but to suspend the Northern Ireland Executive and Assembly. After the suspension of the government on 15 October 2002, the British and Irish Governments stated their joint intention to make the Agreement succeed. President Bush issued a statement in strong support for the British action (White House, 14 October 2002). All three governments emphasised that the need for the IRA to fully decommission.

It should be added that the Republican movement and some Nationalists believe there has been insufficient movement towards demilitarisation, that is, a reduction in forces, facilities and operations by the British military and security forces. From the British point of view, they have already demilitarised to a significant degree, and the UK Government is responsible for security in Northern Ireland in a situation where the other side had failed to live up to its promises to disarm. But the question of demilitarisation is an important symbolic and quality-of-life issue for Republicans and Nationalists, and it is possible that more could be done in this area. Additionally, from the viewpoint of the IRA and Sinn Féin, the Agreement called for decommissioning in the context of the implementation of other aspects of the Agreement. Republicans claimed, for example, that the police reform mandated by the Agreement had not been fully achieved. Democratic parties and many leaders throughout Ireland, and, of course, the US Government and many Irish-American citizens, saw this as an excuse for unjustifiable stalling.

Moreover, opposition by Unionists to the implementation of some aspects of the Agreement greatly complicated the peace process. The Patten Commission, a body with international representation, recommended a series of changes to policing in Northern Ireland designed to legitimise the police and law enforcement processes to alienated sectors of the minority community. The ultimate aim was to have a system of policing acceptable to all sectors of society. Many Unionists and Loyalists adamantly opposed the change of name from Royal Ulster Constabulary to the Police Service of Northern Ireland. This change as well as other reforms have now been implemented.

It is possible that the War on Terrorism may have strengthened the position of the DUP vis-à-vis the UUP. Already noted were the problems created for David Trimble and the moderate leadership of the UUP by the perceived inconsistency in the British Government's handling of terrorist organisations at home and abroad. The DUP's stronger line against British policy would more effectively tap into this discontent. More generally, the threat of terrorism by members of the Al Qaeda movement and the international struggle against it reinforces the appeal of the DUP as being the strongest voice against terrorism within Northern Ireland. Also, the War on Terrorism may make the DUP appear somewhat less extreme to political leaders in the United States and elsewhere. In addition to its electoral victory in 2003, the DUP's initial flexibility into 2004 relative to its earlier positions on issues of political reform and dialogue with Sinn Féin may have given the party both greater power as well as credibility. Although the often noted comparison is overdrawn, the package developed with the DUP and Sinn Féin as the principle players is something like Richard Nixon's recognition of China. As leader of the party further to the right, his concessions in recognising China carried more legitimacy than would have been the case with a Democratic president. Nevertheless, it seems clear that events within Northern Ireland were far more important than the War on Terrorism in explaining the DUP's electoral success.

Although the subject of violence, crime and vigilante justice from violent Loyalist organisations is beyond the scope of this chapter, it should be noted that levels of criminality and vigilantism have been far higher among these groups and that reform has been far less significant than change within the Republican movement. The United States, Republic of Ireland and other external bodies have little positive influence on these groups. Furthermore, it can be noted that Loyalist violence is more of a threat to peace than activities by mainstream Republicans. Attacks by these groups on Nationalist areas, for example, might spark dangerous retaliatory actions.

## Further aspects of American influence on the peace process

The United States continues to be a player in the politics of Northern Ireland. Although the British Government has been the primary beneficiary of the War on Terrorism from the standpoint of maintaining strong support from the American Government on the Northern Ireland issue, other political entities continue to court American public opinion. A dramatic example of this was the decision of Sinn Féin to advertise on the op-ed page of the *New York Times*. This advertisement listed Sinn Féin's views on the failures of the police reform in Northern Ireland. Among the complaints specified were a failure of the British to turn over control of policing, the continuation of collusion with Loyalist death squads and the failure to establish democratic accountability (15 March 2004, p. A25). The advertisement drew a harsh rebuke from President Bush's special envoy to Northern Ireland, Mitchell Reiss, indicating strong solidarity by the US Government with its British ally. The implicit 2005 St Patrick's Day snubbing of Gerry Adams by the Bush administration and the probable political decision to delay Adams' entry into the United States for St Patrick's Day 2006 further illustrates the American role in lending support to the British Government and the peace process.

American support for the British Government and pressure on Sinn Féin can be seen as positive for the peace process in that it strengthened the joint efforts of the British and Irish Governments to elicit compromise from the respective parties to the conflict, particularly Sinn Féin and the IRA. The more fully the Republican movement becomes democratic, a change that ultimately requires support for policing, the ending of vigilante justice and criminal activity, the greater the likelihood of an enduring set of accommodations being achieved. Whether or not Sinn Féin's complaints about policing and security policy may be overstated or unfounded, it seems clear that the Republican and Nationalist communities may have legitimate concerns in the area of security policy. The fact that the British Government has recognised the importance of continued demilitarisation illustrates this point.

Thus, it is also helpful to the peace process if the Republican and Nationalist movements have support for legitimate concerns within the Catholic community, in addition to that provided by the Republic of Ireland. As one example, the statements of the Catholic Archbishop Seán Brady about the negative impact of the Catholic community's

concerns about collusion between the security forces and Loyalist paramilitaries lend credence to the importance of movement on these issues
(Brady, 2004; Stevens, 2003). Of course, Archbishop Brady is strongly
opposed to violence. The recommendations of Judge Peter Cory for
an independent commission to investigate the murder of civil rights
attorney Pat Finucane, a demand advanced by many in the Catholic
community, are another illustration of serious concerns (Cory, 2004).
Judge Cory, speaking at a hearing of the US Helsinki Commission,
an independent government body comprised of members of the US
Congress, voiced concern that delaying the establishment of an investigative body might reduce the ability of that body to gather sufficient
evidence (Commission on Security and Cooperation in Europe, 5 May
2004). Such hearings further indicate that the American Governmental
influence on the Northern Ireland issue is not determined solely by
the executive branch of government. Although the president and his
administration have predominant power and voice in these matters,
other sectors of the US political system and society provide a counterbal-
ance that is more sympathetic to the Nationalist community of Northern
Ireland.

## Conclusion

From several perspectives, it is clear that since September 11 the War on
Terrorism has had a significant impact on the Northern Ireland peace
process as well as upon the relationship between the United Kingdom
and the United States. Most fundamental have been the constraints
placed on Sinn Féin and the IRA. While these constraints are not limitless,
they create a strong disincentive for the IRA to reinstitute its campaign
of bombing and other acts of violence. Attacks on the island of Britain
or other external targets would produce especially intense reaction, and
even a return to bombing and other attacks on the state within Northern Ireland would strongly erode support for the Sinn Féin and the IRA.
The Republican movement has depended on the assistance of American supporters, and the great majority of these supporters would after
September 11 equate IRA violence as similar to the actions of radical
Islamic terrorists.

Implicit in this chapter has been the assumption that the close relationship between the Bush and Blair administrations is beneficial to each
country. The overall positive and negative consequences of the Bush
administration's War on Terrorism are beyond the scope of this chapter.
It should be acknowledged, however, that some critics in the United

States and the United Kingdom argue that the attack on Iraq was neither justified nor wise and that it has compounded the problem of the threat from the Al Qaeda movement. From this perspective, the support and encouragement of the British Government helped encourage and facilitate a dangerous military adventure. In any event, whatever decisions might occur with respect to Iraq, the next leaders of the United States and the United Kingdom are likely to maintain a close relationship between the two countries.

The War on Terrorism has increased the influence of the United Kingdom on the United States. The fact that the United States is now in a fight that is in some ways more dangerous and difficult to prosecute than the Cold War has meant that British support once again has become a primary resource for the United States in its military and diplomatic strategies. The staunch support of the British Government makes it a particularly important ally and gives the British the credibility and stature to advise and to quietly disagree where necessary. To be sure, depending on leadership changes in the United States and Britain, the degree of cooperation as well as British influence on the United States could recede somewhat. Yet the British Government gains influence on international politics to the extent that it can help influence the politics of the world's only superpower. Thus, continued cooperation would bring benefits to both the United States and Britain. Furthermore, the two countries have similar interests with respect to Northern Ireland. Any future American administration would be strongly committed to the ending of terrorism in Northern Ireland and be aware of the connection and collaboration among international terrorist organisations.

In sum, the impact of the War on Terrorism on the peace process in Northern Ireland appears to have been largely positive, contributing to pressures on the IRA to refrain from returning to full-scale military action and strengthening the hand of the British Government in supporting democratic forces within Northern Ireland. Yet it also complicated the position of the British Prime Minister in his dealings with the Unionist community, among other things because of the apparent inconsistency in his tough position on international terrorism and his much more accomodationist position vis-à-vis the Republican movement.

A broader lesson of the dilemmas confronting the British Government in Northern Ireland is that communal violence unleashes forces that are very difficult to constrain. The higher the levels of violence and the longer the duration of the conflict the more difficult it becomes to build trust and to achieve compromise. It should be remembered that the United Kingdom and the Republic of Ireland are viable, respected democracies. If the politics of accommodation is so difficult in this setting, the complexity of bringing peace and stability, not to mention democracy, to places such as Afghanistan, Iraq and Pakistan should be apparent. Although Northern Ireland presents a set of circumstances and constraints very different from those in less modern societies, the Troubles and the peace process can be an instructive case for international efforts to create viable political systems in war-torn and deeply divided societies. In particular, the effort to find a power-sharing settlement in Northern Ireland helps highlight key stumbling blocks to one of the major strategies for resolving conflict in deeply divided societies (Kerr, 2005; O'Flynn and Russell, 2005).

To the extent that conflicts in other settings may be amenable to such techniques, the role of international actors will be crucial to their development and implementation, as they have been in Northern Ireland. In any case, September 11 and the War on Terrorism have made much more unlikely a return to violence by the Republican movement, however difficult the achievement of accommodation may continue to be.

## Note

1. This article is a revised version of my chapter entitled 'The Impact of September 11 on Terrorism and Peace Processes in Northern Ireland', in W. Crotty (2005) (ed.) *Democratic Development and Political Terrorism*. Boston: Northeastern University Press. The author wishes to thank Adrian Guelke of Queen's University, Belfast and Joshua Spero of Merrimack College, North Andover, Massachusetts for suggestions on earlier versions of this chapter. Any remaining errors of fact or interpretation are, of course, the responsibility of the author.

## Bibliography

The Agreement: Agreement Reached in the Multi Party Negotiations (Belfast Agreement; Good Friday Agreement) (1998) Belfast: Northern Ireland Office.

Allison, G. and P. Zelikow (1999) *Essence of Decision: Explaining the Cuban Missile Crisis*. 2nd edn. New York: Longman.

Arthur, P. (2000) *Special Relationships: Britain, Ireland and the Northern Ireland Problem*. Belfast: Blackstaff Press.

Brady, S. (2004) *Faith and Identity: A Catholic Perspective on Northern Ireland*. London: St Ethelburga's Centre for Peace and Reconciliation.

Commission on Security and Cooperation in Europe (US Helsinki Commission) (5 May 2004) *Hearing: Northern Ireland Update: Implementation of the Cory Reports and Impact on the Good Friday Agreement.*

Cory, P. (1 April 2004) *Cory Collusion Inquiry Report: Patrick Finucane.* HC 470. London: Stationery Office.

Cox, M. (2000) 'Northern Ireland after the Cold War', in M. Cox, A. Guelke and F. Stephen (eds), *A Farewell to Arms? From 'Long War' to Long Peace in Northern Ireland.* Manchester: Manchester University Press, pp. 249–62.

Drumbell, J. (2001) *A Special Relationship: Anglo-American Relations in the Cold War and After.* London: Macmillan.

English, R. (2003) *Armed Struggle: The History of the IRA.* Oxford: Oxford University Press.

Finnegan, R. (2002) 'Irish-American Relations', in W. Crotty and D.E. Schmitt (eds), *Ireland on the World Stage.* Harlow, England: Longman, pp. 95–110.

Gordon, P. (2006) 'The End of the Bush Revolution', *Foreign Affairs*, 85:4, 75–86.

Guelke, A. (2002) 'The International System and the Northern Ireland Peace Process', IBIS Working Paper No. 21. Dublin: Institute for British-Irish Studies, University College.

Hennessey, T. (2000) *The Northern Ireland Peace Process: Ending the Troubles?* Dublin: Gill & Macmillan.

Huggler, J. (2006) 'McGuinness on Peace Mission to Sri Lanka', *Belfast Telegraph*, 5 July 2006.

Independent International Commission on Decommissioning (26 September 2005) *Report of the International Commission on Decommissioning.* Belfast.

Independent Monitoring Commission (20 April 2004) *First Report of the Independent Monitoring Commission.* HC 516. London: Stationery Office.

Independent Monitoring Commission (24 May 2005) *Fifth Report of the Independent Monitoring Commission.* HC 46. London: Stationery Office.

Independent Monitoring Commission (26 April 2006) *Tenth Report of the Independent Monitoring Commission.* HC 1066. London: Stationery Office.

Kerr, M. (2005) *Imposing Power-Sharing: Conflict and Coexistence in Northern Ireland and Lebanon.* Dublin: Irish Academic Press.

Knox, C. and R. Monaghan (2002) *Informal Justice in Divided Societies: Northern Ireland and South Africa.* New York: Palgrave Macmillan.

Maloney, E. (2002) *A Secret History of the IRA.* New York: W. W. Norton.

Majority Staff, Committee on International Relations, U.S. House of Representatives (25 September 2002) 'Summary of IRA Links to FARC Narco-Terrorists in Columbia'.

Naím, M. (2004) 'Meet George W. Kerry', *Foreign Policy*, 142, May/June, 96–7.

O'Flynn, I. and D. Russell (2005) *Power Sharing: New Challenges for Divided Societies.* London: Pluto.

O'Hanlon, M., Gunter, D., Destler, I.M., Ivo H. Daalder and James B. Steinberg (2002). *Protecting the American Homeland.* Washington, DC: Brookings Institution Press.

Shultz, G. (1993) *Turmoil and Triumph: My Years as Secretary of State.* New York: Scribner's.

Sinn Féin, Advertisment, *The New York Times*, 15 March 2004, p. A 25.

Stevens, J. (17 April 2003) *Stevens Enquiry: Overview & Recommendations.* Available at: http://cain.ulst.ac.uk/issues/collusion/stevens3/ stevens3summary.htm.

U.S. Commission on National Security/21st Century (Hart-Rudman Commission), Reports (1999, 2000, 2001) Available at: http://www.nssg. gov.

White House (14 October 2002) Office of the Press Secretary, 'Statement by the President on Northern Ireland'.

White House (September, 2002) *The National Security Strategy of the United States*.

White House (March, 2006) *The National Security Strategy*.

# 3
# The Lure of the Miracle? The South African Connection and the Northern Ireland Peace Process

*Adrian Guelke*

In March 2006, the BBC broadcast three programmes under the title, 'Facing the Truth'. These brought together victims and perpetrators from the era of Northern Ireland's Troubles. In the final programme of the three, the notorious Loyalist paramilitary killer, Michael Stone, was brought face to face with the widow and the brother of one of his victims. The programmes were chaired by Archbishop Desmond Tutu in conscious imitation of South Africa's Truth and Reconciliation Commission (TRC). The success of the programmes revived the idea that a truth and reconciliation mechanism similar to that adopted by South Africa should be tried in Northern Ireland. Such a course has periodically been advocated in Northern Ireland ever since the South African TRC first attracted international attention as a result of its televised public hearings. The prospect that Northern Ireland would follow South Africa's example appeared strongest in 2004. In that year, calls were made by both the Chairman of the Northern Ireland Police Board, Professor Desmond Rea, and the Chief Constable of the Police Service of Northern Ireland (PSNI), Hugh Orde, for the creation of a truth and reconciliation mechanism in Northern Ireland. The idea also received serious consideration from the then Secretary of State for Northern Ireland, Paul Murphy, who visited South Africa at the end of May 2004 on a fact-finding mission to study how South Africa had approached the issue of dealing with the past. This prompted a wide-ranging debate on the appropriateness of a Northern Ireland TRC during the course of 2004. This is examined further below, along with the reasons why interest in the concept waned towards the end of the year.

## The Northern Ireland–South African comparison

Consideration of the South African TRC as a possible model for Northern Ireland is connected to a much more general interest in South Africa's transition as offering lessons for other deeply divided societies such as Northern Ireland. This interest has remained high in Northern Ireland in spite of the divergence in the paths of the two societies since South Africa's transition to democracy in 1994. South Africa's political settlement took hold after the country's first democratic elections in 1994 and, despite social difficulties, including high crime rates and the pervasive impact of the AIDS pandemic, the country has remained politically stable ever since. By contrast, the period since the achievement of the Good Friday Agreement in April 1998 has been marked by continual political difficulties, as a consequence of which the devolved government that the Agreement provided for has operated only in fits and starts. Part of the reason why, nonetheless, there has continued to be interest in South Africa in Northern Ireland has been revelations about past links between the two societies during South Africa's apartheid era. In particular, Sinn Féin has made much of the information that has come to light about the role that agents of the apartheid regime played in the activities of Loyalist paramilitary organisations, a dimension bound up with the larger issue of the extent of state collusion with the Loyalists in combating the IRA's long war. For example, the nexus of the Loyalists, apartheid regime and the British state was at the heart of a book by an investigative reporter, Paul Larkin, published in 2004 (Larkin, 2004).

To put these issues into context, it is necessary to provide some background on the comparison between South Africa and Northern Ireland and the role it has played hitherto in the peace process, as well as on the South African TRC itself. A century ago, it was common for the Irish struggle for home rule to be compared to the Afrikaners' quest for independence from the British Empire (Suzman, 1999). Thus, for the first half of the last century, the assumption was Afrikaner nationalism was a rough equivalent of Irish nationalism and that was reflected in the attitudes adopted by both sets of Nationalists and, for that matter, by their radical sympathisers. The imposition of apartheid after the National Party's victory in the South African general election of 1948 reduced sympathy for the Afrikaner nationalist cause, but the old alignments continued to retain a measure of influence on both political behaviour and attitudes. When the Unionist government turned down a request by the British Government that the South African High Commissioner should be invited to open an exhibition in Belfast to celebrate the achievements of the British Commonwealth, it was the Republicanism of the National Party government that the Unionist ministers objected to. This was in 1960. However, one of them (Brian Faulkner) did foresee that the greater danger for Unionism of association with the South African Government than the taint of Republicanism was that comparisons would be made between sectarianism in Northern Ireland and apartheid (Follis, 1996, 172).

The civil rights movement in the late 1960s drew attention to a comparison a South African cabinet minister had made between the Northern Ireland Special Powers Act and the introduction of detention without trial in South Africa. However, the analogy was of limited significance, since the primary comparison for the civil rights movement in Northern Ireland was quite naturally the movement led by Martin Luther King in the United States. Nevertheless, the era of the civil rights movement helped to establish the notion that the position of Catholics in Northern Ireland was comparable to other subordinate communities that had been denied their rights by the majority or, in the case of Southern Africa, by powerful minorities. These lines of sympathy were reinforced by a tendency among Unionists to identify with the cause of other groups at odds with world opinion. Consequently, there was considerable sympathy among Unionists for Ian Smith's rebellion in Southern Rhodesia that was reflected in editorials of the *Newsletter*.

However, the initial impact of the Troubles was to diminish rather than to enhance interest in the specific comparison of South Africa and Northern Ireland. This was in part because the Provisional Republican movement saw scant value in developing the comparison. Under its socially conservative Southern leadership, the movement identified with other regionally based Nationalists in Europe and entertained notions of Celtic solidarity but was generally much more suspicious of similar movements in the Third World, particularly if they were supported by the Soviet Union. In fact, during the 1970s and particularly after the Soweto uprising in 1976, there was greater interest in the comparison of South African and Northern Ireland in South Africa than Northern Ireland. What attracted South African interest in Northern Ireland was the search for an alternative to apartheid that avoided majority rule. The initial interest came from the white opposition to the government on the calculation that the white electorate could not be persuaded to support a nonracial franchise under South Africa's existing Westminster-style system of government. In short, its leaders accepted that white consent for one-person-one-vote in single-member constituencies could not be achieved.

This was the context in which Progressive Party politicians, such as Frederik van Zyl Slabbert who became leader of the party in 1979, discovered the writings of Arend Lijphart on consociationalism (Slabbert and Welsh, 1979). The relevance of Northern Ireland was that it was an example of a deeply divided society, like South Africa, and in Northern Ireland's case there appeared to be a broad consensus that an alternative to simple majority rule was required. As it became apparent even to the National Party government that apartheid had failed, government ministers too started to promote the concept of a consociational solution to South Africa's political impasse. However, the scheme they ultimately adopted in the early 1980s was denounced by the opposition and by Lijphart himself as sham consociationalism. This was because the tricameral constitution excluded the African majority from central government and the element of power-sharing in the arrangements involving the Coloured and Indian minorities was constructed in such a way as to prevent an alliance between these minorities and the white opposition.

The basis for the revival of interest in the comparison of the two societies in Northern Ireland in the 1980s could hardly have been more different. The Provisional Republican movement underwent a process of fundamental change in the late 1970s and early 1980s. Northern radicals, most prominently Gerry Adams, took over the leadership of the movement. The expectation that violence alone would bring about a British declaration of intent to withdraw from Northern Ireland was abandoned. The strategy of the long war was adopted. Its basis was that the Provisional IRA's campaign of violence would have to be sustained for a number of decades in order for the movement's objective of a united Ireland to be achieved. The implication of that was that the Provisional IRA would need to husband its resources so as to be able to sustain its campaign over a long period. Further, it was accepted that there would have to be political campaigning running alongside the IRA's activities so as both to give meaning to violence at a lower level than in the 1970s and to exert pressure on the government in a different way.

The new strategy, as well as the impact of the hunger strike crisis of the early 1980s, provided the context of the Provisional Republican movement's radicalisation and politicisation. A significant dimension of the new approach was that Sinn Féin much more explicitly identified the conflict in Northern Ireland with a global struggle against imperialism. Hostility towards Communism, which had been a feature of the Provisional Republican movement at its inception, largely disappeared, especially where the Communists in question were Third World revolutionaries. There was strong identification with two particular cases, the struggle of the Palestinian Liberation Organisation (PLO) for the recognition of the right of Palestinians to self-determination and the struggle of the African National Congress (ANC) against apartheid. It became increasingly common for the IRA to be compared to the ANC and the PLO on the wall murals that sprung up during the hunger strike crisis and in its aftermath. A widely publicised wall mural of the early 1980s compared the words of Bobby Sands with those of an ANC martyr executed in South Africa, the message underlined by the description of the location of the mural as being Anti-apartheid Corner on RPG Avenue. The analogy between Northern Ireland and South Africa, in particular, was a constant theme in the writings and speeches of the Sinn Féin President, Gerry Adams (Adams, 1986, 5, 27, 28, 113, 118).

The continuation of the Troubles in Northern Ireland through the 1980s, the further internal unrest in South Africa in the mid 1980s and the intifada in Israel-Palestine in the late 1980s reinforced the view that the three cases provided examples of intractable conflict deserving of special study by social scientists. So comparison of the three cases received the added benefit of academic endorsement of its validity (Giliomee and Gagiano, 1990). Ironically, the main basis of these academic comparisons, the hopelessness of the three cases, was rapidly overtaken by events in the 1990s. In February 1990, the South African President, F.W. de Klerk, announced the unbanning of the ANC and other proscribed organisations, including the South African Communist Party. At the same time, Nelson Mandela was released from prison. It was evident that the South African Government was committed to the achievement of a new political dispensation through negotiations with the ANC. However, not merely did the shape of a new dispensation remain very much in doubt, but it was by no means clear that the negotiations would reach a successful outcome.

The liberalisation of the South African political system and the abandonment of the policy of apartheid were followed in 1993 by agreement between the Israeli Government and the PLO on a Declaration of Principles. Northern Ireland seemed to be lagging behind the other two cases of 'intractable' conflict. From Sinn Féin's perspective, there appeared to be a danger that it would be hoist with its own petard. That is to say, the comparison with the ANC and the PLO no longer served to legitimise the IRA's long war. Sinn Féin needed a peace process if the credibility of the comparison of Northern Ireland with the other two cases was not to be lost. In fact, in any event, the leadership of the Republican movement was already contemplating movement away from the armed struggle. Evidence that the movement was searching for an alternative to the long war could be detected in the party's 1992 publication, *Towards a Lasting Peace in Ireland*, though at the time this statement of policy did not attract the attention it deserved. Consequently, the argument can certainly be made that events in South Africa and the Middle East as such were not responsible for the peace process in Northern Ireland on the grounds that a separate trajectory towards the peace process already existed.

Be that as it may, it was certainly the case that the leadership (and especially Gerry Adams) made very full use of the comparison, and most particularly that with South Africa, to justify the peace process within the wider Republican community. One factor that helped to sustain the analogy with South Africa was that South African politicians across the political spectrum were willing to validate and to encourage the comparison. By contrast, there was much less interest in any comparison with Northern Ireland in the Middle East. Another factor, though one that understandably also prompted strong resistance to the analogy in many quarters in Northern Ireland, was that insofar as it suggested some sort of equivalence between Republicans and the ANC, it cast the former in an extraordinarily flattering light. Whereas the ANC had secured over 60 per cent of the vote in South Africa's first fully democratic elections in April 1994, Sinn Féin at this point represented a minority of the minority community in Northern Ireland. Its support in the Republic placed it among the smaller of the polity's minor parties. The comparison carried the valuable implication for the party that it was indispensable to any political settlement of the Irish Question.

By the time of the first paramilitary cease-fires in 1994, Nelson Mandela had already become President of a post-apartheid, non-racial South Africa. Inevitably as a consequence of what South Africa had already achieved, much of the emphasis of the comparison was on what lessons Northern Ireland might learn from South Africa's transition. This was a dimension of the comparison that was of interest to a much wider spectrum of opinion than Republicans. For example, a booklet, *The South African Experience – Lessons for Northern Ireland?*, was put out on the subject by a group with a broadly liberal perspective on what might be learned from the South African negotiations and their outcome (*South African Experience*, 1995). Indeed, it may reasonably be argued that this dimension of the comparison was not the primary concern of Republicans who looked to South Africa more as a way of legitimising their own struggle and the turn towards negotiations than as a model for Northern Ireland's political evolution. The themes of political accommodation and of reconciliation, which made South Africa appear such an attract-ive model of political change to the British and Irish Governments and the middle ground in Northern Ireland, did not have the same import-ance for Republicans as pursuit of the equality agenda. In fact, insofar as Mandela could be accused of abandoning the objective of the radical redistribution of wealth on racial lines for the sake of reconciliation, South African policies were vulnerable to criticism from a Republican perspective. Critics of Adams' leadership of the Republican movement, such as Brendan Hughes, latched on to this issue to criticise the move-ment's peace strategy. Hughes stated the following: 'I look at South Africa and I look at here and I see that the only change has been in appearances' (*Fourthwrite*, 2000).

Mandela himself was inclined to view the conflict in Northern Ireland in anti-colonial terms and consequently his comments on the situ-ation often reflected that fact, much to the delight of Republicans and the dismay of their opponents. For example, in an interview with Christopher Farrington on 5 February 2004, a Sinn Féin politician described the endorsement of the party by Nelson Mandela, whose moral credibility was 'absolutely unquestioned', as 'hugely valuable'. However, at the same time, Mandela was an Anglophile who greatly admired British constitutional practice. He took a very favourable view of the Labour Party and its role in bringing an end to colonialism and supporting the anti-apartheid cause. The warm relationship between the Labour Party and the ANC encouraged the Labour government that was elected in May 1997 to draw on the experience of the South African transition in the steps it took to advance the peace process. An example was the adoption of the rule of sufficient consensus in the multi-party negotiations that led up to the Good Friday Agreement. Admittedly, what had been borrowed from South Africa was the label rather than the principle. The notion that government in Northern Ireland required majority support among both Protestants and Catholics was hardly a new one and formed a basis of the British Government's approach to a political settlement that went back to the early 1970s. Shorn of the link with the South African transition, it was known as the principle of parallel consent. But calling it sufficient con-sensus gave it added legitimacy by associating it with South Africa's suc-cessful negotiations. Another example was the re-labelling of the Royal Ulster Constabulary (RUC) as the PSNI. This followed the example of the remaking of the South African Police as the South African Police Service.

Sometimes the deference shown to South African experts and institu-tions by their Northern Irish counterparts was excessive and took little account of differences between the two societies, including South Africa's relative poverty compared to Northern Ireland. However, the appeal of South Africa's example across a range of fields did not simply rest on the understanding that as a deeply divided society, South Africa's experience naturally tended to have relevance for Northern Ireland as another deeply divided society. It also rested on a perfectly knowing recognition that invoking what South Africa did carried a large measure of legitimacy with it. In this context, Sinn Féin did not have a mono-poly of the South African connection. Others, including the PSNI, could invoke South African experience to justify their actions. Indeed, in some respects, Sinn Féin found itself wrong-footed by different interpretations of the South African miracle and what it did or did not legitimise. In fact, nearly everyone jumped on the anti-apartheid bandwagon, with, for example, the Orange Order insisting that in striving for the right to march down the Garvaghy Road, it was combating apartheid in Ulster.

## A Truth and Reconciliation Commission for Northern Ireland?

It is often mistakenly imagined that the establishment of the TRC was a direct result of South Africa's negotiated settlement. This was not the case. What the parties agreed to in the negotiations prior to the 1994 elections was that 'amnesty shall be granted in respect of acts, omissions and offences associated with political objectives and committed in the course of the conflicts of the past'. They did not agree on the mechanism that should be employed to achieve this end. The epilogue to the interim constitution of 1993 mandated the parliament elected in April 1994 to determine how the clause on amnesty should be implemented. The lead-ers of the ANC favoured the mechanism of the TRC for two reasons. First, they believed that the ANC would largely escape criticism because its limited 'armed struggle' had been conducted outwardly at least in accordance with international norms. Secondly, they believed that the process would be damaging to the National Party, which had emerged from the 1994 elections as the ANC's main rival. Both the National Party and the Inkatha Freedom Party (IFP) expressed serious reservations about the creation of the TRC during the passage of legislation to set it up and were even more hostile to it in practice.

The calculation by ANC leaders that the process would damage politic-ally anyone associated with government during the apartheid era proved correct. The TRC hearings and report did much to discredit the former rulers of South Africa. They contributed to a collapse in support for the

National Party's successor, the New National Party, and paved the way for it to be replaced by the Democratic Party as the principal opposition party in the general election of 1999. However, the other calculation of the ANC that the TRC would gloss over violations of human rights by the 'liberation movements' was confounded. Mandela recognised that the credibility of the TRC depended on its applying the same set of criteria to all parties and accepted the criticism with good grace, but that was not true of the party as a whole. A factor that angered members of the ANC even further was that F.W. de Klerk had forced the TRC Commissioners to remove many of their criticisms of his tenure of office from their report. De Klerk achieved this objective by the sheer volume of the material he submitted to the TRC in rebuttal of criticisms that would have otherwise appeared in the report. As a result of a legal ruling, the TRC had been obliged to inform those it intended to criticise of the terms of any criticism ahead of the report's publication. A full evaluation of de Klerk's objections would have necessitated delaying the report's scheduled publication, a course of action the Commissioners decided against.

However, notwithstanding the political calculations involved in the creation of the TRC, it can be argued that it was a necessary process. A remarkable feature of South Africa's transition was constitutional and legal continuity between the old order and the new. The interim constitution under which South Africa held its first fully democratic elections was enacted by the institutions that had been created under the apartheid regime. A consequence of constitutional and legal continuity was that both the actions of those fighting apartheid and the excesses of the security forces in combating the forces of revolution remained violations of the law that could be the subject of prosecution in the absence of an amnesty. Further, if an amnesty was not to encompass criminally motivated actions on either side, there had to be a mechanism to establish that the beneficiaries of amnesty had acted in accord with the political objectives of a recognised organisation. To this requirement was added a requirement of proportionality and full disclosure of their actions on the part of those applying for amnesty. It is worth underlining that applicants were not required to demonstrate that they regretted their actions or to express any kind of remorse.

In any event, in the climate of opinion in which public hearings into gross violations of human rights took place, few would have expected members of the ANC to say that they regretted what they had done, since the country's transition to democracy seemingly justified anything they might have done. By the same token, there was an expectation

that their victims should accept their *bona fides*. A number of cath-
artic moments of reconciliation did occur during the TRC's hearings.
They usually involved victims forgiving perpetrators whose actions were
accepted as having been directed at freeing the country from apartheid.
However, while it may be claimed that in these individual cases, the TRC
facilitated a healing process, these responses were by no means typical
of reaction to the hearings. Opinion surveys after the publication of the
TRC report highlighted that respondents of all races believed that the
TRC's revelations about past atrocities had deepened the country's racial
divisions.

Generally, uncritical reporting of the TRC by foreign correspondents
took little account of these polls. They also tended to ignore other
limitations of the process. Thus, the failure of the TRC to address
external connections of the apartheid regime so as not to embarrass
countries with which post-apartheid South Africa wished to have good
relations hardly registered. Even more significantly, scant regard was
taken of the fact that the TRC secured little co-operation in its invest-
igations outside the ranks of those who were convicted of offences or
against whom there was such substantial evidence that they had good
reason to fear prosecution. Admittedly, investigating specific crimes
and granting amnesty was not the only function of the TRC. It was
also given the task of inquiring into the 'causes, nature and extent'
of the conflict. In short, part of the TRC's remit was to produce an
official history of apartheid after 1960. However, given the notoriety
of apartheid, producing an account that in broad outline, if not in
some of the detail, was generally accepted did not present too many
difficulties.

Two aspects of the TRC made it particularly appealing as a model to
policy makers in Northern Ireland. First, it was seen as a factor in South
Africa's achievement of reconciliation following the country's political
settlement. This was in sharp contrast to the quite evident absence in
Northern Ireland of a spirit of reconciliation after the Good Friday Agreement was endorsed by the electorate. Secondly, the perceived success of
the TRC in closing the book on the apartheid era was attractive to those
wanting to find a way of drawing a line under the past in Northern
Ireland. This was the context in which the Chief Constable of the PSNI,
Hugh Orde, mooted the setting up of a Northern Ireland version of the
TRC in Northern Ireland's Troubles in the course of speeches in 2003
and 2004. In particular, Orde proposed that a truth and reconciliation
mechanism might be used to address the issue of the large number of
unsolved murders that remained on the police's books from that era.

Orde accepted that convictions in most of the 1800 cases involving loss of life were unlikely, but by working with the families of the victims, he hoped that some myths that had developed over how they had originally been investigated might be dispelled.

The then Chairman of the Police Board, Desmond Rea, backed by his deputy, Denis Bradley, supported Orde's idea and elaborated on it. In an interview with BBC Radio Ulster on 18 February 2004, Rea suggested that it should involve an amnesty for the perpetrators of Troubles-related crimes, including the unsolved murders referred to by the Chief Constable. Rea argued that a truth commission could prove more useful than a series of judicial inquiries.

> There are people on both sides who have lost lives. There are people who have been injured, and there is a deep sense of hurt. Therefore a commission is the proper way to take account of that hurt, but also to seek to find a way forward that is a more productive way forward than the road that we appear to be embarking [sic].
>
> (Keenan, 2004)

Rea was alluding to the very high cost of the Bloody Sunday inquiry and to the fact that the pressure was building up for further judicial inquiries into state collusion with Loyalist paramilitaries, the Claudy bombing, Bloody Friday and the La Mon bombing of 1977.

Reaction to Rea's comments was largely negative. Unionist hostility centred on the issue of amnesty, as did those of some of the victim groups. Ian Paisley Jnr proclaimed: 'Professor Rea has now lost the confidence of ordinary Unionists through his outrageous comments.... What the chairman of the Policing Board is saying is that he has no confidence in the police to capture the perpetrators of 30 years of violence' (*Belfast Telegraph*, 19 February 2004). Arlene Foster, who had defected from the Ulster Unionist Party (UUP) to the Democratic Unionist Party (DUP) after the November 2003 Assembly elections, declared: 'The last thing Northern Ireland needs is a truth commission and an amnesty for terrorists. We could never be confident that a truth commission would get at the whole truth' (ibid). The fact that the British had not as yet published the findings of Judge Cory on the Finucane, Hamill, Nelson and Wright cases was the primary influence on Nationalist reaction. Gerry Kelly of Sinn Féin suggested that the proposal was a stalling device to prevent the truth from emerging. The Social Democratic and Labour Party (SDLP) accepted that a mechanism was needed to help society move away from the past. However, the party emphasised that the proposal should not be used to defer any recommendations made by Cory. The Alliance Party also was willing to give the proposal for a truth commission further consideration, but its deputy leader made plain the party's opposition to any amnesty for criminal offences.

Despite the largely negative reaction, Hugh Orde repeated his claim that some sort of truth and reconciliation forum was needed to deal with unsolved murders of the Troubles, which he argued the PSNI simply did not have the funds to reinvestigate, in an interview with *The Guardian* (Chrisafis, 2004). His comments were strongly attacked by the DUP and Sinn Féin. The most overheated reaction was from Catriona Ruane of Sinn Féin who accused Orde of

> deliberately and very cynically entering a debate around truth recovery and inquiries in a bid to protect senior members of the PSNI from having their past role within the RUC investigated. He knows that many of these individuals are human rights abusers and were centrally involved in organising a campaign of genocide against the nationalist community.
>
> (*The Irish Times*, 24 February 2004)

This did not dissuade the British Government from continuing to promote the possibility of a truth and reconciliation commission for Northern Ireland. At a press conference in Downing Street on 1 April, the Prime Minister, Tony Blair, explained why the government was still considering the question.

> I do not know whether necessarily a truth and reconciliation commission is the right way to do it, but I think there needs to be some way of trying to both allow people to express their grief, their pain and their anger in respect of what has happened in Northern Ireland without the past continually dominating the present and the future, and that is what we will try to do.
>
> (*The Irish Times*, 6 April 2004)

However, it was not the case that the government simply disregarded all criticisms of the concept of a Northern Ireland TRC. One of the most common objections was that the establishment of such a body was premature. The point was made forcefully by Dennis Kennedy in an article in *The Irish Times*. He argued that two key elements present in South Africa were missing in the Irish case. One of these was that in South Africa, 'the argument was over, the dispute was settled' (Kennedy, 2004). Kennedy went on:

> The National Party conceded that apartheid had to end, and that majority rule was inevitable. The ANC took power on foot of their democratic majority, and white minority rule was over. In Northern Ireland the argument is not over; everyone may give lip service to the consent principle, but Sinn Fein and the SDLP both continue to insist that Irish unity is their prime political goal. Nationalism continues to assert that partition was unjust and remains unjustifiable. Violence continues, though at a mercifully reduced level. Illegal armies have not gone away.
>
> (ibid)

In his comments on the possibility of establishing a truth and reconciliation commission, the Secretary of State for Northern Ireland, Paul Murphy, has acknowledged this point. The most recent example was in an article for *The Irish Times* to mark his fact-finding mission to South Africa. After discussing the publication of a new edition of *Lost Lives* (2004), a catalogue of those killed during the Troubles, Paul Murphy reiterated three prerequisites for dealing with the past. The first of these dealt directly with Kennedy's point: 'First, the conflict must truly be over. There must be no more additions to *Lost Lives*, no more young people mutilated in "punishment" attacks by loyalist and republican paramilitaries' (Murphy, 2004).

Murphy's third prerequisite was the need for a shared vision of the future. This addressed another of the objections raised by Dennis Kennedy, that missing in the Irish case was 'acceptance of a common moral view of the situation' (Kennedy, 2004). In South Africa, there was a consensus that apartheid had been wrong and that the quest for majority rule was justified in terms of democratic principles. As Kennedy put it:

> This retrospective viewpoint on ANC use of violence made it easier, though by no means easy, for Afrikaners to close the chapter. The fact that the crisis had been resolved in a clear-cut victory for one side, and the immediate end of minority rule and of apartheid, made it easier for the black majority to move on without systematic pursuit of those guilty of crimes in the name of the apartheid regime. Nothing like that applies in Northern Ireland. As John Hume repeatedly said, there was no moral cause to justify any violence.
>
> (ibid)

Murphy's second prerequisite was whatever methods were finally adopted to deal with the past 'must come from the whole community and enjoy a consensus of support' (Murphy, 2004).

When Murphy's piece was published, it seemed unlikely that any of his prerequisites would be met any time soon. In particular, there had been no softening of Unionist opposition to the concept. When the Chief Constable once again raised the issue of an amnesty for Troubles-related crimes, mentioning both South African and Peruvian experience, the *Newsletter* responded with an angry editorial entitled 'No banana republic ways here, Mr Orde' (*Newsletter*, 31 May 2004). Nationalists were scarcely less sceptical. The *Irish News* reported on its front page the reaction of Brian Feeney, one of the co-authors of *Lost Lives*, to the announcement of Murphy's fact-finding trip to South Africa.

> Is Tony Blair using it as a pawn to try and break the political logjam, because if he is, it won't work?
>
> There have been about 40 truth and reconciliation processes around the world in places like South Africa and Peru. The only time they have worked is when the conflict has definitively come to an end. That is not the case here.
>
> (McCaffrey, 2004)

Feeney expressed his concern that the idea of a truth and reconciliation was being used to block inquiries into controversial killings.

> Does Paul Murphy expect people to believe the British government will be an honest broker in a truth process when they were one of the key combatants in the conflict?
>
> Does anyone believe either the paramilitaries or security forces are going to turn up at a truth hearing and admit to everything that went on? Each party will try and score points from what the other side says.
>
> Families will support this process in the hope that they can get something positive from it. But the reality is that if this truth process is established it will just be used as another part of the conflict.
>
> (ibid)

In April 2004, the government accepted Judge Cory's recommendation that there should be inquiries in three of the four cases he investigated. However, the government deferred a decision on an inquiry in respect of the Finucane case.

Suspicion of the government's motives was one of the factors that undermined support for the idea among both Unionists and Nationalists. Consequently, the government was forced to accept that there was little prospect that Murphy's second prerequisite would be met. This political reality was evident in the fact that the idea found no place in the proposals the British and Irish Governments put forward for a settlement in December 2004. The fact that the two governments had come close to getting the agreement of both the Democratic Unionist Party and Sinn Féin to these proposals also carried the implication that these would form the basic template for any future settlement. Consequently, others, including the Chief Constable of the PSNI, Hugh Orde, were also forced to come to terms with the fact that the necessary political support within Northern Ireland for a TRC along South African lines was lacking. Orde's response was to propose another solution to the problem of the unsolved murders from the Troubles. This was for the PSNI itself to take the initiative in uncovering the truth about past events after the necessary funding for this approach had been secured. It led to the setting up of the Historical Enquiries Team, a specially funded group of detectives with a mandate to re-investigate the murders that took place as a result of the security situation from 1969 to 1998. It began its work in 2006, starting with murders that had taken place at the beginning of the Troubles. This effort is expected to last at least seven years and involves more than two hundred detectives and other staff.

Despite the fact that Murphy's exploration of the possibility of creating a Northern Ireland TRC in 2004 in the end came to nothing, interest in the idea has by no means disappeared, as was indicated at the start of this chapter. In 2004 the British Government seems to have envisaged that this idea might provide a way of tying up a number of loose ends in the context of an overall deal. It hoped that the inducement of a final, historic settlement might persuade the political parties in Northern Ireland to drop their objections to the idea. The attraction was in part the South African connection itself. As the government appreciated, any model derived from the country's miraculous transition to democracy tended to be imbued with a large measure of legitimacy in Northern Ireland. At the same time, the high standing in Northern Ireland of Archbishop Desmond Tutu, who chaired the South African TRC, was another reason for believing that the association would be both a beneficial and an appealing one to many people in the province. Admittedly, a weakness of the South African analogy was that it by no means assuaged Unionist fears that a Northern Ireland TRC would be biased against them. This was no doubt why the Chief Constable invoked the experience of Peru in addition to South Africa in seeking once again to promote the notion that there needed to be a mechanism to achieve closure over deaths during the Troubles. However, as the *Newsletter's* dismissive and contemptuous reference to a banana republic underlines, the citing of other cases by no means removed Unionist doubts.

## Conclusion

The British Government has not been alone in being drawn to the lure of the South African miracle. In the early years of the peace process, of all the parties to the conflict in Northern Ireland, Sinn Féin had the greatest stake in the comparison with South Africa. In particular, the comparison with the ANC flattered a party with relatively limited popular support. As support for the party has grown to the point where it is the largest Nationalist party in Northern Ireland and has a strong presence in Southern Irish politics, this reason for advancing the analogy with South Africa has lost some of its force. There now seems to be a greater emphasis on using the connection between Loyalists and apartheid and between the British state and Loyalists, hence connecting all three, to delegitimise their opponents. The issue of collusion has also provided the party with a useful means for diverting attention away from the Republican movement's misdeeds, past and present, and on to the conduct of the security forces, as well as assisting Sinn Féin to resist giving its full support to the PSNI outside of an overall settlement that restores devolved government.

An opinion survey in Northern Ireland in 2005 that formed part of a study of truth commissions by researchers at the University of Ulster found a considerable measure of popular support for the idea of Northern Ireland TRC, though there was stronger support for the idea among Catholics than Protestants (University of Ulster news release, 2005). And not merely does the idea enjoy support among the general public in Northern Ireland, it also has the backing of many non-governmental organisations campaigning on the issues of truth recovery and reconciliation. Nevertheless, there are good reasons why support for the idea in principle tends to evaporate when it is subjected to closer examination. In particular, there are significant practical objections to the idea. One of the functions that Murphy identified in 2004 as one that might be performed by a Northern Ireland TRC, providing an opportunity for victims to tell their stories, has in fact been fulfilled in large part already without the government's imprimatur through initiatives of the BBC and others. Further, the release of paramilitary prisoners under the terms of the Good Friday Agreement has substantially limited any need for the creation of special arrangements for the granting of amnesty. It is also difficult to imagine any circumstances in which both Unionists and Nationalists would be ready to endorse the concept, let alone the content, of an official history of the Troubles.

But more important than these practical objections is the misconception that underlies most references to the South African TRC in Northern Ireland, which is that it was through the TRC that South Africa achieved reconciliation after apartheid. The poignancy of this observation stems from the very evident truth that Northern Ireland has been unable to achieve the same measure of reconciliation after its Troubles, as was evident in post-apartheid South Africa. Thus, it has become common to refer to the relative tranquillity Northern Ireland has enjoyed since the paramilitary ceasefires as a cold peace. However, if the advocates of a Northern Ireland TRC have been correct in diagnosing what the province lacks, they have been wrong in their assumptions about how South Africa achieved reconciliation. The person of Nelson Mandela and his conduct in the office of South Africa's first democratically elected President were far more important agents of reconciliation than the TRC. Northern Ireland's tragedy is that no remotely comparable figure exists in the province who could fulfil the role that Mandela assumed in the years immediately following the South African transition. However, in fairness to Northern Ireland's politicians, it should also be acknowledged that the different nature and structure of Northern Ireland's divisions constituted a profound obstacle to the emergence of such a figure. The South African analogy is helpful in underlining the importance of reconciliation to peace processes and transitions, but it is less helpful as an example of how it can be achieved in the case of Northern Ireland.

## Bibliography

Adams, G. (1986) *The Politics of Irish Freedom*. Dingle: Brandon.

Chrisafis, A. (2004) 'Police Chief Calls for Truth and Reconciliation in Ulster', *The Guardian* (London), 23 February 2004.

Follis, B.A. (1996) 'Friend or Foe? Ulster Unionists and Afrikaner Nationalists', *Southern African-Irish Studies*, 3, 171–89.

*Fourthwrite* (2000)1, Spring, Belfast.

Giliomee, H. and J. Gagiano (eds) (1990) *The Elusive Search for Peace: South Africa, Israel and Northern Ireland*. Cape Town: Oxford University Press.

Keenan, D. (2004) 'Amnesty and NI Truth Commission Proposed', *The Irish Times*, 19 February.

Kennedy, D. (2004) 'The Problem with Tidying Away the North's Raw Past', *The Irish Times*, 15 April.

Larkin, P. (2004) *A Very British Jihad: Collusion, Conspiracy and Cover-Up in Northern Ireland*. Belfast: Beyond the Pale Publications.

McCaffrey, B. (2004) 'Truth Process would be "Part of Conflict"', *Irish News*, 31 May.

McKittrick, D. (with S. Kelters, B. Feeney, C. Thornton and D. McVea) (2004) *Lost Lives: The Stories of the Men, Women and Children Who Died Through the Northern Ireland Troubles*. 2nd edn. Edinburgh: Mainstream Publishing.

Murphy, P. (2004) 'Hearing the Stories of the Troubles is Part of Building a New Society', *The Irish Times*, 2 June.

Slabbert, F. van Zyl and D. Welsh (1979) *South Africa's Options: Strategies for Sharing Power*. Cape Town: David Philip.

*The South African Experience – Lessons for Northern Ireland?* (1995) Belfast: An Ad Hoc Group on South Africa, Belfast.

Suzman, M. (1999) *Ethnic Nationalism and State Power: The Rise of Irish Nationalism, Afrikaner Nationalism and Zionism*. Basingstoke: Palgrave Macmillan.

University of Ulster news release (2005) 'Cautious Support for an Irish Truth Commission', 11 July.

# 4

# From the European Union in Northern Ireland to Northern Ireland in the European Union

*Elizabeth Meehan*

The title of this chapter reflects the beginnings of a transition from a situation where many people saw the European Union (EU) as an actor – for better or worse – in Northern Ireland to one in which a new Northern Ireland might play a more active part on the EU stage. The first part of the story is dealt with only briefly as it has been told before. The chapter concentrates on efforts to become what the Northern Ireland Executive called *Northern Ireland as a Forward and Outward Looking Region*. This was the title of the strategy initiated by the First Minister and Deputy First Minister and overseen by the other ministers in the Office of the First Minister and Deputy First Minister (OFMDFM), Denis Haughey and Dermot Nesbitt. The initial steps have been faltering – unavoidably, because of the periodic and, since 2003, lengthy suspensions of the devolved institutions. However, Direct Rule Ministers have attempted to continue the process, albeit in a context of problems, not peculiar to Northern Ireland, about how the component parts of the United Kingdom can or cannot contribute to the centre's approach to policy-making in the EU.

The chapter begins with a summary of the earlier period. It then discusses institutional issues and relationships relating to the elucidation of Northern Ireland's EU interests and the construction of the UK 'line'. These involve coordinating arrangements within Northern Ireland and channels that are simultaneously vertical, through the UK Government, and horizontal given the North–South and East–West axes of the Good Friday/Belfast Agreement. Thirdly, the chapter deals with Northern Ireland's ability to interact horizontally with other regions in the EU. Finally, the chapter draws attention to a particular policy area where Northern Ireland (and, perhaps, Scotland) could put to test the UK 'line'; that is over the euro. The conclusion is necessarily inconclusive; in the absence of devolution, it was difficult to tell how effective Northern Ireland is, or could be, as a *Forward and Outward Looking Region*.

## The European Union in Northern Ireland

From the beginning of UK and Irish membership of the then European Economic Community, there was a little contemplation of the implications for the border between north and south (Laffan, 2006; Meehan, 2000). As EU regional policy developed from the 1970s to the present, its philosophy of partnership seemed to promise a new tool with which to attempt to reform social and political relationships across the border and within Northern Ireland (Hodgett and Meehan, 2003; Laffan, 2006; McCall and Williamson, 2000). The European Parliament's interest in the 1980s in Northern Ireland's problems was regarded by Unionists as an illegitimate extension of external interference from economic to internal political affairs. But this interest contributed to a new initiative in the Commission for special funding in the 1990s (Peace and Reconciliation) for Northern Ireland. This innovation was promoted throughout its manifestations by Nationalist and Unionist Members of the European Parliament (MEPs), who have cooperated to ensure its continuation in the 2000s (Hainsworth, 1999; Laffan, 2006).

The increased mutual familiarity of Irish and British civil servants and politicians, occasioned by EU meetings and policy-making processes, contributed to their ability to cooperate with one another, and to see that cooperation was necessary to finding a settlement in Northern Ireland (Gillespie, 2000; Laffan, 2006; Meehan, 2000). Finally, the experience of governments and local politicians of an evolving idea of sovereignty and familiarity with the workings of EU institutions can be seen in the design of the institutions agreed in Belfast on Good Friday 1998 (Laffan, 2006; Meehan, 2000; O'Donnell, 1999).

Given levels of violence and the vociferousness of protest, one could hardly say that Northern Ireland was in these 30 years a passive part of the EU. But it was a recipient or beneficiary of policy initiatives rather than a self-motivated definer and pursuer of its own interests. This began to change in the early 2000s.

## Institutional issues and relationships

### Northern Ireland's own arrangements for pursuing EU policy interests

At the turn of 1999–2000, Northern Ireland emerged from a preliminary period in which new institutions were in 'shadow mode' to full devolution. Since then, arrangements for handling EU interests have been criticised by both academics (Kennedy and Murphy, 2001; McGowan and Murphy, 2003; Murphy, 2002; Phinnemore, 2003) and Members of the Legislative Assembly (MLAs) (Official Record, 18 February 2002, 4 March 2002, 19 March 2002, 8 April 2002). Criticism was directed at:

- an alleged incapacity of the OFMDFM and Ministerial Departments to oversee the volume of work;
- the Assembly itself for not having a dedicated European Committee;
- the absence for too long of an official Northern Ireland Office in Brussels (there was, of course, Northern Ireland Centre in Europe[1]);
- then, when the Executive Office in Brussels was established in 2001, at its remit and the resources at its disposal compared to the task in hand;
- the relative infrequency in Northern Ireland (compared with Great Britain) of seconding civil servants to EU institutions, leading to less familiarity than elsewhere with European policy-making and exclusion from significant networks;
- the absence of coordination – indeed, a seeming lack of awareness for its need – amongst all Northern Ireland's actors in Brussels; MEPs, the Executive, members of the Committee of Regions and of the Economic and Social Committee, as well as people from civil society working on European issues;
- the absence of Northern Ireland MPs from EU scrutiny committees in the House of Commons (at the time, only one Northern Ireland MP served on just one of the several committees; Phinnemore, 2003); and, finally,
- the apparently smaller interest in Northern Ireland (than Scotland in particular) to be part of UK delegations to the Council of Ministers.

The protracted absence of formal institutions means that criticisms of the Executive and Assembly could not be addressed, though it should be noted that, from the beginning, two former Commission officials were appointed as advisors in the OFMDFM (Laffan, 2006, 181).

Despite the absence of a devolved Executive, improving coordination began to be tackled. In December 2003, all the UK and Irish delegates to the Committee of the Regions met in Belfast (Executive Press Release, 8 December 2003; and see later). The meeting was hosted by Belfast City Council's newly established European Unit and addressed by its Chair (and of the Council's Development Committee), Councillor Ian Crozier, and Ian Pearson, Direct Rule Minister for, among many other things, Europe.

Since February 2004, there have been monthly meetings of all those involved in EU institutions. Indeed, Ian Pearson spoke at a lunch to mark the first occasion. People in Northern Ireland with EU interests began to report that the OFMDFM (which remains as a department even under direct rule) and the Northern Ireland Executive Office in Brussels were very helpful in briefing politicians from the region (QUB/DD[2] European Liaison seminar on 22 March 2004). All the same, the suspension of the Assembly was much regretted, as the absence of somewhere to report back gave rise to a sense of isolation amongst those operating in EU institutions (Alban Maginness (SDLP) at the seminar, and Jim Nicholson (UUP), BBC interview during the last European Parliamentary election). In the context of the re-establishment of the Assembly, there is likely to be a strong demand for it to introduce a specialist European committee – as there is elsewhere.

In the summer of 2004, the OFMDFM launched a consultation document, *Taking Our Place in Europe: Northern Ireland's European Strategy 2004–2006* (OFMDFM, 2004). One place where it was discussed was at a meeting of the European Liaison Group (see note 2). While recognising that the OFMDFM was hampered by uncertainty over whether or not devolution would be restored, the meeting felt that greater vision was required. The document needed to be clearer about where Northern Ireland was and more concrete in its strategy and objectives.

The meeting raised specific questions about issues that recur in this chapter: how Northern Ireland should relate to the EU through the United Kingdom, with specific reference to 'demystifying' the Joint Ministerial Committee (JMC) system; what might be the roles of the North/South Ministerial Council (NSMC) and British-Irish Council (BIC); and the fact, seemingly overlooked in London, that this part of the United Kingdom shares a land border with another EU state, one that is in the euro zone. The meeting also drew an unfavourable comparison between the Northern Ireland Executive Office in Brussels and the Scottish arrangement for combined civic and official representation (see note 1).

The closing date for responses to the document was the end of September 2004, the same time as further talks at Leeds Castle on the future of devolution; the results seem to have been submerged under the continuing attempts to restore devolution. A further consultation is underway – initiated by the UK Government for the whole state – to identify strategic priorities for structural funding between 2007 and 2013 (Department of Finance and Personnel News Release, 28 February 2006).

## The UK channel to the EU for the devolved administrations

In the year before the institutions were first suspended in October 2002, the two previously mentioned Ministers, Denis Haughey and Dermot Nesbitt, with responsibility for EU matters and Mark Durkan, as Minister for Finance and Personnel and, later, Deputy First Minister, increasingly spoke of the confidence and self-awareness that devolution gave the region in being a proactive member of the EU and of the importance of cooperating with the other devolved administrations in the United Kingdom in contributing to the construction of the United Kingdom's EU policy (e.g. Executive Press Releases, 9 May 2001, 22 May 2001, 25 June 2001, 28 March 2002, 4 September 2002, 20 September 2002).

There are interlocking formal mechanisms for coordination of all policy, including EU policy, under devolution – Memorandums of Understanding, Concordats and the JMC system. JMCs are supposed to meet in sectoral format, according to subject – health, transport and so on. Often, however, as in the case of agriculture, meetings are not actually called JMCs but are a continuation of pre-devolution practice. Equally, a good deal of discussion takes place outside the formal framework at what may be sporadic meetings. Cooperative outcomes often depend on pre-existing networks of goodwill.[3] Attendance at JMCs imposes a burden of secrecy on ministers from the devolved administrations about any matter of dispute with the centre. There is little public information about the outcomes of meetings. For these reasons, the system was criticised by the House of Lords Select Committee on the Constitution (2002, paras. 36, 37, 187; Meehan, 2006, 154–6) – which compares it unfavourably with reporting processes that followed, when the Assembly existed, from meetings of the NSMC and BIC.

The Select Committee (House of Lords, 2002, para. 177) is better disposed to the special JMC for the EU which, according to the evidence submitted to it, functions satisfactorily. The Committee noted, however, that satisfaction might stem from recognition that formal relations within the EU are a matter for central government; difficulties may be more likely where particular policies straddle levels of governance and come within the purview of sectoral committees. Moreover, the JMC Europe does bring devolved ministers into contact with the most senior ministers of central government, including members of the main cabinet committee on the EU (Trench, 2001, 155–68). In the case of Northern Ireland, this is particularly important. Elsewhere, tensions between the devolved capitals and London were eased by the coexistence of governments that were broadly of the same ideological outlook – which, of course, is not, and cannot be, the case in Belfast. This point is reinforced by a contrast between Scotland and Northern Ireland. That is, according to *The Scotsman* (1 March 2001), there is cynicism in Scotland that all JMCs (Europe or otherwise) are about the 'repatriation' of powers. Conversely, Ministers in Northern Ireland, even Nationalist ones, suggest that they and/or interlocking mechanisms can be useful. For example, the SDLP's Mark Durkan, when Minister of Finance and Personnel, endorsed the Concordat with the Treasury on public procurement as providing a channel of influence (Executive Information Services, 11 April 2001).

Another route that can be exploited as a means of placing Northern Ireland's EU interests on the wider agenda is to secure a place on the UK negotiating team at meetings of the Council of Ministers – as was possible before for the territorial Secretaries of State. At face value, this is not necessarily advantageous. Decisions about who can attend, and, perhaps, speak, on behalf of the United Kingdom, are taken by the lead UK minister and attendance is permitted only if the matter under discussion has a significant impact on the powers and work of the devolved administrations. Moreover, the role of the delegation and its speaker is to 'support and advance the single UK negotiating line' (Hazell, 2000, 173). On the other hand, attendance provides opportunities to advance the informal links that are permitted between ministers in devolved administrations and commissioners and their *cabinets* about distinctive interests (House of Lords, 2002, para. 175). In the early days, Scotland was the most assiduous of the devolved administrations in lobbying to be included, sometimes in the face of reluctance on the part of the UK Government (Hazell, 2000, 173). Wales began to catch up. Devolved ministers in Northern Ireland seemingly saw little need to attend but, in periods of suspension, Direct Rule Ministers did attend meetings of the Council of Ministers (for example, agriculture and fisheries; Executive Press Releases, 5 June 2003, 8 March 2006, 20 June 2006) and did attend meetings of the Convention on the Future of Europe (see below).

Despite noting defects in the JMC system and the limits of being part of a ministerial delegation, the House of Lords Committee argues that, overall, devolved administrations in the United Kingdom have better opportunities to influence both the UK 'line' and to advance their own interests than regions in other member states. That it is right that regions should be heard in the EU is supported by Secretary of State, Peter Hain (see later on the Convention on the Future of Europe). But, in view of the new leadership of the Labour Party, it may be of interest to note at this point an alternative view from the centre which seeks to downplay the importance of a direct regional voice in the EU.

## A view from the centre of devolution and regional EU interests

The House of Lords Select Committee on the Constitution had considered how the drafting of EU legislation could take account of the rationale of devolution – reflecting and permitting diversity within a state – in the context of common, EU-wide policies. In March 2003, the British Government produced a consultation document on UK regional policy in which it, too, pursued the theme of the autonomy of the devolved administrations (UK Government, 2003; see also Gordon Brown, 'As the EU expands, we must repatriate some of the power from Brussels', *Times*, 6 March 2003). The document proposed a new role for the EU, suggesting that it should concentrate on defining a framework of high-level policy priorities towards which all its members and regions should work. The idea is that the EU would have a much reduced role in financing the delivery of the priorities, determined by the principle of subsidiarity. That is, it should become involved only where financing and delivery could not be done at member state level. Thus, the document envisages some continued EU funding for cross-border initiatives such as INTERREG and networking under the EQUAL programme to promote good equal opportunity practice. The document also noted that some version of Peace funding might continue in Northern Ireland but that this should take place separately from the proposed EU Framework. If budgetary support for regional policy were to be repatriated, according to the document, there would be more money for the devolved administrations in the United Kingdom. And, if detailed policy powers were allocated to them, solutions could more readily be tailored by local people to meet local needs (subject to not widening disparities).

The London-based press focused mainly on how the proposals would be seen in the EU, in view of tensions between the then Chancellor, Gordon Brown, and the Commission over the stability and growth pact. The London press also discussed the government's proposals in the light of the United Kingdom's increased net contribution (under an unreformed EU regional policy) arising from enlargement and the adverse impact on regions in the United Kingdom hitherto in receipt of EU support.[4]

In Northern Ireland, the proposals were welcomed by local economic commentator and one-time member of the Committee of the Regions, John Simpson,[5] as 'the freshest piece of government thinking' seen for some time. Gordon Brown, John Prescott and Patricia Hewitt had 'cut through a maze of confused thinking' and provided 'a clearer vision of how to allow regions to develop their own policies' (within reasonable restraints). 'Gone', he suggested, 'will be the need for tedious submissions' and the 'maze of transferring money to Brussels to allocate it back to regions'. Simpson called his readers to scrutinise the proposals closely and to respond to them positively. He urged this, not only upon parties, but also upon the business and community sectors on the ground that attitudes to the proposals would be a test of the intent of a devolved government and of the claim that devolution was advantageous.[6]

### The Republic of Ireland as a channel to the EU for Northern Ireland?

Under the Northern Ireland Act, the NSMC has the power to identify common North–South interests in the EU and to find ways of these being communicated to the Council of Ministers. Laffan (2006, 182) argues that the wording of the Agreement (giving rise to the Act) was deliberately ambiguous,

> offering the prospect either that the views of the Council on EU matters could simply be noted by the relevant channels, or that at some future date members of the NSMC might participate in Irish delegations...

Before suspension, a plenary meeting of NSMC decided that, at each sectoral meeting of the NSMC, ministers might consider the EU dimension of North–South cooperation in that sector and that the European working group should bring forward an assessment of any EU issues that were likely to emerge. It deferred – to 'a date to be confirmed' – consideration of how the views of the NSMC could be reflected at EU meetings (Executive Press Release, 11 October 2002). Five days later, suspension intervened. Though the NSMC continued, it did so on a 'care-taker' basis.

In the Assembly, Dr Paisley, MLA, had argued that such a development would weaken the status of Northern Ireland as a separate entity from the south, prevent Northern Ireland from making its own case in association with the rest of the United Kingdom, and could be seen as an agenda driven by the Irish Government to promote reunification (Official Record, 2 July 2002; see also OR, 8 April 2002). The Deputy First

Minister pointed out that Northern Ireland's interests varied from being distinctive, to being similar to those of Ireland or similar to those of the United Kingdom. All possible channels must be used, including the MEPs, the JMCs, direct influence on UK ministers, and attendance with them at EU meetings. The NSMC added one more layer of advocacy (Official Record, 2 July 2002). Another potential layer may lie on the East–West axis.

### The beginnings of a two-island approach?

With or without devolution, there is the possibility of a two-island approach. Despite the collapse of devolved institutions, a way was found to retain the BIC in something more than 'care-taker' mode. It had the authority to discuss EU matters of common interest. It chose not to do so explicitly, though, inevitably, aspects of its work programme overlap with EU issues, particularly the environment (including Sellafield[7]).

The previously mentioned Belfast meeting in December 2003 of the 81 UK and Irish delegates to the Committee of the Regions was to enable all of them to learn about the priorities of the Irish Presidency and to discuss shared interests and cooperation on the future of the EU's cohesion policy. Their host, Councillor Ian Crozier, emphasised the importance of local government in the delivery of many EU initiatives and noted Belfast's aim to foster and maintain international alliances to promote the development agenda. Mr Pearson, as Minister for Europe, stressed the importance of a cohesive approach amongst those with similar interests and concerns, not only in the context of the two islands, but also through wider inter-regional links and pan-European networks (Executive Press Release, 9 December 2003).

Three-way coordination is most evident in the field of agriculture. Under devolution, the devolved Minister of Agriculture, Brid Rodgers, always operated in this manner – which led to a distinctive and successful containment of Northern Ireland from foot and mouth disease (according to the House of Lords, 2002, para. 23, inspite of rather than because of formal mechanisms). A direct rule example is that of Mr Pearson, this time as Minister of Agriculture (Executive Press Releases, 8 January 2004, 22 January 2004). He attended a regular meeting in January 2004 of UK counterparts, co-chaired by Mr Ben Bradshaw MP, Minister for Nature Conservation and Fisheries, and Lord Whitty. He briefed his colleagues on consultation in Northern Ireland over the 2003 CAP Reform Agreement. Equally, CAP reform was on the agenda at his meeting a few days later with the Irish Minister for Agriculture and Food, Mr Joe Walsh TD. They agreed to set up a joint working group to work on issues arising from CAP reform. They also discussed animal health issues, noting the development of complementary approaches to preventing the introduction of new diseases and policy convergence over Scrapie, BSE, contingency planning, cross-border fraud and a range of related actions. They announced their ultimate goal of an all-island animal health strategy to enable the free movement of animals, subject to EU rules.[8]

Another potential channel for a two-island approach lies in the British-Irish Inter-Parliamentary Body (BIIPB). Its meeting in Killarney in 2006 was unusual in leading to a public report of proceedings (BIIPB, 2006). Many issues with an EU dimension were discussed, including agriculture (see note 8), energy, environment (including Sellafield, see note 7), an Ireland-Wales INTERREG programme and a proposed new one involving Ireland, Scotland and Northern Ireland. However, despite the historic attendance of the DUP at part of the Killarney meeting and its indication that, under the right circumstances, it would become a full member, Unionist parties continued to boycott the BIIPB.

## Northern Ireland and the wider EU

### Northern Ireland initiatives in becoming more forward and outward looking

Over the years, Northern Ireland has taken a number of steps to promote itself on a wider stage. For example, soon after the establishment of the Executive, the First Minister, Deputy First Minister and departmental ministers visited President Chirac and German Foreign Minister, Joschka Fischer, to discuss new possibilities for inward investment. As indicated in the earlier reference to Belfast City Council's European Unit, local government also attempts to be more outward looking. The town of Bangor (North Down Borough Council), close to Belfast, hosted on 12 June 2003 the European 'Edge Cities' Conference. 'Edge Cities' partners include, not only Bangor, but also Helsinki, Stockholm, Lisbon, Athens, Fingal/Dublin, Croydon/London, Madrid and Copenhagen (Executive Press Release, 12 June 2003).

Enlargement was greeted with celebrations, not only in the Republic of Ireland (then holder of the EU Presidency) but also in Belfast. In the latter, a major exhibition was staged in St George's Market on 26–27 April 2004 with music, dance, language lessons and a video-link with Lithuania. At a gala reception in the Waterfront Hall on 27 April, a booklet, *The Amber Road: A Journey Through the New Countries of the European Union*, was launched.

A few days after the Bangor event, on 17 June 2003, the OFMDFM, in partnership with QUB, held a conference on *Forging Regional Links in Europe*. It was opened by Ian Pearson MP, who had to leave after his speech for a meeting of the Convention on the Future of Europe (see later). His speech addressed Northern Ireland's ability to operate effectively in the EU and to exchange ideas and build relations with other regions in other member states (Executive Press Release, 17 June 2003). Other speakers included the heads of the Northern Ireland and Scottish executive offices in Brussels, as well as the head of the Catalan office (a more civic body) in Brussels. The latter two presented a range of activities and practical partnerships with other regions that imply the need for an ambitious programme for Northern Ireland.

Perhaps with this and criticism of the absence of a 'civic' dimension to the Executive Office in Brussels in mind, Northern Ireland recently invested – jointly with Ireland and the private sector[9] – in the further refurbishment of the Louvain Institute. This is a former Franciscan College which, when first taken over in the 1980s, provided a place for people from Northern Ireland (and elsewhere) to learn about the EU. In its new development, it is to be 'an active resource contributing [along with the Brussels Office] to Northern Ireland's strategic policy objectives and raising the region's profile in Europe' (OFMDFM News Release, 8 June 2006).

### The Convention on the Future of Europe

The Assembly's criticisms of Northern Ireland's arrangements for handling EU affairs included concern about the capacity of the executive to develop a view internally and to have an impact on the wider debate about the future of Europe. On 29 May 2002, the Assembly Committee on the Centre (which 'shadowed' OFMDFM) decided to concentrate its attention on:

> a possible simplification of the Treaties; the delimitation of competences; subsidiarity; the status of the Charter of Fundamental Rights; how to achieve greater democracy in the EU; whether the Commission should have an elected President; and whether the European Council should meet in public. (Official Record, 29 May 2002)

The OFMDFM organised a public policy forum on 27 June. The keynote speaker, Minister Denis Haughey, emphasised the intention of OFMDFM to initiate a series of fora aimed at developing the debate on Northern Ireland in the EU. But a few months later, suspension intervened.

Northern Ireland's MEPs were conspicuous by their absence during the progress of the Convention. None of them was among the delegates or alternates. Only one of the thousand submissions had a Northern Irish name as a signatory, Jim Nicholson, MEP (Phinnemore, 2003). He was one of 18 signatories (including Jens-Peter Bonde, Georges Berthu and Dana Rosemary Scallion) of the Earl of Stockton's[10] Contribution to the Convention (European Convention Secretariat, 2003a). This criticised the Convention for failing to entrench the position of the nation state as the means of bringing democracy closer to the people. It contrasted with the aims of the Flanders Declaration, signed by 'constitutional regions', including Scotland, to secure acknowledgement of the regions in the EU and with one of the submissions by the UK Government.

### The constitutional treaty and regions

The UK proposals on the sections in the draft Constitutional Treaty dealing with regions were submitted to the Convention by the Minister for the Convention and Secretary of State for Wales, Peter Hain (European Convention Secretariat, 2003b). They were drawn up in consultation with the Scottish Parliament and the Welsh Assembly and Northern Ireland Executive and presented to the Convention in a Contribution by Peter Hain. Even though Northern Ireland institutions were suspended at the time, local politicians were consulted.

The Contribution proposed a strengthened role for regional influence in respect of any initiatives that had to be implemented at a regional level. As a result of representations by the United Kingdom and others, the draft Constitutional Treaty, published in May 2003, did refer to regional and local authorities in its reference to subsidiarity (Title III: Union Competences and Actions). It also strengthened the Committee of the Regions by, among other things, allowing it to go to the European Court of Justice when it believed that EU legislation was inconsistent with the principle of subsidiarity. However, in requiring the Commission to take account of regional and local authorities, the onus was put on national parliaments to consult regional parliaments and it is for the former to give notice when it was thought that subsidiarity has been violated (Protocol on the Application of the Principles of Subsidiarity and Proportionality).

The Draft Constitutional Treaty became a Treaty when it was signed by Heads of Government on 29 October 2004 but, though ratified in many states, 'no' votes in referendums in two founding states, the Netherlands and France, mean that it has not come into effect. Had it done so, the points above about the primacy of national parliaments would have meant but a modest impact on an increased capacity of Scotland, Wales and Northern Ireland to act in the EU (Lodge, 2003). In Lodge's view, the effects would be felt more in those countries whose regions are, as noted by the House of Lords, less well positioned than those in the United Kingdom. But, as also noted by the House of Lords, the reasonably smooth way in which things have worked so far may depend too much on informal relationships. In conclusion, this chapter turns to a policy area where both those relationships and the formal arrangements could be put to the test.

## Policy on the euro as a potential test of devolution

It was an aim in the first Programme of Government that the Northern Ireland Executive would have a unified policy on the single currency, or the euro. Had the Executive had a longer life, it may have been difficult to maintain unity. There are different party attitudes and, as noted earlier, Northern Ireland has a distinctive position as the one part of the United Kingdom to share a land border with another state which is in the euro zone. Indeed, newspaper reports on the introduction of the euro to Ireland in 2002 were headlined by such examples as: 'You can keep the UK out of the euro but you can't keep the euro out of the UK' (Nicola Byrne, *Scotland on Sunday*, 13 January 2002). Similar headlines appeared the following January (Chris Ashmore in the *Irish Times*, 4 January 2003).

### Party positions and government actions

In December 2001, Jane Morrice of the Women's Coalition put a motion to the Assembly calling for it to ask the UK Government to permit Northern Ireland to operate a voluntary dual currency system. On this occasion – at the point of transfer from 'shadow' to full devolution – Sinn Féin was silent. But since then it has been more explicit. In its *Ard Fheis* (annual conference) on 28 March 2003, it passed two motions, one in favour of something like Jane Morrice's proposal. The language of the motions was different from hers – more suitably Republican. They noted the real preference for 'Irish monetary autonomy' and an economy democratically controlled by Irish people. At the same time, they recognised the 'reality for the foreseeable future' of the euro in 'the 26 County area'. One, therefore, proposed the euro as a 'co-equal' (with sterling) currency for the 'Six County area' and the other a 'yes' vote in the future UK referendum.[11]

The SDLP favours the euro as does the Alliance Party, provided entry is at the right exchange rate. Officially, the UUP is against, though some individual members differ. The DUP robustly opposes it. Dr Paisley described a visit to Belfast by the then Foreign Secretary, Jack Straw (in connection with the Convention on the Future of Europe) as a 'touting exercise' for the Prime Minister's 'backdoor agenda' to bring in the euro and lead the United Kingdom into a 'centralised super state' (*Newsletter*, 28 September 2002).

In September 2003, Ian Pearson, as Direct Rule Minister for both Europe and Finance and Personnel, chaired the first meeting of the Northern Ireland Standing Committee on Euro Preparations. The establishments of the Committee followed from the statement by the Chancellor of the Exchequer on 9 June about the stepping-up of preparatory work for potential membership of the euro zone. The committee comprises representatives of business and finance sectors, some voluntary organisations and local and regional government personnel; that is:

Confederation of British Industry, NI;
NI Chamber of Commerce and Industry;
NI Bankers' Association;
Institute of Directors;
Federation of Small Businesses;
Institute of Chartered Accountants (Ulster Society);
NI Tourism Industry Confederation;
NI Centre for Competitiveness;
Chartered Institute for Marketing;
NI Committee of the Irish Congress of Trade Unions;
General Consumer Council for NI;
NI Council for Voluntary Action;
NI Local Government Association;
Head of the NI Civil Service, and Officials from the Departments
    of Agriculture and Regional Development, Enterprise Trade and
    Industry, Finance and Personnel and HM Treasury.

The Secretary of State for Northern Ireland sits on the UK Standing Committee on Euro-Preparations which is overseeing UK-wide preparations, while the local Committee's role is to oversee preparations in Northern Ireland and to formulate Northern Ireland's response to the Chancellor's National Changeover Plan.

## Public opinion on the euro

As noted earlier, the EU context of territorial politics in the United Kingdom works satisfactorily, less because of formal arrangements, than because of the dominance of the same party at the centre and in Scotland and Wales – though not, of course, in Northern Ireland in the periods of non-suspension. But, though distinctive, Northern Ireland may not be alone, even in the context of Labour dominance throughout Great Britain, in sharing with Scotland, in particular, a slightly different view on the euro from that of the centre.

Research (Northern Ireland Life and Times Survey, 2002) on public attitudes shows that, though there is not a majority of public opinion in favour of the euro as a single currency, there may be less scepticism than in England. In Northern Ireland, 47 per cent of people would like to keep the pound as the only UK currency. Fewer – 35 per cent – would like the euro as a single currency. But 13 per cent would like a dual system which, added to those who are pro-euro, is a point more than those in favour of the pound alone. 50 per cent of those in the age group 18–24 wanted a shift to the euro and 12 per cent of them wanted both to be there.

Prior to the Chancellor's statement in June 2003 on the five tests, the Northern Ireland branch of the Britain in Europe movement was active in trying to pre-empt what was widely expected; that the Chancellor would say the tests had not been met – in effect delaying entry and ruling out a referendum until the next parliament. Members of the suspended Assembly, including a UUP member, wrote to the Secretary of State for Northern Ireland, stressing the importance to the regional economy, noting majorities in favour of the euro among people in key sectors and urging him to persuade the cabinet that there should be a referendum 'on this momentous question' in the current parliament. In Scotland, the then Secretary of State for Scotland, Helen Liddell became the first cabinet minister to criticise the Treasury, arguing in the *Sunday Telegraph* on 11 May 2003 and in a speech in Edinburgh that 'such a momentous decision' should be taken by the whole cabinet. She also argued that not entering the euro zone would have an adverse impact on the Scottish economy (Lodge, 2003). A Scottish National Party MSP tabled a motion calling on the government to publish its evidence and conclusions about the euro 'specifically in relation to Scotland and the other nations and regions of the UK' (Lodge, 2003).

It may be because of such pressures that the Chancellor was more upbeat about the topic than most people had expected, allowing both those for and against the euro to claim that his view reflected theirs.

## Conclusion

As noted, the Agreement bears the hallmarks of the EU design. Robin Wilson notes that 'after three decades of membership of the European Union, Northern Ireland is inextricably entwined in a "variable geometry" of relationships with the rest of Ireland, the rest of the UK and the rest of Europe. Either/or "sovereignty" choices are now remote from reality' (*Irish Times*, 5 March 2003). Though local political discourse is still too often dominated by zero-sum game understandings of what is at stake, these interconnections were recognised by Des Browne, then Parliamentary Under-Secretary of State responsible for equality issues. In welcoming the panel of experts appointed to advise on the development of Northern Ireland's single equality bill, he noted that the aim was 'to harmonise the legislation as far as practicable, taking into account developments in the EU, GB and the Republic of Ireland' (Executive Press Release, 19 February 2003). He, of course, was a Direct Rule Minister. Only time will tell whether a devolved Northern Ireland Government can benefit from the opportunities outlined by the House of Lords to promote interests, participate in wider developments and to engage with other regions in the EU.

## Notes

1. The Northern Ireland Centre in Europe (NICE) was what Sloat (2001, 444) calls a 'membership organisation', distinguishing such offices from official ones with diplomatic status. NICE was created in 1991 by a coalition of the Law Society, Chamber of Commerce, most district councils (on a cross party basis), employers, trades unions and the voluntary sector. It was closed in 2001 when the Executive Office opened. It might be noted that the House of Lords (2002) noted the advantages to a region of a situation in which diplomatic and non-diplomatic delegations shared the same building and where the diplomatic delegations had close links with the office of the UK representative to the EU (UKREP) (see also Laffan, 2006; Meehan, 2006; Trench, 2001).
2. That is, Queen's University Belfast and Democratic Dialogue, a Northern Ireland think tank – which, together, set up this forum for groups and individuals with an interest in EU policies and programmes as they affect Northern Ireland.
3. From devolution until 2007, the UK governing party, Labour, was in power (alone or in coalition) in Scotland and Wales. Reliance on pre-existing networks of goodwill may not be possible when governments of different colours are elected at the centre and in the devolved administrations.
4. For example, 'Brown wants EU to hand back £20bn to regions', *Times*, 6 March 2003; 'Brown calls for EU aid funds to be repatriated', *Independent*, 6 March 2003.

5. 'An overdue plan to modernise regional policy', *Belfast Telegraph*, 17 March 2003; see also Robin Morton, 'Wind of change for EU funding', *Belfast Telegraph*, 17 March 2003.
6. In another of his articles, however, he seems less sceptical of devolution; 'Scots have a clear lead!', *Belfast Telegraph*, 17 March 2003. Here, he says the document offers 'a very revealing comparison of the state of current regional policies in Scotland Wales and Northern Ireland'. The summary by Scotland's devolved Executive of its policies is presented in 'language that spells out innovation, energy and imagination'. But, 'sadly, the very short summary of policies in Northern Ireland is so brief as to be unhelpful', appearing to have been written as a 'filler'. 'Where', he asks, 'was Ian Pearson, [direct rule] Minister for all economic issues, when this was proofed in his departments?'
7. The Irish Government (and others) wants Sellafield to be closed down. The EU, too, is worried with the Energy Commissioner, Loyola de Palaccio, warning the UK Government in 2004 of stiff penalties when the plant again failed to comply with standards for the disposal of nuclear waste (*Belfast Telegraph*, 23 April 2004, 8 May 2004).
8. However, when members of the BIIPB asked about the possibility of a common North–South policy on CAP to alleviate the challenges faced by small farmers, they were told that this was not possible because of different systems of farm subsidies in Ireland and the United Kingdom (BIIPB, 2006, 65). Also, the United Kingdom seems not greatly excited by agriculture; the only disappointment expressed at the meeting was that the work of the Agriculture Committee of the BIIPB was seriously hampered by the fact that the UK members had 'no interest in the farming situation whether good bad or indifferent' (Seymour Crawford, TD, BIIPB, 2006, 68).
9. NI's contribution was 16 per cent of the total cost, Ireland's 41 per cent, with the remaining 43 per cent coming from private sponsorship (OFMDFM News Release, 8 June 2006).
10. The Earl of Stockton, MEP was an alternate member of the Convention.
11. The author is grateful for a sight of the texts to John Farrell, then director of the Northern Ireland branch of the Britain in Europe campaign.

# Bibliography

British-Irish Inter-Parliamentary Body (2006) Official Report of Thirty-Second Plenary Conference of the British-Irish Inter-Parliamentary Body, 24–25 April 2006. Dublin: TSO. Available at Norwich: The Stationery Office.

Coakley, J., B. Laffan and J. Todd (eds) (2006) *Renovation or Revolution? New Territorial Politics in Ireland and the United Kingdom*. Dublin: University College Press.

Cox, M., A. Guelke and F. Stephens (eds) (2000) *A Farewell to Arms? From 'Long War' to Long Peace in Northern Ireland*. Manchester: Manchester University Press.

European Convention Secretariat (2003a) Stockton, 'Reaffirming the Aims of the Laeken Declaration', Contribution 365 by the Earl of Stockton, Alternate Member of the Convention, to the Convention on the Future of Europe,

CONV 808/03. Brussels: The European Convention, 16 June 2003. Available at www.europeqan-convention.eu.int.

European Convention Secretariat (2003b) 'Europe and the Regions', Contribution 221/03 by Mr Peter Hain, Member of the Convention. Brussels: European Convention, CONV 526/03, 3 February 2003. Available at www.europeqan-convention.eu.int.

Gillespie, P. (2000) 'From Anglo-Irish to British-Irish Relations', in M. Cox, A. Guelke and F. Stephens (eds), *A Farewell to Arms? From 'Long War' to Long Peace in Northern Ireland*. Manchester: Manchester University Press, pp. 180–98.

Hainsworth, P. (1999) 'Northern Ireland in the European Community', in M. Keating and B. Jones (eds) *Regions in the European Community*. Oxford: Clarendon Press, pp. 109–32.

Hazell, R. (2000) 'Intergovernmental Relations; Whitehall Rules OK?', in R. Hazell (ed.), *The State and the Nations: The First Year of Devolution in the United Kingdom*. London: The Constitution Unit/Imprint Academic, pp.149–82.

Hodgett, S. and E. Meehan (2003) 'Multilevel Governance in the European Union: the Case of Northern Ireland', in J. Magone (ed.), *Regional Institutions and Governance in the European Union*. Westport: Praeger, pp. 135–52.

House of Lords Select Committee on the Constitution (2002) Devolution: Inter-Institutional Relations in the United Kingdom. Session 2002–03, Second Report. HL Paper 28, 17 December. London: The Stationery Office.

Keating, M. and B. Jones (eds) (1999) *Regions in the European Community*. Oxford: Clarendon Press.

Kennedy, D. and M. Murphy (2001) 'Plus ca change: Stormont, Devolution and the European Union'. Paper presented at European Liaison Seminar. Belfast: QUB and Democratic Dialogue.

Laffan, B. (2006) 'The European Context: A New Political Dimension in Ireland, North and South', in J. Coakley, B. Laffan, and J. Todd (eds) *Renovation or Revolution? New Territorial Politics in Ireland and the United Kingdom*. Dublin: University College Press, pp. 166–84.

Lodge, G. (2003) 'Devolution and the Centre'. Quarterly Report for ESRC/Leverhulme funded programme, Nations and Regions. The Dynamics of Devolution. London: The Constitution Unit.

McCall, C. and A. Williamson (2000) 'Fledgling Social Partnership in the Irish Border Region: European Union "Community Initiatives" and the Voluntary Sector', *Policy & Politics*, 29:3, pp. 397–410.

McGowan, L. and M. Murphy (2003) 'Northern Ireland Under Devolution: The Challenge of Institutional Adaptation to EU Policy Formulation', *Regional and Federal Studies*, 13:1, 81–99.

Magone, J. (ed.) (2003) *Regional Institutions and Governance in the European Union*. Westport: Praeger.

Meehan, E. (2000) 'The Europeanisation of the Irish Question', in M. Cox, A. Guelke and F. Stephens (eds), *A Farewell to Arms? From 'Long War' to Long Peace in Northern Ireland*. Manchester: Manchester University Press, pp. 199–213.

Meehan, E. (2006) 'The European Context: Changing Forms of Territorial politics in the United Kingdom', in J. Coakley, B. Laffan and J. Todd (eds), *Renovation or Revolution? New Territorial Politics in Ireland and the United Kingdom*. Dublin: University College Press, pp.147–65.

Murphy, M. (2002) *The European Union Dimension to Devolution in Northern Ireland*. PhD Thesis submitted at QUB.

Northern Ireland Life and Times Survey (2002) Europe Module. Available at www.ark.ac.uk/nilt/2002/Europeecuview2.html.

O'Donnell, R. (1999) 'Fixing the Institutions', in R. Wilson (ed.), *No Frontiers: North-South Integration in Ireland*. Belfast: Democratic Dialogue, pp 70–3.

Office of First Minister and Deputy First Minister (2004) *Taking Our Place in Europe: Northern Ireland's European Strategy 2004–2006*. Belfast. Available at www.ofmdfm.gov.uk/europe.pdf.

Phinnemore, D. (2003) 'The Draft Treaty Establishing a Constitution for Europe'. Paper presented at a conference on From Convention to Constitution: Northern Ireland and the Future of Europe, QUB. 18 September.

Sloat, A. (2002) 'Reconfiguring Scottish Politics: Domestic Governance v. European Influence', *Northern Ireland Political Quarterly*, 53:4, 435–55.

Trench, A. (2001) 'Intergovernmental Relations a Year On; Whitehall Still Rules UK', in A. Trench (ed.), *The State of the Nation 2001: The Second Year of Devolution in the United Kingdom*. London: The Constitution Unit/Imprint Academic, pp.153–74.

United Kingdom Government (2003) *A Modern Regional Policy for the United Kingdom*. London: Stationery Office.

# Part II
# Civil Society

# 5
# Models of Civil Society and Their Implications for the Northern Ireland Peace Process[1]

*Christopher Farrington*

In the search for an explanation of a negotiated settlement to an apparently intractable ethnic conflict, several authors looked beyond the political elites in Northern Ireland. They argued that, as the political elites had not changed (in either personnel or ideas) over the course of about 20 years, we must look to other social and political actors and other structural changes in order to explain the successful conclusion of the negotiations in 1996–98. One of these was the international environment and actors (discussed in the first section of this book) and the other was civil society within Northern Ireland, which is the subject of this second section. Guelke, in particular, has stressed the importance of two civil society initiatives in the 1990s: the Opsahl Commission of 1992 and the 'Yes' Campaign for the 1998 referendum (Guelke, 2003). However, since the Agreement was concluded, civil society seemed less prominent in agitating for political change. An obvious question that was raised was, if civil society was important in the successful conclusion of the Agreement, then how has it influenced or failed to influence the crises of the implementation of the Agreement? It is this question which this chapter seeks to answer.

At the outset it must be stressed that the contribution of civil society to the peace process has been 'indirect rather than direct, gradual rather than dramatic... The role of such organisations has been osmosis-like, and almost imperceptible in its effect' (Cochrane and Dunn, 1997). Even those who are most enthusiastic advocates of the position outlined above do not credit civil society with causal importance. As one member of an Intermediary Funding Body stated: 'the worst-case scenario is that we created the mood music for progress to be possible'.[2] Thus, civil society contributed to the environment in the 1990s which led to the Agreement but was not a determining factor. It must also be pointed out that the role of civil society is infrequently considered in academic analyses of the peace process, as these tend to rely heavily on accounts of journalists, who have underplayed the role of civil society organisations and formulated a highly elitist account of the process. The attempt to extend the narrative of the peace process to include civil society has, however, been made at the expense of maintaining a narrow and elitist view of the peace process. This view is maintained by the focus on the relationship between civil society and the formal political process but this has been at the expense of a proper understanding of the contribution of these civil society initiatives and the wide array of functions and roles which it performs. The Opsahl Commission's contribution to Northern Ireland was in the development, if not creation, of a public sphere. This contribution was then continued by organisations inspired by this process, such as Democratic Dialogue and Community Dialogue.[3] The 'Yes' Campaign, while connected in terms of personnel and motivations, can be seen as part of an activist discourse connected to ideas within civil society about their connection to the peace process and the democratic process.

However, even these civil society-centred accounts fail to account for civil society in its totality. There must be a holistic account of civil society's role in Northern Ireland in order to appreciate its impact and influence on the practice of politics. In some instances this may seem unrelated to the formal peace process conducted behind the gates of Leeds Castle, Weston Park or St Andrews but that process became elitist in the extreme and the practical import of that elitist approach affected civil society groups, which altered their thinking on their role within the political system. Indeed, there is a disjuncture between the legal and administrative framework of devolution, which necessitates a high level of civil society input, and the political negotiations, which deliberately sought to exclude as many people as possible.

The central argument of this chapter is that political change is important to civil society and is an explanatory factor in the seemingly diminished role of civil society in the Northern Ireland peace process. This can be seen by examining a variety of different ideas of civil society and their corresponding outlets in Northern Ireland. In this way, the Agreement is shown to be an important juncture not merely for its significance as an historical deal between Unionism and Nationalism and the respective implications but because it fundamentally altered the administrative framework and necessitated a fundamental change within civil society in terms of how it interacted with political institutions and political actors.

## Discourses of civil society

The concept of civil society can be thought of in two ways: 'civil' as an adjective to 'society' or 'civil society' as a noun. The first is the concern of much of the theoretical literature on civil society and is linked with historical and theoretical notions of 'civility' and 'barbarity' (see essays in Keane, 1988) and is connected to the question of violence within society (Keane, 1998).[4] The second idea, civil society as a noun, is more complex and includes a range of philosophical and empirical definitions and problems. It is well noted that the concept had fallen into disuse but was revised by movements in Eastern Europe during the collapse of communism, most notably Solidarity in Poland. Since then the concept has become utilised as an explanatory factor in the study of democracy, ethnic conflict, globalisation and public policy. It is this second notion which will be the concern of this chapter.

The definition of civil society depends much upon which area is under investigation. The common definition is that which appears in the *Oxford Dictionary of Politics*: the 'set of intermediate associations which are neither the state nor the (extended family); civil society therefore includes voluntary associations and firms and other corporate bodies' (McLean, 1996, 74). This is obviously an exceptionally wide definition and encompasses virtually all avenues of social, economic and political life and, as Michael Edwards observes, 'an idea that means everything probably means nothing' (Edwards, 2004, 3). Political theorists who have addressed the abstract connotations of civil society have also been unable to effectively narrow the subject. Michael Walzer, for instance, echoes the dictionary definition: 'The words "civil society" name the space of unco-erced human association and also the set of relational networks—formed for the sake of family, faith, interest and ideology—that fill this space' (Walzer, 1991, 293). Within this it is possible to discern several further analytical distinctions. Charles Taylor, for instance, argues that there are three modes of civil society: a minimal sense, where civil society is not under the tutelage of state power; a stronger sense, where civil society exists where society can structure itself and co-ordinate its actions through such associations; and as a supplement to the second, where the ensemble of associations can significantly determine or inflect the course of state policy (Taylor, 1990, 98).[5] It is important to make these distinctions because definitions are crucial to assessing the influence or otherwise of civil society in political processes.

Mary Kaldor and Michael Edwards have independently argued that there are several different discourses of civil society, which rarely engage with each other. These discourses are mirrored by discourses within Northern Ireland, although they are frequently not expressed as such. Moreover, the case of Northern Ireland necessitates an integration of these approaches because it problematises many of the underlying assumptions. Kaldor identifies five versions: *societas civilus* (civil as an adjective), *bürgerliche Gesellschaft* (Hegel and Marx's ideas that civil society included all organised life between the state and the family), activist (civil society is about political emancipation and is connected with Eastern European and Latin American notions), neoliberal (associational democracy) and postmodern (civil society as an arena of pluralism and contestation and includes elements of incivility as well as civility) (Kaldor, 2003, 6–12). These theoretical discourses of civil society are also complemented by vernacular discourses. In particular, two are relevant in Northern Ireland: civil society as a site of conflict transformation and the 'third way' discourse on civil society's role in public policy. This chapter will address four discourses which are relevant:

- The neoliberal discourse – civil society (broadly defined) is important for the promotion of democracy.
- The activist discourse – civil society is in tension with the state and has the possibility to be an important agent of change.
- The public sphere discourse.
- The conflict transformation discourse.

It should be acknowledged that these categories are far from exclusive and that a strong notion of the role of civil society would integrate these discourses (see Edwards, 2004) and, indeed, activists and practitioners within Northern Ireland frequently do integrate these ideas. The distinctions are therefore analytical. In addition, the noticeable feature of the interviews for this study is the consensus exhibited about where civil society is situated and its role in the political process, although clearly not about specific issues, which is the result of a long process of dialogue and discussion.

## The neoliberal discourse

The neoliberal discourse derives from Putnam's writings on the connection between civil society and associational life. Putnam defines civil society in the broadest possible sense, as associational life (Putnam, 2000); and several of the respondents from various sections of civil society who were interviewed for this study also defined civil society in this way. Putnam argues that associational membership creates social capital, which is the bond of trust and reciprocity generated by the positive benefits of group membership, and this has real value. I am going to discuss one particular institutional critique of Putnam's work in order to analyse how civil society and the peace process have interacted with each other.

The institutional critique argues that Putnam fails to appreciate the relationship of the state and civil society. For instance, Lowndes and Wilson (2001) argue that he overlooks the state's role in creating and promoting social capital. Putnam's initial work on Italy argued that strong associational life led to a better quality of democracy (Putnam, 1993). However, the experience of Northern Ireland is that civil society is more dependent on the state than vice versa. In particular, during the periodic suspensions of the Assembly, civil society was essentially reactionary.

> Well for the community sector obviously, I think almost unanimously, people will respond that that's pretty bloody disastrous, irrespective of the political slant of individuals within the community sector but that does not necessarily reflect the feelings of wider society and that's a very important statement to make because the community sector has its own particular agenda and a concern not just for what's happening in wider society but for its own future. The stop-start nature of this process spreads confusion widely throughout our sector that makes planning for the future extremely difficult and it has an impact on funding hence employment.[6]

Moreover, there is a strong argument that if civil society can support democracy, it can also be used to undermine it (Foley and Edwards, 1996). We can see this from Berman's work on the Weimar Republic, which found that Germany at this time had a strong associational life but which ultimately ended in a totalitarian dictatorship. Berman thus suggested that it was not civil society *per se* that was important but that it may help if political institutionalisation was strong and neutral or even a hindrance if political institutionalisation was weak, as happened in Germany (Berman, 1997). In Northern Ireland, democratic ideals have been enshrined within the political culture and the political parties, thus ensuring that totalitarian dictatorship was an unlikely outcome. For example, one author has claimed that politics in the 1970s was marked by strong claims to democratic ideals, despite the ongoing political violence (Bourke, 2003). However, since the proroguing of Stormont in 1972, there have been no real local representative political institutions and therefore the Assembly which was established in 1998 was essentially a new institution.

Northern Ireland therefore seems an ideal test case; it has a strong civil society but with new political institutions. It is worth briefly reflecting on the monumental changes that the Agreement introduced to the governance of Northern Ireland. Indeed, the Agreement was as big a change to the governance of Northern Ireland as the proroguing of Stormont in 1972. There is perhaps an argument to be made that it introduced governance *per se* into Northern Ireland. The direct rule structures, while assuming the appearance of permanency, were imperfect, highly unaccountable, undemocratic and ultimately designed to be short term and temporary. As Peter Hain argued: 'Direct Rule was a 1970s solution to a 1970s problem.'[7] Moreover, the governmental framework of Northern Ireland was not designed for direct rule structures and therefore there was a very weak local government system, a proliferation of quangos, very little scrutiny of legislation and part-time ministers. The Agreement, if it was about nothing else, was nothing short of a major overhaul of this system. Nearly 30 years of political behaviour had to be changed, quite dramatically and quite quickly, in all parts of the administration of Northern Ireland. Institutional rules and conventions disappeared; old relationships were rendered meaningless and new ones had to be constructed. Moreover, for many civil society groups which were connected with the political parties, the dynamics of those relationships changed: politicians now had power and responsibility and were no longer in the same position as those in civil society, whose position on the outside of government had not altered. In addition to the changing status of relationships and the changing situation of civil society groups, the Agreement also heralded significant changes to the *practice* of government through Section 75 of the Northern Ireland Act and the establishment of various other institutions such as the Northern Ireland Human Rights Commission, the Equality Commission and the Civic Forum.

Civil society, in all its forms, was affected by these changes, perhaps to a greater degree than the political parties. As one interviewee described the situation before devolution:

> Civil society played a more advanced role in the governance of Northern Ireland than I think would be the case in other areas. I think it really did fill for a long time that democratic deficit whereby

Northern Ireland most of the way through direct rule has really been a technocracy—basically . . . run by civil servants with some oversight from British ministers.[8]

Another described the change:

The changeover was challenging. We probably had an easier ride under a direct rule administration because those ministers had much less time to spend here . . . and needed to find out what the situation was and what was going to work and what wasn't going to work and what hadn't worked in the past; a lot of civil servants were quite approachable in that it was easier for them to do their job if they were actually finding out from us what we knew and what we would suggest and so changing from that to what was a slightly more . . . potentially suspicious environment with politicians that we probably hadn't paid a great deal of attention to before. Some organisations worked very closely with local councils on local issues but political representatives who weren't working on social and economic issues at local council level were very much focused on constitutional and security issues at Westminster and there was no meeting point for us there, it was only when they started to turn their eyes towards the actual governance of Northern Ireland that we came into their radar and they came into our radar.[9]

What then was civil society's effect on the new devolved institutions? First, a comprehensive assessment requires a different research project, which would look to track suggestions and proposals from civil society into the legislation. Anecdotally, there is evidence to suggest that civil society was important in initiatives such as the Children's Commissioner. However, it could be hypothesised that civil society's existing relationship with direct rule institutions would not provide the required support for the new institutions established under the Agreement. This hypothesis, however, is not confirmed by this research. Civil society has shown itself to be flexible and adaptive, if nothing else, during the periodic suspensions and, by most accounts, politicians and members of civil society had developed good working relationships and the progress of those relationships were frustrated by suspension.

### Relationships and policy

What is significant about the nature of the relationships between civil society and the politicians is that they centred on policy issues, as opposed to the broader political issues involved in getting to the Agreement in the first place. This change was entirely due to the changing context created by the institutionalisation of the Agreement but it is worth bearing in mind that it was merely a change in the relationship between civil society and politics rather than a change in the role of civil society. One of the legacies of direct rule has been that civil society has developed sophisticated public policy experience, which the political parties have not.

> What we are trying the do is try to feed into the nascent political process the social policy expertise on social and economic issues that we have built up over the years. Because we're not elected, we will always have a role in a democracy but we're not the politicians and it was never our intention to provide an alternative political process. What we want to be able to do is to step back into our role as the healthy watchdog voice and allow politicians to take over their jobs. There's a certain amount of hostility and suspicion there but there's no denying that a great deal of the policy expertise resides in this sector rather than in the political sector in Northern Ireland because a lot of people came to work in the sector rather than move into mainstream politics. So, there's been a rebalancing of relationships post Agreement and a lot of pro-active work trying to influence politicians and gear them up to specific issues and on the other side sometimes a great willingness to learn and to see what policy needs to be undertaken and, sometimes, a great suspicion kind of 'oh, well hands off, the professionals are here now; we don't need to hear that from you'.[10]

This was particularly noticeable when the policy manifesto of the Northern Ireland Council for Voluntary Action (NICVA) is compared with the manifestoes of the political parties.[11]

It is the policy role of civil society in Northern Ireland, which links the neoliberal discourse on civil society to the 'third way' ideas, that came to prominence in Europe in the 1990s. Whereas Putnam saw the lines of influence reaching from civil society into politics, Giddens argued that the lines of influence ran in both directions: 'State and civil society should act in partnership, each to facilitate, but also to act as a control upon, the other' (Giddens, 1998, 79). Civil society was the mechanism by which the state could 'democratise democracy': 'Downward democratisation presumes the renewal of civil society' (Giddens, 1998, 77). This discourse on civil society is perhaps more conservative than the radical and optimistic versions contained within the Eastern European discourse and is closer to what theorists such as Taylor or Young would understand by the concept. Here, the relationship with the state is kept in focus; civil society is not about replacing or providing opposition to the state as it is recognised that the state is the most important player in allocating resources and in adjudicating between various factions within society. Instead, civil society is able to influence state policies and goals through a variety of mechanisms. When theorists were analysing the possibilities for such influence in the 1990s, media campaigns and lobbying were the most effective avenues for civil society groups. However, the context has changed since the late 1990s; Tony Blair's Labour government and his ideological 'third way' project have placed additional emphasis on the input from civil society. This has been built upon by devolution in the United Kingdom, which has altered the legislative framework of public policy decision-making; the government is now legally obliged to consult with all relevant groups when it is making legislation.[12]

## The Civic Forum

The one exception to the benign relationships which were being developed was the Civic Forum. The Forum was initially the subject of much excitement and attention. As one interviewee noted, there had been 'bizarrely more debate about the Forum than the Assembly or the Executive'.[13] The blame for the failure of the Civic Forum can be laid at many doors – the politicians, the members of the Forum, the various sectors that were represented on or nominated to the Forum, the civil service – but the arguments of many is that the Forum failed, at least in part, because civil society was ambivalent about it. The Civic Forum was the institution established by the Agreement, over which civil society was able to have a direct influence. It was proposed by the Women's Coalition, a party firmly informed by a civil society ethos (Fearon, 1999), and was effectively left to its own devices by the politicians when it was established. This is not to underestimate the effects of the politicians when they were given tasks in relation to the Forum, specifically constructing the composition: 'Well it wasn't a perfect design. It was given to us in its current form. We wouldn't have selected people from our sector under the 18 categories that were handed down to us by the First and Deputy First Minister.'[14] In addition, there were wildly different ideas as to how it should function. Members of civil society had discussed the possibilities of the Forum:

> After the Agreement the thing I was involved in was the idea of a Civic Forum and New Agenda drew up a consultation document, got some key people together to talk about it...and we got some responses from people which basically proposed a Civic Forum, as we

described it, based on a model of negotiated governance ... but what actually emerged was ... a different animal which was somehow about representing all works of civil society life. Whereas ... in my mind representation came through voting not through something like this so ... basing it on section 75 groups and PAFT [Policy Appraisal and Fair Treatment] and that kind of thing; there was a lot of talk of those kinds of equalities and representations and so on, which to my mind didn't make an awful lot of sense. I think as a result Business, for example, didn't take it seriously or didn't take it as the most serious Forum for them to be involved in, where they would sit down with trade unions and others and hammer out what it is that society needs; they'll do their negotiating elsewhere and there is an Economic Development Forum which is run by the DETI and that was a shame I thought because it was a missed opportunity.[15]

The chair of the Forum described the process:

Through Democratic Dialogue there was a group of people meeting who obviously discussed the aftermath of any agreement that we came to and I think it was through that. And the idea of a Civic Forum came through the Women's Coalition who took that up and put it into play politically. So it came in from left field if you like to the negotiations and almost at the 11th and the half hour if you look at the record. So it was an idea which was around that civic society needed some connectivity with the new political scene and with the new assembly and with the new devolved government and administration.[16]

The Democratic Dialogue discussions came to the conclusion that any Civic Forum should aim to embody principles of negotiated governance, providing the Executive with information and inputs from people affected by the policies it was implementing.[17] While civil society appeared to be well versed in this rationale, the politicians – even those favourable towards the institution – did not appear to buy into (or be involved in) these discussions. Ideas on its role varied from including all relevant sections of society, which led to some meaningless categories, to providing ownership of the process for civil society to providing some kind of unformulated opposition in the absence of an opposition in the Assembly.[18] In the end, the Forum did none of these things. It was affected more than any other institution by suspension. While North–South bodies and the Assembly were given funding under care and maintenance legislation, the Forum was treated crudely and had its resources pulled immediately. Some members argued that the Forum should be put into the same status as the North–South bodies but this suggestion was not endorsed by all members.

However, the Forum became entangled in a wide array of vested interests, some of which were from civil society. The prominence of the community sector clashed with its established lines of influence. The community sector representatives were not those with the greatest political clout and those individuals continued to have access to ministers (direct rule and devolved). Moreover, the importance of the Forum was compromised by the consultation process under Section 75 of the Northern Ireland Act 1998, which almost negated the need for such a body. Civil society was thus offered a wide variety of possible avenues of influence, of which the Civic Forum was the least attractive. Therefore, while the Forum had its own internal divisions, the politicians may have been suspicious and the civil service awkward, the Forum ultimately failed because civil society found other ways of fulfilling the role which they had assigned to it and which did not involve their interests being mediated through a body which they did not control.

## The activist discourse

The emergence of civil society in Eastern Europe in the 1980s was a cause of great excitement and enthusiasm for the possibilities of civil society. The Eastern European discourse influenced a number of inter-related areas. Some authors have suggested that Eastern Europe, and particularly Hungary, demonstrates how private business is a force for political change by horizontally integrating civil society and therefore empowering it *vis-à-vis* the state (Wank, 1995, 60). Others, examining Poland, have argued that there was a political programme underlying Solidarity which had a holistic critique of the Communist system and also a communal ideology (Wesolowski, 1995, 113). The actual nature and development of civil society in Eastern Europe is perhaps less easily generalised to places where the state is more benevolent to civil society[19] but the Eastern European example showed the possibilities of civil society as an agent of social and political change. Civil society was seen as providing a plural space in tension with hierarchical forms of government and therefore intrinsically deepening democracy. In Eastern Europe, the very existence of civil society groups provided an alternative locus of political power and an intrinsic challenge to the state. This has been taken even further by the Zapatistas in the Chiapas region of Mexico, who have formulated a radical conception of democracy based solely on civil society and involving the removal of the state (Baker, 2003). Academics are also prone to endorsing this optimistic view of civil society; as John Keane points out, many who work in or study civil society are uncritical optimists about its potentialities and tend to privilege it over ideas of the state (Keane, 1998). The Eastern European model can be seen as the originator of much of this optimism, which was continued by some of the modest but important successes of trans-national civil society groups (Florini, 2003, 119–42). However, there are other ways in which civil society can be influential and an important agent of change without necessarily being in opposition or tension with the state. Civil society bodies can be agents for change within the society they operate.[20] In this version of the civil society discourse, we are primarily discussing how civil society can change the political system, rather than wider societal change.

Northern Ireland experienced civil society activity on this level during the civil rights campaign but the subsequent polarisation meant that the tension between the state and society was not mediated by civil society groups but descended into violence. During the course of the Troubles any peaceful tensions that existed between society and the state were focused on sectional and not on plural interests. In the 1990s, elements of civil society began to utilise the Eastern European example and challenged the prevailing notions of the conflict and the interpretations by political elites and paramilitaries. This was done through a variety of ways. Initiatives such as the Opsahl Commission were the beginnings of altering the public sphere in Northern Ireland, while a variety of other organisations formed the G8. These bodies created public pressure for a peace process and a conflict resolution process which was independent of political machinations. It has also been crucial in giving ownership of the peace process to 'the people' of Northern Ireland (Oliver, 2002). For those who credit civil society with an important role in the Northern Ireland peace process, this has been the primary role which it performed (Guelke, 2003).

Civil society's ability to be an agent for change is also severely circumscribed by the type of political change it envisages and the methods by which this change is to be realised. Civil society is as divided as the society within which it is embedded. Those elements of civil society actively lobbying for an agreement between Unionism and Nationalism had two main avenues to pursue: they could publicly agitate for an agreement or they could privately lobby for an agreement. The private role was perhaps more significant than the public role. Various civic society organisations, such as Evangelical Contribution On Northern Ireland (ECONI) and

Democratic Dialogue, were involved in track two diplomacy, organising meetings between political parties and between Unionists and Nationalists, to encourage dialogue and to alter perceptions. Some of this took place on an international level but equally private discussions occurred in Northern Ireland. The intensity of this private role appears to have diminished over the course of implementation:

> It comes down to some pretty stark things about who's going to trade off what with whom and I think there are maybe some in the background...some individuals and so on outside of politics who are helping to lubricate things along but I think they've got all the contacts they need. If the Ulster Unionists want to speak to the IRA or whatever it is that's all there really and it's not as though we don't really know what the answers are. I think now it is well clear to most people what the nature of how are we going to move forward it's just getting them to that point and it seems to be an...issue entirely for the political parties.[21]

One person who was involved in such initiatives stated:

> Once we got up and running, all the crisis over Patten, policing, would Sinn Féin join the Policing Board and Weston Park, we constantly get sucked back into those things. We kept saying: 'they'll get on with it now, they'll talk to each other' and then we get a phone call saying 'can we help?' Certainly over the last year we've been less involved in that sort of stuff as the sort of stalemate because no one is going anywhere and I suppose we, at the moment, feel ourselves we sit ready to serve as needed those who know we're there know we're there and...we don't go knocking and pushing but people know who to phone and we're always there to help so in the long-term no our role hasn't changed.[22]

The public role was much less than a maximalist 'people power' argument might suggest. The agreement was essentially a political deal concluded by elites in 'smoke-filled rooms'. Civil society may have provided some lubrication for the process through public discussions, billboard campaigns and an active campaign in support of the Agreement for the referendum but the limits of its input are shown by the reduction of the scope of the 'Yes' campaign from its initial optimism of cross-community public support to a more limited and strategically targeted campaign (see Couto, 2001). This has been reflected in the role of civil society since the Agreement in relation to the implementation of the Agreement. Many interviewees expressed frustration with the politicians for effectively closing off avenues to participation, echoing Chris Gilligan's analysis of the peace process (pre-Belfast Agreement) as a 'pacification process' (Gilligan, 1997). Implementation has been focused at elite level to a much greater degree than even the negotiations. The lack of transparency, the confusion over deals and the general cynicism at the whole process prompted several to remark that there were two peace processes going on – one for the politicians and one for the community.

> It's like two things happening at the same time. Two very different things and I'm not sure those two things are going to meet properly...even though I think there's very good work being done on the ground. We're an inter-community project so this is our job to talk across the wall but not all projects are like that but I still think they are creating a stability and creating development and capacity within organisations and then you have the politicians making new structures at Stormont, which I'm not sure how that will translate on the ground...I think there's two actually different processes going on and I think I hope at least in our area...that the work that has been done on the ground can then feed into the political level so that we can at least have a some sort of relationship locally with the politicians that can influence their parties to cease in the sectarian dynamic that keeps going on, to work with us, keep supporting our good work that is being done here. We would have activists that...are taking a lot of risk and some of the things are a secret and some other things are quite public right now and then those hush-hush things become more public as they develop here on the ground. Those things are feeding into a political level into parties. How much then is translated into the political arena I'm not sure that's happening very well so I am not sure there's a lot of link-up between the two processes.[23]

This is in marked contrast to a discourse on civil society which stresses potentialities of a civil society when it is connected with political processes.

However, the activist role of civil society goes beyond this. Many peace and conflict resolution organisations, as discussed in the next section, would see themselves as part of this discourse but there is also a wide array of other NGOs lobbying for political change of various descriptions.

The human rights sector draws out some of these themes. The activist discourse within civil society has also included a normative drive on issues such as human rights and equality that have been part of the discourse of global civil society. Thus, there have been a significant number of groups which have taken on an advocacy role, as opposed to the large amount of service provision in which civil society is involved. Kaldor has argued that the international NGOs (INGOs) involved in advocacy roles in the rest of the world are now tamed new social movements. They are tamed insofar as 'the authorities open up access to social movements and even take on some of their demands, and movements become institutionalised and professionalized' (Kaldor, 2003, 145). A similar process can be seen in some of the more activist strains of civil society in Northern Ireland, particularly in the human rights advocacy groups. The Campaign for the Administration of Justice (CAJ), for example, has seen the mainstreaming of human rights and the creation of a quasi-governmental human rights watchdog body. The creation of the Northern Ireland Human Rights Commission was something for which they had lobbied and many members and former members applied to and were appointed onto the Commission. However, it simultaneously neutered the cutting edge of some of the demands and agitation of the human rights organisations. The problems of the Commission notwithstanding, it is yet another example of how the establishments of the institutions of the Agreement fundamentally changed the context of civil society groups. In the case of some of the advocacy groups, which had been vociferous in their criticism of the state, they were brought into a much closer relationship.

## The public sphere discourse

Civil society cannot be divorced from the idea of the public sphere, as formulated by Jürgen Habermas (Edwards, 2004). However, the public sphere is not synonymous with civil society; it attempts to go beyond civil society 'and to introduce a discussion of the specific organisation within civil society of social and cultural bases for the development of an effective rational-critical discourse aimed at the resolution of political disputes' (Calhoun, 1993, 269). The peace process has been littered with attempts and initiatives to expand the public sphere; it has already been noted that the Opsahl Commission was the most important but this has been a preoccupation of civil society throughout the process and the lack of transparency about political deals and negotiations is a constant cause of frustration. As one interviewee argued:

I think there is a big problem because one of the things that . . . was helpful about the initiatives that took place over the Nineties was that it did have some kind of public character, as anything civic in some sense has to have. Now things weren't, I'm not being romantic about this, the deliberations that took place in the New Agenda network, for example, including particularly discussions with the parties were quite sensitive and were under the Chatham House rule but those deliberations led to . . . a public advertising campaign to hopefully encourage wider debate and the Opsahl Commission, one of its greatest strengths was the public hearings which took place over 17 days plus 2 days . . . for sixth-form school students; those were open to the media and the public and I think that was actually very helpful and obviously the 'Yes' campaign was very public . . . and you can't really expect to treat people as foot soldiers who you deign to bring on the stage when it suits you. If people are going to be engaged, they've got to be engaged and can't be treated in that way and that has been a problem.[24]

Whether the Opsahl Commission stimulated the public sphere in Northern Ireland or not, there has been a significant development of public forums of everyday debate on agendas driven by the public during the 1990s. The importance of *Talkback* on Radio Ulster or Stephen Nolan's phone-in show on Belfast CityBeat should not be underestimated. Similarly, *Slugger O'Toole*,[25] as an Internet cybersalon, fulfils the criteria for a non-hierarchical public space. The print media have also provided forums for the expansion of the public sphere. Journals such as *The Other View* or *The Blanket* provide regular forums with the explicit rationale for the expression of divergent views and for the debate between Republicans and Loyalists.[26] Moreover, as the title of Colin Irwin's book, *The People's Peace Process*, suggests, there were people outside the formal political process working to sell the process and the Agreement and also providing an input for 'the people'. Irwin's opinion polls, formulated in conjunction with the political parties, were an attempt to bring the public into the secret deliberations of the multiparty talks, even if they were unaware of it (Irwin, 2002). This does not quite satisfy the conditions for a public sphere but the efforts to publicise the results are the closest that the negotiations came to a public process.

Members of civil society connect the public nature of politics with participation in political decisions. Almost all the interviewees for this research stated, unprompted, that civil society offered mechanisms for participative democracy. Participative democracy appears to be understood in the context of structured input into policy-making, rather than the more classical sense of direct democracy:

> There's no doubt about that because with the absence of ordinary politics a kind of participative democracy arose, which meant that there was a fair degree of influence on policy by voluntary community sector organisations and I think that continued right through until the assembly came on and then it was one of the key phases which the assembly and the sector had to get to grips with the change of relationships and think that was quite difficult for people to let go. I think there was a big willingness in the voluntary and community sector to let the politicians have their day and get on and really do the business in terms of a representative democracy but I think then there were some problems too.[27]

Participation is thus understood to provide an adjunct to representative democracy and the changing balance between representative democracy and participative democracy is significant in how democracy, and thus civil society, functions in Northern Ireland.

> I think the battle was starting to be won these days that democracy is not purely representative that participative democracy is an important part of governance and so there will often be space at the table for social partners stroke civil society where big decisions are being made when your talking about PFI or any of those things; still not when your talking about political process so still not during the review, they're still not saying we need to broaden this out to civil society in terms of how the review is going to work but the Opsahl Commission started to put a foot in that door, started to say 'well we're not going to prescribe what the way forward for Northern Ireland is but here are some suggestions from people who are actually living and working in areas close to the ground who have thoughts about these things'. So, I think the Opsahl Commission is a bit of a watershed moment in that; that's when the politicians started to say 'oh these people actually have something to say'. Not so much our local politicians but certainly the British and Irish governments started to say 'hmmm clearly there's some expertise resident here that we need to tap into', which is why I think the 'Yes' campaign eventually came about.[28]

Some even stated that Northern Ireland was more advanced than other places in the avenues it offered for participation:

> My sense is that there is a growing awareness in the modern world should Northern Ireland become more normal in inverted commas. Should we have elections every few years, it's not enough to just let politicians decide; it's very useful to have this complementary process to make sure politicians really are informed about the views across their electorate and that people who don't ever consider voting for them and that that influences the decision-making. It's a more complex decision-making process but I think it is representative and participative democracy working hand-in-glove and that's why it, again, I think Northern Ireland is ahead of the game and we could dump the participative approach by saying No. We might be able to have normal politics but I think that would be a loss. We actually have something that we should be exporting to other people and similarly I would feel very strongly that it's not a question that everybody should be at the table and therefore you don't need elected politicians.[29]

It should be noted that it is participation rather than deliberation which is the central concern here. Nevertheless, it seems that the establishment of the Assembly in 1998 was seen by all as a real opportunity for normal democratic politics involving political representation and policy debates to operate in Northern Ireland. For civil society, this opportunity meant the widening of the public sphere and more opportunities for political participation. In terms of public policy and social and economic issues, this was possible; but where issues pertaining the political process were concerned, the public sphere and the avenues for political participation narrowed and this has created apathy and disillusionment.

## The conflict transformation discourse

Mary Kaldor argues:

> Civil society has an important humanitarian role to play in conflicts. But civil society can only be sustained in the framework of a rule of law ... Moreover, the effects of new wars, and Bosnia is a good example of this, is to destroy civil society. Because new wars represent a form of political mobilization, extremists are generally strengthened in war and civil society greatly weakened.
>
> (Kaldor, 2003, 135)

There are two corollaries to this. First, a key part of transforming conflicts lies in rebuilding civil society. Second, civil society is uniquely placed to address relationships between communities at an individual level. The ethnic conflict literature on civil society attaches great importance to its potential to alleviate or prevent conflict. Perhaps the most systematic treatment of the two subjects is Ashutosh Varshney's study of riots in India. His conclusion was that civil society was an explanatory factor in presence or absence of Hindu–Muslim riots in Indian cities. Where Hindus and Muslims were involved in the same formal organisations and had everyday contact with the other community, riots did not happen (Varshney, 2001). His research has prompted some in Northern Ireland to suggest that cross-community work is therefore more likely to be beneficial than single-identity work (Bryan, 2003); but Varshney's work is not as conclusive as that reading would suggest. Indeed, I would contest that all Varshney demonstrates is that in certain Indian cities Hindus and Muslims are integrated to a degree which prevents conflict. His understanding of the possibilities of cross-community work to integrate communities after conflict is not clear and Northern Ireland actually presents a better case study in that sense than India. However, what Varshney does raise is the relationship between bridging and bonding social capital in divided societies. For example, church attendance, which is a major source of social capital in Putnam's America and is exceptionally high in Northern Ireland, is one of the major markers of communal division (see Mitchell, 2006). As Nelson, Kaboolian and Carver argue: 'bonding social capital, which connects similar individuals and lubricates action within a social network, can simultaneously reinforce the differences and social distance between members of the network and "others"' (Nelson *et al.*, 2003).

This is a fairly commonplace critique of Putnam's neoliberal version of civil society. Putnam does not consider the possibility that the *type* of civic engagement is important rather than just the *fact* of them. Research on Britain suggests that it also has high levels of associational life and social capital (Hall, 1999) and, although there is no specific data on Northern Ireland, it would seem likely that it would follow British trends. It is forgotten too often that Northern Ireland has a network of Rotary Clubs, Lions Clubs, Credit Unions, St John Ambulance Divisions, charity shops, local football, rugby and cricket clubs, Gateway Clubs and so on. However, these have little or no direct impact upon political developments connected with the high politics of the peace process. It is therefore necessary to distinguish between types of civic engagement.

Here it is then necessary to integrate a normative idea into the definition of civil society, which links associational life with other notions of democracy and the 'good society'. Holding a wide and undifferentiated definition can lead to the inclusion of uncivil groups, such as the Ulster Defence Association (UDA) or IRA (Cochrane, 2005). However, this is not necessarily the case, as such groups are not involved in 'voluntary association' and do not create social capital. A more ambiguous case would be the Gaelic Athletic Association (GAA) or the Orange Order and this leads to the second problem: the distinction which Putnam only makes in passing, between bridging and bonding social capital, is of acute relevance in Northern Ireland, as it is in other divided societies (see Varshney, 2003). One critic made the distinction between social and unsocial capital (Levi, 1996), while another has argued that it is important to contextualise the relationship between civic engagement and social and political outcomes (Cochrane, 2005). Perhaps the most useful distinction has been drawn by Chambers and Kopstein (2001), who distinguish between civil society organisations that promote a particularist idea of democracy and those that promote a universalist idea. This allows us to distinguish between bonding organisations that are good for conflict resolution and bonding organisations that are not.

Can civil society provide integration of communities? The literature on ethnic conflict resolution, while not giving a resounding 'yes', does privilege civil society over political structures. A consociational system of government is subject to particular criticism but there are differences between the criticisms. Donald Horowitz, for example, would remedy the deficiencies he would see with the system by way of other political structures, particularly the electoral system (Horowitz, 1985). However, others would argue that consociationalism reifies identities which should be deconstructed. Political structures are unable to do this and this necessitates an approach based on the transformative capacities of civil society (Taylor, 1994, 2001). There are initiatives within civil society which are actively working towards integration, with integrated schooling as the best example (O'Connor, 2002). Most of the projects funded by European Peace and Reconciliation money are funded to work on the individual and micro-community level to alter attitudes between and among communities, to break down the system of sectarianism. Frequently this sort of work builds on psychological and not political concepts (see, for example, Francis, 2002). In Northern Ireland, the tendency has been to pursue both types of conflict resolution approaches at the same time, for instance the British Government sponsored both talks on political structures and the development of civil society approaches at the same time (Bloomfield, 1996).[30]

Nevertheless, civil society in Northern Ireland is as divided as the wider society and reflects the divisions within that society and, while the peak organisations hold to integrative tendencies, this is not necessarily the case of all groups:

> In my own view...civil society got hijacked by a number of key players ...and it's still very difficult to be not pro-agreement; and I'm not even saying anti-agreement [but] to be not pro-agreement because the main sources of money for the community development sector ...[is] peace and reconciliation money [and that is]...clearly about peace building, all the horizontal principles; all the application process is all about how you're going to, one, address the legacy of the conflict and [two] to take opportunities arising from the peace, which I have an issue about as well. So you've got to buy in. Other people who are in stronger positions say: 'if you can't buy into what we think, don't bother'. We have to administer that. If you put...that up against something like the money we have...for the ex political prisoners, they get the money on account of being groups of...political ex-prisoners...so they are brought in immediately and they get the money because of who and what they are. Now we have some influence on their workload but surprisingly little....  [Ex-prisoners] bridges everything through the UVF [Ulster Volunteer Force] side [to] the UDA side (there's no LVF [Loyalist Volunteer Force] side because we didn't go and talk to them). So those are the kind of small decisions you're making so you're not overtly saying 'you've got to buy into the peace scheme' but, if you only talk to X, Y and Z, you're moving the goalposts. So I suppose if you have to analyse it we are pro agreement but not a big player in the formation of consensus I would argue. ...I cannot see where civil society played a big role and I can't see where civil society was supposed to play a big role, or any role. This is consociationalism; it is about elites. I think the war weariness, people's desperation for an end to the conflict and their hopes post' 94 for some sort normality meant you've got to be a fool not to mobilise that sort of body of opinion.[31]

As those who advocate an elite-driven solution for Northern Ireland and are sceptical of the social transformation approach argue, with a certain amount of glee:

> It is not even true that the political preferences of Northern Ireland's 'civil society', that is, its large numbers of civic associations, differ from

those of its political parties. The most popular civil society organisations in Northern Ireland, the Orange Order and the Gaelic Athletic
Association, are solidly unionist and nationalist, respectively.

(McGarry and O'Leary, 2004, 21)

This is slightly facetious, as, while the Orange Order and the GAA may
be two of the largest associational organisations in Northern Ireland,
neither is representative of the type of work which is conducted under
the ambit of the community sector. However, the question as to how to
work with existing community structures is a serious one for peace and
conflict resolution organisations and one which has been unsatisfactorily
answered. The sector is informed by a vernacular communitarianism;[32]
this is perhaps unsurprisingly called the 'community sector', but there is
a lack of definitional rigour enshrined in this terminology. Perhaps the
most coherent exposition of the rationale of the sector, which illustrates
many of the themes throughout this chapter, comes from NICVA's policy
manifesto of 2002:

> The voluntary and community sector is a major force for change in
> Northern Ireland. What the sector has to offer is a profound experi-
> ence of civic life — of a world where everyone is equally valued as an
> individual, where individuals come together for the common good,
> and where the everyday concerns of 'normal' politics are to the fore.
> A vibrant civic culture is critical to a well-functioning, inclusive soci-
> ety. Civic associations have the capacity to achieve virtuous circles
> of growing trust, confidence and cohesion. Government increasingly
> depends on NGOs (non-governmental organisations) in complex soci-
> eties where it can neither know nor do everything. Research shows
> that NGOs enjoy greater trust on the part of citizens than gov-
> ernments or the private sector. If supports are not put in place to
> enable excluded groups to participate in democracy, then inequal-
> ities are exacerbated. The voluntary and community sector fulfils
> this role through providing such supports. The not-for-profit ethos
> of the sector means that it actively seeks to build collective or com-
> munity profit (capital) within economically and socially deprived
> communities when it is delivering services. The sector's ethos—
> treating everyone as an individual, involving users and constantly
> evaluating—can offset the dangers of one-size-fits-all bureaucracy and
> stagnation that many big state organisations suffer. The voluntary
> and community sector also has a role to play in reconciling Northern
> Ireland's divided society. Strong civic networks can offset sectarian

divisions and work at community level has the potential to encourage outward-looking and outward-reaching development rather than inward-looking competitive communities.

(NICVA, 2003, 4–5)

Community is obviously, for NICVA and others, a positive concept, bound up with many of the notions which define social capital but it is not clear from the statement above what relationship between bridging and bonding social capital is envisaged. For example, the GAA or the Orange Order are not considered part of the community sector and yet there are many comparable organisations which are. Community can mean small localities, 'the Lord Street community'; larger estate size communities, 'the Short Strand community'; even larger constituency size communities, 'the East Belfast community'. It can mean non-territorially defined communities, 'the working class community of West Belfast'; it can mean the 'traditional' communities, 'the Nationalist community'; it can mean several of these definitions at the same time, 'the Protestant community of East Belfast', 'the Catholic community of East Belfast'. Rarely are any of these communities thought of in a cross-community fashion. They are always thought of as positive and embodying close social bonds between members; areas where there are few 'community organisations' are referred to as areas with 'weak community infrastructure' and these tend to be rural or Protestant areas. We have already confronted the problems with assuming that social networks can alleviate problems and it seems that the community sector is unable to resolve these issues because communities are allowed to define themselves and with the level of social segregation, locality becomes synonymous with communal identities. Indeed, this is the major difficulty that Elizabeth Fraser has identified with communitarian projects; she argues that communities should be thought of as territorial and not psychological areas because of the potentials for in and out groups which the latter creates (Fraser, 1999, 141–72).

Where this conflict transformation discourse links with the activist discourse is in the women's movement. The women's sector in Northern Ireland in particular has seen civil society as a plural space where concerns that could not be articulated in the formal, male-dominated political arena could be addressed and discussed. Indeed, the women's sector did what civil society in general discussed prior to 1998 and formed a political party.[33] Moreover, the women's sector represents a move away from ideas associated with community and embodies what a social movement which Ernest Gellner might describe as 'modular', that is, allowing a variety of identities to coexist (Gellner, 1996). The literature on the women's sector in Northern Ireland is increasing in volume but the integrationist approach is a central part of its agenda and one which is not theoretically muddied by the prominence of bonding social capital (See Chapter 6).

In addition, there are strong class elements to the conflict resolution organisations. This correlates with the class dimensions of the conflict and is reflected in a variant of standpoint theory which informs this sector. Marxist standpoint theory stated that only the proletariat had access to the truth because they were oppressed and therefore uniquely situated to see the structures of oppression in society, while the feminist variant on this replaced the proletariat with women. In Northern Ireland, there is the assumption that those who lived with the conflict are in a better position to understand the structural sectarianism and inequalities in society and therefore are better able to address those issues. Because community development and community relations work address the issues of conflict within these areas, it therefore sees itself as the most progressive element of Northern Irish society, frequently expressing frustration with politicians. Indeed, politicians are seen as the bearers of sectarian politics in Northern Ireland, uninterested in addressing sectarianism and the causes of the conflict. Indeed, for such groups the tension is not on the state–civil society axis but rather the civil society–political society axis.

John Paul Lederach has argued that a successful reconciliation process must include dialogue and connections between politicians, civil society and the masses. Lederach's work in particular has become popular in Northern Ireland and he suggests that resolving conflict should involve all sections of society and can be thought of in terms of a triangle. Civil society provides the important secondary level, which can, if lines of communication are properly developed, negotiate and communicate to both the political leaders (at the top of the triangle) and the grass roots (at the bottom; Lederach, 1997). Overall, it is difficult to argue that civil society has consistently played this role. Civil society has played an important role in translating difficult political decisions taken at an elite level to the ground on a number of occasions: the ceasefires, the 'Yes' campaign. Moreover, ex-prisoner groups would be the most proactive in providing the conduit between elites and their constituents. However, because civil society interprets its interests as jeopardised by those of the politicians, frustration rather than dialogue is the result.

## Conclusion

In order to understand the impact of civil society on the peace process (including negotiation and implementation), it is necessary to appreciate two aspects. The first is civil society's world view, which is bound up in notions of openness, transparency, participation, empowerment and plurality. The second is to understand the nature of political change in Northern Ireland from a civil society perspective. The elite peace process embodies few of the ideas which encompass civil society's world view and there has been a genuine and perceptible disconnection of civil society with the political process. On the other hand, the framework for the role which civil society has played during the period of direct rule has fundamentally altered, offering a more expansive and influential role than previously but changing the rules of the game. The result is that civil society has an ambiguous relationship with the political institutions; it is simultaneously supportive and critical. It is only when we examine the conflict transformation role of civil society that we can see an unambiguous and primary role. However, if we are to maintain a focus on the relationship between civil society and the formal political process then a proper contextual analysis is needed.

## Notes

1. This article was written with ESRC funding, grant number: RES-223-25-0045.
2. Interview with Intermediary Funding Body (IFB) representative, Belfast, 11 February 2004.
3. Representatives of Democratic Dialogue and Community Dialogue both described their origins in the Opsahl process; see http://www.democraticdialogue.org/aboutus.htm.
4. This is the sense in which the phrase is used in the title of NIVT (1999).
5. A similar distinction between private, civic and political associations is made in Young (2000) and in Kymlicka (2002).
6. Interview with member of cross-community group, Belfast, 10 May 2004.
7. Statement made by the Secretary of State in the House of Commons on Tuesday 18 April 2006, http://www.nio.gov.uk/media-detail.htm?newsID=12974.
8. Interview with member of community education group, Belfast, 10 May 2004.
9. Interview with IFB representative, Belfast, 11 February 2004.
10. Interview with IFB representative, 11 February 2004.
11. For NICVA's manifesto see NICVA (2003, 2006); the political parties' manifestoes can be found at http://cain.ulst.ac.uk/issues/politics/election/manifestos.htm.
12. For an examination of the process of consultation in Wales, see Hodgson (2004). Interestingly, Hodgson's research demonstrates a remarkably similar experience of consultation in Wales and Northern Ireland.

13. Interview with member of policy and research group, Belfast, 19 April 2004.
14. Interview with IFB representative, Belfast, 11 February 2004.
15. Interview with member of New Agenda, Belfast, 5 May 2004.
16. Interview with Civic Forum representative, Belfast, 14 January 2004.
17. See Democratic Dialogue (1999). Academic analysis also tended to stress the potential role of the Civic Forum in the governance of Northern Ireland; see McCall and Williamson (2001).
18. See the debates in the Northern Ireland Assembly, available at www.niassembly.gov.uk.
19. For an examination of the role of the state and its treatment of civil society, see Hadenius and Uggla (1996).
20. I take this from Young (2000).
21. Interview with member of New Agenda, Belfast, 5 May 2004.
22. Interview with member of a civil society group, Belfast, 19 January 2004.
23. Interview with cross-community group, Belfast, 9 February 2004.
24. Interview with member of policy and research group, 19 April 2004.
25. www.sluggerotoole.com.
26. See *The Other View*, or *The Blanket*, http://lark.phoblacht.net.
27. Interview with member of community education group, Belfast, 3 February 2004.
28. Interview with IFB representative, Belfast, 11 February 2004.
29. Interview with member of human rights group, Belfast, 12 January 2004.
30. Bloomfield argues that these two approaches are complementary but this is not widely endorsed in the literature.
31. Interview with IFB representative.
32. For a discussion of this see Fraser (1999). It seems more appropriate to call it vernacular communitarianism as it does not have any of the rigour of the philosophical or political communitarianism.
33. Interview with member of New Agenda, Belfast, 5 May 2004.

# References

Baker, G. (2003) ' "Civil Society that so Perturbs": Zapatismo and the Democracy of Civil Society', *Space and Polity*, 7:3, 293–312.

Berman, S. (1997) 'Civil Society and the Collapse of the Weimar Republic', *World Politics*, 49, 401–29.

Bloomfield, D. (1996) *Peacemaking Strategies in Northern Ireland: Building Complementarity in Conflict Management Theory*. Basingstoke: Palgrave Macmillan.

Bourke, R. (2003) *Peace in Ireland: The War of Ideas*. London: Pimlico.

Bryan, D. (2003) 'An Examination of the Obstacles and Challenges to Development in Northern Ireland'. Paper delivered to 'Working Together for Sustainable Peace: The Challenges for Community and Political Action', 4–5 December 2003, Templepatrick, Northern Ireland. Report from the conference available at http://www.ksg.harvard.edu/justiceproject/northernirelandnew.htm.

Calhoun, C. (1993) 'Civil Society and the Public Sphere', *Public Culture*, 5, 267–80.

Chambers, S. and J. Kopstein (2001) 'Bad Civil Society', *Political Theory*, 29:6, 837–65.

Cochrane, F. (2005) 'The Limits of Civil Society in a Divided Society: The Case of Northern Ireland', in S. Roßteutscher (ed.), *Democracy and the Role of Associations: Political, Organizational and Social Contexts*. London: Routledge.

Cochrane, F. and S. Dunn (1997) *People Power? The Role of the Voluntary and Community Sector in the Northern Ireland Conflict*. Cork: Cork University Press.

Couto, R.A. (2001) 'The Third Sector and Civil Society: The Case of the 'Yes' Campaign in Northern Ireland', *Voluntas: International Journal of Voluntary and Nonprofit Organisations*, 12:3, 221–38.

Democratic Dialogue (1999) *DD Papers: The Civic Forum and Negotiated Governance*. Available at http://www.democraticdialogue.org/working/negotiated-goverance.htm.

Edwards, M. (2004) *Civil Society*. Cambridge: Polity Press.

Fearon, K. (1999) *Women's Work: The Story of the Northern Ireland Women's Coalition*. Belfast: Blackstaff.

Florini, A. (2003) *The Coming Democracy: New Rules for Running a New World*. Washington: Island Press.

Francis, D. (2002) *People, Peace and Power: Conflict Transformation in Action*. London: Pluto Press.

Fraser, E. (1999) *The Problems of Communitarian Politics: Unity and Conflict*. Oxford: Oxford University Press.

Foley, M.W. and B. Edwards (1996) 'The Paradox of Civil Society', *Journal of Democracy*, 7:3, 38–52.

Gellner, E. (1996) *Conditions of Liberty: Civil Society and its Rivals*. Harmondsworth: Penguin.

Giddens, A. (1998) *The Third Way: The Renewal of Social Democracy*. Cambridge: Polity Press.

Gilligan, C. (1997) 'Peace or Pacification Process?', in C. Gilligan and J. Tonge (eds), *War or Peace? Understanding the Peace Process in Northern Ireland*. Aldershot: Ashgate, pp. 19–34.

Guelke, A. (2003) 'Civil Society and the Northern Ireland Peace Process', *Voluntas: International Journal of Voluntary and Nonprofit Organisations*, 14:1, 61–78.

Hadenius, A. and F. Uggla (1996) 'Making Civil Society Work, Promoting Democratic Development: What Can States and Donors Do?', *World Development*, 24:10, 1621–39.

Hall, P.A. (1999) 'Social Capital in Britain', *British Journal of Political Science*, 29:3, 417–61.

Hodgson, L. (2004) 'The National Assembly for Wales, Civil Society and Consultation', *Politics*, 24:2, 88–95.

Horowitz, D. (1985) *Ethnic Groups in Conflict: Theories, Patterns and Policies*. Berkeley: University of California Press.

Irwin, C. (2002) *The People's Peace Process*. Basingstoke: Palgrave Macmillan.

Kaldor, M. (2003) *Global Civil Society: An Answer to War*. Cambridge: Polity Press.

Keane, J. (ed.) (1988) *Civil Society and the State: New European Perspectives*. London: Verso.

Keane, J. (1998) *Civil Society: Old Visions, New Images*. Cambridge: Polity Press.

Kymlicka, W. (2002) 'Civil Society and Government: A Liberal-Egalitarian Perspective', in N.L. Rosenblum and R.C. Post (eds), *Civil Society and Government*. Princeton: Princeton University Press, pp. 79–110.

140    *Models of Civil Society*

Lederach, J.P. (1997) *Building Peace: Sustainable Reconciliation in Divided Societies.* Washington, DC: United States Institute of Peace Press.

Levi, M. (1996) 'Social and Unsocial Capital: A Review Essay of Robert Putnam's *Making Democracy Work*', *Politics and Society*, 24:1, 45–55.

Lowndes, V. and D. Wilson (2001) 'Social Capital and Local Governance: Exploring the Institutional Design Variable', *Political Studies*, 49:4, 629–47.

McCall, C. and A. Williamson (2001) 'Governance and Democracy in Northern Ireland: The Role of the Voluntary and Community Sector after the Agreement', *Governance: An International Journal of Policy and Administration*, 14:3, 363–83.

McGarry, J. and B. O'Leary (2004) *The Northern Ireland Conflict: Consociational Engagements.* Oxford: Oxford University Press.

McLean, I. (1996) *Oxford Concise Dictionary of Politics.* Oxford: Oxford University Press.

Mitchell, C. (2006) *Religion, Identity and Politics in Northern Ireland: Boundaries of Belonging and Belief.* Aldershot: Ashgate.

Nelson, B.J., L. Kaboolian and K.A. Carver (2003) *The Concord Handbook: How to Build Social Capital across Communities.* Los Angeles, CA: School of Public Policy and Social Research. Available at http://concord.sppsr.ucla.edu/concord.pdf.

NICVA (2003) Policy manifesto. Belfast: NICVA.

NICVA (2006) Policy manifesto. Belfast: NICVA. Available at http://www.nicva.org/index.cfm/section/article/page/NICVAPolicyManifesto.

NIVT (1999) *Towards a Civil Society: A Report of Conference Proceedings* . Belfast: The Foundations for a Civil Society and NIVT.

O'Connor, F. (2002) *A Shared Childhood: The Story of Integrated Education in Northern Ireland.* Belfast: Blackstaff Press.

Oliver, Q. (2002) 'Developing Public Capacities for Participation in Peacemaking', in C. Barnes (ed.), *Owning the Process: Developing Public Capacities for Participation in Peacemaking.* Available at http://www.c-r.org/accord/peace/accord13/pedev.shtml.

Putnam, R.D. (1993) *Making Democracy Work: Civic Traditions in Modern Italy.* Princeton: Princeton University Press.

Putnam, R.D. (2000) *Bowling Alone: The Collapse and Revival of American Community.* New York: Simon and Schuster.

Taylor, C. (1990) 'Modes of Civil Society', *Public Culture*, 3:1, 95–118.

Taylor, R. (1994) 'A Consociational Path to Peace in Northern Ireland and South Africa', in A. Guelke (ed.), *New Perspectives on the Northern Ireland Conflict.* Aldershot: Avebury, pp. 161–74.

Taylor, R. (2001) 'Northern Ireland: Consociation or Social Transformation?', in J. McGarry (ed.), *Northern Ireland and the Divided World: Post-Agreement Northern Ireland in Comparative Perspective.* Oxford: Oxford University Press, pp. 36–52.

Varshney, A. (2001) 'Ethnic Conflict and Civil Society: India and Beyond', *World Politics*, 53, 362–98.

Varshney, A. (2003) *Ethnic Conflict and Civic Life: Hindus and Muslims in India.* New Haven: Yale University Press.

Walzer, M. (1991) 'The Idea of Civil Society: A Path to Social Reconstruction', *Dissent*, Spring, 293–304.

Wank, D.L. (1995) 'Civil Society in Communist China? Private Business and Political Alliance, 1989', in J.A Hall (ed.), *Civil Society: Theory, History, Comparison.* Cambridge: Polity Press. pp. 56–79.

Wesolowski, W. (1995) 'The Nature of Social Ties and the Future of Postcommunist Society: Poland after Solidarity', in J.A. Hall (ed.), *Civil Society: Theory, History, Comparison.* Cambridge: Polity Press, pp. 110–35.

Young, I.M. (2000) *Inclusion and Democracy.* Oxford: Oxford University Press.

# 6
# Women, Civil Society and Peace-Building in Northern Ireland: Paths to Peace through Women's Empowerment

*Michael Potter*

Women have long been conspicuous in organisations promoting peace and reconciliation and have been at the forefront of peace-building efforts. Indeed, there are women's groups the world over whose main focus and rationale is furthering or bringing about peace. This chapter aims to examine this phenomenon in the context of Northern Ireland.

While linkages between women and peace-building have been well established in theory, this chapter will analyse this relationship in the context of women's integration into theories of civil society, the identification of women's networks with the nature of social capital and the role of civil society in post-conflict reconstruction. The example of women's empowerment projects under the European Union Programme for Peace and Reconciliation in Northern Ireland is used to illustrate these linkages between women and peace via civil society involvement.

## Women and peace

Examples of women's organisations engaging in the process of urging, making or building peace are a global phenomenon. Specific studies of peace movements have highlighted the centrality of women to the concept, such as the Derry Peace Women in Northern Ireland, the Women's Unarmed Uprising Against War in Sweden, the Women's Peace Union in the United States or the Greenham Peace Camp in the United Kingdom, to name but a few (Alonso, 1997; Andersson, 2003; Hammond, 2002; Harford, 1984). There are also specific studies of women in the context of a conflict area, such as Northern Ireland, or profiles of individual women taken from a variety of conflict areas (Henderson, 1994;

Morgan, 1995). While the promotion of peace is frequently the *raison d'être* of many women's groups worldwide, the same cannot be said of groups of men. Women, therefore, appear to be more conspicuous in the pursuit of peace.

In the international context, the United Nations Security Council passed Resolution 1325 in 2000 to increase the participation of women in all UN field operations and ensure a gender element in all peace-building initiatives. Clearly, the association of women with peace is considered strong and is internationally recognised, or at least the need to include women more effectively following conflict. The argument for specific gender perspectives in post-conflict situations is put succinctly by Woroniuk and Schalkwyk, stating that gender relations in pre-conflict situations often set the stage for women's and men's options during conflict, women and men experience conflict in very different ways, social structures mainly sustained by and relied upon by women are thrown into confusion during conflict and women and men tend to be involved in building peace in different ways, women being involved more in grass roots peace-building and men in formal political processes (Woroniuk and Schalkwyk, 1998, 1). Women's integration into all peace-building efforts is therefore essential, particularly in the reconstruction of society following conflict.

One explanation of the relationship between women and peace has been that women are naturally more peaceful. Women, writes Johann Galtung, have innate qualities that make them more peace-loving. High in empathy, their characters are horizontal and centripetal, making them more prone to peaceful relationships, combined with the chemical programming of the cyclical and complex oestrogen and high levels of mono amino oxidase, the chemical responsible for controlling violence (Galtung, 1996, 40, 43). Young girls, writes Brock-Utne, tend to share and co-operate, whereas young boys compete (Brock-Utne, 1989, 99). Alonso affirms this notion, insisting that 'almost every group has portrayed women as more sensitive, more caring, more thoughtful and more committed to producing a more humanistic and compassionate world than men as a whole' (Alonso, 1993, 11).

In contrast, men are portrayed as makers of war and perpetrators of violence. Galtung cites the low empathy, vertical, centrifugal, expansionist character of man, pointing out that 95 per cent of direct violence is committed by men (Galtung, 1996, 40-1). Something in the nature of men makes them fight, as Skjelsback and Smyth point out:

Some of the violent acts perpetrated by men in armed conflicts are perpetrated precisely because the men have become convinced that that is the way to show their masculinity.

(2001, 3)

It is the male value system that creates war, and it is women who suffer, as Brock-Utne notes: 'Women pay for the male priorities of this world' (Skjelsback, 2001, 65; Brock-Utne, 1989, 15). Military thinking, adds Ruddick, is imbued with male values (Ruddick, 1990, 145). These views move from the innate qualities of 'warlike men' and 'peaceful women' to acknowledgements that a degree of social conditioning drives men to fight.

But Moser and Clark are not satisfied with this explanation:

Stereotypical essentialising of women as 'victims' and men as 'perpetrators' of political violence and armed conflict assumes universal, simplified definitions of each phenomenon.

(2001, 4)

Karam is equally critical, suggesting the literature on women and conflict 'tends to view women as victims rather than as active actors, largely as a result of patriarchal structures' (2001, 22). Other voices of dissent concord with a view that women are not as peaceful as they are portrayed nor men as warlike, as Reardon explains, women 'are not predisposed by their hormonal balance to pacifism any more than men are predisposed to warmongering' (Ruddick, 1990, 151; Reardon, 1993, 15). Women, by this view, are being squeezed into a pervasive model that portrays them as peaceful and men into one of violence through a process of socialisation that accords with prevailing gender roles.

The association of women with peace, if not innate, may derive from women's experience. UN Secretary General Kofi Annan stated: 'Existing inequalities between women and men, and patterns of discrimination against women and girls, tend to be exacerbated in armed conflict' (Annan, 2002). Alonso has also attested that in war, women 'were the ones to suffer most, both in the perpetual violence against women during the occupation and through the deaths of sons, husbands, lovers, brothers and fathers' (1993, 57). Moser and Clark add that women suffer severe forms of victimisation and men are overwhelmingly the perpetrators (2001, 8). If women generally experience conflict disproportionately to men, an affinity with peace is unsurprising; so women have more reason to oppose war if a major by-product is their abuse, defilement and destitution.

Hammond (2002) writes that the Derry Peace Women were driven by civil rights aspirations as well as 'maternalist motivations'. Indeed, Sara Ruddick argues that women's experience of being mothers makes them better suited to peacemaking. Daily, mothers think out strategies of protection and nurture towards their children, qualities that women extend to the community (Ruddick, 1990, 23, 80). Maternal thinking, adds Ruddick, which is opposed to military thinking, does not result from an innate maternal peacefulness, but the fact that 'maternal practice is a "natural resource" for peace politics' (ibid, 150–7). While Ruddick's argument is convincing, it cannot explain how childless women are involved in peace movements, or those who have rejected the mothering role. Likewise, the fact of women's active involvement in conflict clashes with Ruddick's thesis on the mothering effect. Nevertheless, the image of women socialised into caring for the welfare of others may well contribute to an anti-war ethos among women.

The association of women with peace leads to a logical assumption that a higher percentage of women in decision-making positions would lead to less hostile activities on the part of the state in question. 'Critical mass' theory defines a certain percentage of women in national legislatures to influence policy positively. This figure differs according to source, but Gierycz suggests 30–35 per cent to make a difference (2001, 25). Virginia Woolf has been quoted as stating that there can never be peace until women's values in private life are included in international decision-making, suggesting that women possess values of passivism the effects of which are impeded by their exclusion from public life (Oldfield, 1989, 3). Brock-Utne is more direct, stating that more women rulers would lead to fewer wars (Brock-Utne, 1989, 90). However, studies by Caprioli and Boyer find that no conclusions can be drawn about the relationship between female leaders and international crisis violence (2001, 516). One explanation of this is that female politicians often imitate men in order to succeed in a system designed for 'male' attributes. The presence of women in powerful positions over a period of time would therefore be needed to have any impact on changing the nature of politics in terms of ethos.

Research by Regan and Paskeviciute suggests that violent conflict has more of a relationship with birth rates than gender. By this thesis, younger populations tend to engage more in conflict and the apparent prevalence of women in public life in states with lower levels of violent conflict is more to do with the family planning measures that enable them to be there, leading to older population profiles (Regan and Paskeviciute, 2003, 287). Huntington makes a particularly convincing case that 'young people are the protagonists of protest, instability, reform and revolution', in which he identifies 'youth bulges' in populations of ages 15–24 in incidences of militancy (2002, 117–8). High birth rates, then, contribute to the incidence of violent conflict. Birth control not only limits the violence perpetrated by a state, but enables women to participate more fully in public life, creating the coincidence of peacefulness and women's representation.

While essentialist perceptions about 'violent men' and 'peaceful women' are unhelpful, there is clear evidence that there is a gender differential in the pursuit of peace or in the construction of a peaceful society following conflict. Socialisation may well play a major role in creating female nurturers, but the fact of men being in the majority of perpetrators of violence, women and girls being the main targets of non-combat violence and exploitation and women being the de facto primary sustainers of the social fabric holding families and communities together makes a major role for women in all areas of peace-building essential.

## Women and civil society

Notions of 'civil society' and 'social capital' have received much attention in connection with how a state and its constituent population interact. To understand how women fit into this concept, it is necessary to trace how the ideas of civil society and social capital have developed, how they are defined or measured and their relationship with ideas of democracy and civil participation. A critique of how these theories are formed in relation to gender can then be made and an analysis formulated on how this affects notions of how women are integrated – or not – into participative processes.

One approach is to define what civil society is not. Baker's analysis of African countries where the state has ceased to function has revealed that anarchy does not prevail, as in Thomas Hobbes' account of nature, but sub-state structures appear to endure (Baker, 1999, 131). Civil society could therefore be defined as where the state is not.

For Kumi Naidoo, Chief Executive of the international civic society organisation CIVICUS, civil society is more of a relationship or state that 'enables all citizens to contribute' (Naidoo, 2003). The concept is therefore quite nebulous. Such lack of consensus has led Trentmann to conclude:

Rather than crystallising into a single master definition...the modern history of civil society is an unfolding dialogue between different imaginaries of the social.

(2000, 7)

Given these difficulties in defining or measuring civil society, the idea of 'social capital' has been developed to describe the qualities of human interaction indicative of civil society or the 'basic raw material' of civil society (Onyx and Bullen, 2000, 24). In short, 'the core idea of social capital theory is that social networks have value' (Putnam, 2000, 19).

Robert Putnam has been an influential figure in defining social capital. He notes that 'the touchstone of social capital is the generalised principle of reciprocity', that is, a society characterised by people who are willing to do things for others, not for immediate return, but with the confidence that others would do the same for them (Putnam, 2000, 135). In addition to reciprocity, Putnam adds 'trust' and 'networks of civic engagement' as essential components of social capital, and highlights how societies with high levels of social capital are more efficient, more prosperous economically and carry general benefits to its members (Putnam, 1993, 170,173, 157; 2000, 21). There are also dimensions to social capital that need to be emphasised, insists Putnam. One of these is the difference between 'bonding' and 'bridging' social capital, the former being good for the community, but exclusive, and the latter reaching out to other parts of society (Putnam, 2000, 23). The other is the idea of 'vertical' networks, which are hierarchical and 'cannot sustain social trust and co-operation', and 'horizontal' networks, which are more beneficial (Putnam, 1993, 173).

Rather than seeing social capital as a new phenomenon, it is an old idea newly defined. Putnam himself relates the concept to the *fraternité* of the French Revolution (Putnam, 2000, 351). If civic cohesion and relationships are significant indicators of social capital, the roots can be traced in the thought of a range of political thinkers. Aristotle wrote: 'The task of all citizens, however different they may be, is the stability of the association', indicating that all members of the collectivity that is the state have a responsibility to its maintenance (Aristotle, 1991, 179). This being the case, the philosophical notion of 'civic virtue' is comparable to social capital, this being the *virtù* of Machiavelli or the *virtue* of Rousseau or Montesquieu (Foster, 1958, 297; Montesquieu, 1970, 82; Rousseau, 1963, 128; Russell, 1985, 496). Social capital is therefore related to how people inter-relate and how they interact with the structures that administer them.

When the philosophy of civil society is taken into account, it is clear that the relationship with the state in the context of democracy is an important dimension. Finer defines democracy as 'government which is derived from public opinion and is accountable to it' (Finer, 1970, 63). Civil society is a mode of mobilising public opinion and making government accountable, amounting to participative democracy and consultation. Indeed, Harold Laski has written, 'the first great need of the modern state is adequately to organise institutions of consultation' (Laski, 1973, 80). This consultation comprises active participation in policy-making processes by civil society, which 'humanises the bureaucracy and strengthens the capacities of individuals and communities to mobilise and help themselves' (Midgley, 1986, 8).

The disparate nature of civil society and differing definitions of social capital give these notions an uncertain form in current political and social thought. Even more uncertain is how these concepts include women. Considering the role of civil society in ideals of participative democracy, this is a crucial aspect of how citizens influence state decisions about themselves. The exclusion of women from public political processes suggests an alternative route of policy development may serve to bypass some of the barriers that are encountered. Regardless, if democratic principles are based on equality of access and opportunity, the experience of women in the context of civil society is of prime importance.

Historical notions of citizenship and the polity have excluded women from the outset (Carroll and Zerilli, 1993, 55; Jones and Jonasdottir, 1988, 1-2; Pateman, 1989, 1). Observers of the philosophical construction of social capital have noted that Machiavelli's *virtù* equated to 'manliness', Rousseau regarded women as transgressors on a 'male domain' in the polity and the 'socialist fraternity' has been more about 'male bonding' (Phillips, 1993, 8; Pitkin, 1984, 25; Vogel, 1995, 215). Hence, if theories of citizenship are integral to the construction of civil society, the exclusion of women is integral to its fabric.

Ainhorn and Sever indicate that politics are gendered 'male' and the home 'female', with civil society in the middle. But this middle ground is also gendered (2003, 167). However, Rotberg has noted that the definitions of social capital in terms of neighbourliness and assistance linkages reflect the domains of women, and it is in the interests of women to protect and develop social capital (1999, 347). Furthermore, it is in this middle space that women have been able to organise and influence the state; for example, Clemens notes that women gained the vote without having the vote, which is an 'object lesson in the political uses of social capital' (1999, 614). In Keen's research, it has also been found that 'the government's relationship with women's associations...came purely through collective action that sought legislation to protect women and children' (1999, 651). Women have used the opportunity spaces presented by the middle ground of civil society to create the instruments of their own emancipation.

The discussion highlights a wider issue of how women are integrated into the theory of civil society. Women predominate in voluntary and community organisations, for example, comprising 75 per cent of the paid workforce of voluntary organisations in Northern Ireland (NICVA, 2006). These organisations constitute the 'horizontal' relationships that Putnam identifies as important for social capital, community-based networks that comprise both 'bonding' capital within communities and 'bridging' capital between communities on the basis of issues such as equality or domestic violence. The qualities associated with the definitions of high levels of social capital accord with those predominantly practised by women, whether in women's organisations (the 'women's sector') or in wider voluntary and community organisations of which they comprise the largest component. Women's organisations operate on more horizontal structures, with a co-operative ethos that relies more on relationship and personal contact than hierarchy.

While women appear to predominate in 'horizontal' civil social structures, they are not necessarily prominent in positions of influence either in executive roles in civil society structures, public bodies or the more formal political structures, such as political parties or government institutions ('vertical' networks), in Northern Ireland comprising 32 per cent of members of public bodies, 22 per cent of local councillors and 17 per cent of Members of Parliament (DETI, 2006). Therefore, the greater the influence of those involved in civic society organisations in policy-making processes, the greater the participation of women. It is primarily women who are involved in the relationships that have been identified as comprising high levels of social capital.

Anne Phillips has pointed out that feminists have generally avoided the concept of civil society, largely due to the fact that its formation was generally along masculine lines and many interpretations of the idea involve state and civil society competing for the public sphere, not the all-important private sphere (Phillips, 2002, 72, 74). But civil society and feminism have much in common: both are pluralist, both have a looser, more informal structure, both appear natural allies in contest with the state, and if the battle for equality is to be won, it has to happen in civil society, acknowledging the limitations of legislation alone (ibid, 76–9). Yet there are still unattractive elements: civil society forma-tion tends to adopt existing power structures, can be discriminatory due to the lack of regulation and can be used to challenge state benevol-ence in favour of a self-help ethos, resulting in Phillips' assertion that 'celebrating civil society as the sphere of freedom and autonomy is not really an option for feminism, given the inequalities that so often mar the cosy associational world' (ibid, 80–1, 87). However, this view may be overly pessimistic. There are opportunities for women to claim spheres of influence within civil society and use its growing importance to struc-ture an equality agenda. Many areas of civil society are sympathetic to the empowerment of women and others form a powerful platform to have the ideals of equal participation aired in a public, sub-state space. The potential pitfalls need to be juxtaposed with the possible gains.

Conflict resolution has tended to be the preserve of elites, where those who have led their communities to conflict or led them during conflict are often the same ones who are expected to lead them out of it. This means that in many cases elites who derive their power from leadership in conflict are either unable or unwilling to adapt to new roles in terms of making peace and post-conflict reconstruction. Writers such as Voutat and Briquet have noted the phenomenon of 'clientelism', which refers to the hold elites have over societies in conflict where elites express (or exaggerate) fears held by communities under threat in return for their continued status in leadership (Briquet, 1997, 65; Voutat, 2000, 286).

In addition to maintaining lines of conflict, such arrangements exclude alternative discourses, significantly that of women (Fearon, 1999, 2). The possibilities for women's organisations and for individual women are curtailed by conflict discourses, leading to a shortfall in the development of empowerment and equality agendas. By silencing women, elite-led processes jeopardise the possibilities of an equitable and sustainable peace.

The task of building peace has been increasingly associated with the processes of community development, economic development and democratic structures, so it is unsurprising that civil society plays a cent-ral role in developing theories of peace-building. Lederach has identified three levels of engagement in the peace-building process: the top level (elites), the middle range and the grassroots level. While all need to be engaged, the middle range is said to be the most important (Lederach, 1999, 39). This is the realm of the active areas of social groups that make up civil society. Kumar agrees, seeing the creation and involve-ment of civil society as an important part of the rehabilitation of war-torn societies (1997, 2).

Civil society and the development of social capital are essential components in the development of community, economic growth and democratic structures required for peace-building. Women are likewise essential components of civil society. As Reardon exclaims, 'the possibilities for peace rest in large measure on the possibilities for women, for their full emancipation and for the realisation of their visions of peace and security' (1993, 4). For the effective development of a peaceful society after conflict, the empowerment of women is not only important on democratic and equality grounds, but essential to the process of building social capital in civil society to ensure a sustainable peace.

## Peace-building through women's empowerment in Northern Ireland

The recognition of a theoretical link between women's empowerment and peace requires qualification. The analysis of current efforts to build peace in the divided society of Northern Ireland demonstrates this link in practice. In this case, the European Union Programme for Peace and Reconciliation in Northern Ireland and the Border Counties of Ireland indicates how women's participation in civil society and peace-building has a direct relationship with the practicalities of peace-building.

In accordance with EU policy commitments, the establishment of a programme to encourage peace on the island of Ireland retains the principles of gender equality enshrined in EU policies and strategies promoting equality between women and men. The initial Special Support Programme for Peace and Reconciliation included the role of women in Sub-Programme 4: Social Inclusion, Measure 1: Developing Grass Roots Capacities and Promoting the Inclusion of Women, recognising:

> The key role of women in community development, both as a source of new leadership in communities and more widely, in shaping social and economic regeneration.
>
> (European Commission, 1996, 145)

The priorities of what was to become known as 'Peace I' (1996–9) were mainly economic, however (ibid, 36). There was an assumption that empowerment through employment and economic development would deliver peace.

In Peace II (2000–6), the empowerment of women was 'promoted' to Priority 1 Measure 5, intended to 'support activities which improve women's access to and participation in the labour market'

(Special European Union Programmes Body, 2000, 89). Again, women's empowerment has been seen as an economic contribution to the project of peace-building, as well as according to the general principles of gender mainstreaming. However, in addition to the specific measure for women, equality, including that between women and men, is laid down as a 'horizontal principle' with which all operations must comply (ibid, 64).

The Training for Women Network (TWN) has acted as a sectoral partner under Measure 4.1 for Peace I and an Intermediary Funding Body (IFB) under Measure 1.5 for Peace II. 114 projects were funded under Peace I, training women in the areas of information technology, management, non-traditional skills, vocational qualifications, personal development, return to learn, research and other areas, such as progression to employment and qualifications. A total of 34 women's training projects were funded under Peace II (2000–6), targeting specific areas, sectors and activities and communities and groups most affected by the conflict, again with a focus on training for employment. The Peace II Extension (2006–8) has a similar focus on employability training, but with even more provision for reconciliation activities.

The International Labour Organisation acknowledges that 'life skills training is vital in a post-conflict situation, as it addresses skill gaps which impede the economic (re)integration of those affected by the conflict' (ILO, 1998, para. 137). In this way, individuals are empowered to cope with the difficult task of transition and new ways of working with those who had been considered enemies. Therefore, the ability to engage in economic regeneration is coupled with personal development and empowerment processes for participation in the peace-building project and the society beyond. As women have been marginalised in activities in both the economic and political spheres, training in personal development and confidence-building is crucial to constructing peace for an equitable society.

The projects themselves have identified the effects of the conflict as weak business infrastructure, low investment, unemployment, social and economic deprivation, population displacement, segregation or polarisation of communities, isolation and general loss of confidence. This situation impacts on women by closing down their networks, frustrating the addressing of important issues common to women through the primacy of constitutional politics and limiting opportunities for self-development through financial independence. In effect, the dynamics of conflict have appropriated women's lives and confined them to narrow spheres of opportunity.

Opportunities brought by peace identified by projects in their own areas included increased possibilities for inter-communal contact, refocusing of communities from conflict identities, greater investment, economic regeneration, more mobility, a greater sense of security, communities being more open to outside help and the resurfacing of important issues that have been subordinated by the conflict, such as homelessness and domestic violence. While these represent possible routes for women to exert more control over their lives, years of restrictions have left them with a low skills base, fewer qualifications, reduced confidence and an inhibited capacity to redefine themselves. Consequently, the varied contexts and backgrounds of projects in the community have similar themes. These include skills and knowledge required to perform in the labour market, such as information technology, business development, entrepreneurship, vocational training and specific skills acquisition, but at the same time giving the capacity for personal and inter-relational development, confidence-building and basic skills. These personal development processes are coupled with elements of reconciliation and mutual understanding within training programmes and experiences of cross-community working and interaction. Such experiences equip women in areas most affected by the conflict with the necessary elements of economic, social and cultural development credited with moving a society beyond conflict.

A developing discipline less easy to define in quantitative terms is that of assessing 'soft outcomes', as opposed to statistical evidence of attendance, qualifications gained, jobs created or businesses started. These are personal skills and capacities acquired by women through training itself, but mainly through the process of attending training. Recorded soft outcomes include community relations awareness, inclusion, mutual understanding, particular life and vocational skills, capacity-building, attendance or participation, self-management, judgement, assertiveness, self-esteem or sense of worth, confidence, teamwork and personal growth. These are the very skills and experiences that have been disrupted by the mechanisms of conflict and which are required to be restored to enable women to gain or regain control over their lives and allow greater participation in their communities, civil society and public life. While developing these skills, projects attempt to negate the systemic barriers to women's participation through, for example, the provision of childcare, transport and flexible working methods to account for women's individual situations.

An example of this work is the Journey for Women project at East Belfast Community Education Centre. The project is situated in what is generally regarded as a Loyalist area and an area of high unemployment and economic deprivation. Women entering the project receive personal development, confidence-building and life-skills training and development, then embark on a twofold process of acquiring skills and qualifications to enhance employability and a programme of engaging with notions of citizenship, equality and human rights. Participants are thus equipped to contribute to the economy through preparation for entrepreneurship or employment and engage with cross-community activities, in this case, the mainly Republican Short Strand area, where there is a similar project for women run by the Short Strand Partnership. The women are supported throughout this process with, for example, on-site childcare, job-seeking skills and advice.

The formation of a cross-community women's citizenship group has assisted women to engage across community and religious boundaries in an area where the conflict between communities had been particularly severe over the years and where there is sporadic tension between communities in the form of civil unrest, rioting and low-level intimidation. Through exploring issues associated with the conflict and discovering each others' identities, relationships between women have been formed and the empowerment processes from the other components of the project have equipped them to take on roles within their own communities and act as restraining influences in times of tension.

Consequently, the theoretical position of women marginalised by the conflict in Northern Ireland becoming empowered to assume roles within their communities and having a positive effect on the task of building peace in the post-conflict context is realised in such projects. To bring women to this stage of participation, preliminary personal development will have taken place to address issues of low confidence, capacity-building and employability training undertaken to enhance life and economic outcomes and engagement with issues of identity, politics and issues of division, including activities with the 'other' community will have been facilitated. In this way, women who would previously have had limited outlooks on life have been assisted to realise their potential socially, economically and in contributing to the formation of a society without violent conflict as a means of political expression or communal tension.

The provision of opportunities for women to enter public life in positions of political, economic or administrative influence and power is necessary to the project of peace-building. In addition, key influencers in civil society are increasingly called upon to become involved in the transition process from conflict. By equipping women who have been most affected by the conflict with the skills, qualifications and capacity to participate more fully in their communities, civil society, economic life and political structures, the chances of a sustainable peace are enhanced. While the understanding of how informal processes of learning and capacity-building contribute to peace is still under development, examples drawn from women's training projects in the community in Northern Ireland as part of the investment in peace in the region demonstrate a clear connection with the theoretical notions that link the empowerment of women with the process of building peace in a society divided by conflict.

However, even in the Peace Programme, this has not always been recognised. For women to move from a position of marginalisation to one of active participation, there is a need for a process of development to take place in projects specifically designed for the needs of women, with the necessary support structures. Yet the notion of a measure for women's training and development was only included in Peace I after lobbying from women's organisations. While the measure was retained under Peace II, again the argument had to be reiterated after the measure was dropped for the Peace II Extension, being replaced after a successful lobbying campaign. Likewise, support to women's centres, networks and organisations across Northern Ireland, where women's empowerment is nurtured and developed, has been sporadic, ill-coordinated and under resourced. Unless the practice of providing support to organisations and projects that empower women is mainstreamed, the potential impacts of women's contribution to peace-building will remain unrealised.

## Conclusion

The empowerment of women in a post-conflict society is a long and difficult process. Women need to travel from a marginalised position during conflict to one of leadership during peace-building. This has to take place in the form of equal political representation in institutions, influence in leadership structures in civil society and a recognition of the extensive impact of women's involvement in maintaining communities throughout conflict and in transition, as well as healing processes during and after conflict.

The transition from conflict is increasingly associated with democratic and participative processes to give citizens a stake in society. The development of civil society is a key part of this process. As the ways women relate to each other and organise fulfil the descriptors of social capital more than traditional 'male' structures in society, the empowerment of women and support of women's organisations are an essential component for any process of peace-building.

The models and processes developed in women's training and development projects in Northern Ireland demonstrate how with a more appropriate level of investment and support, women can be empowered to fulfil those roles in a post-conflict context that are necessary for a more sustainable transition to a peaceful society. These principles and processes can be applied to other areas of conflict around the world, as on the strategic level, the United Nations has already recognised this need through Security Council Resolution 1325, but the mechanics of empowering women in communities to take charge of their lives and take on leadership roles politically, economically and socially still needs to be developed for the overall project of building peace within and between communities in conflict.

## Bibliography

Ainhorn, B. and C. Sever (2003) 'Gender and Civil Society in Central and Eastern Europe', *International Feminist Journal of Politics*, 5:3, 163–215.

*Agreement Between the Government of the United Kingdom of Great Britain and Northern Ireland and the Government of Ireland*. (1998) Belfast: Stationery Office.

Alonso, H. (1993) *Peace as a Women's Issue: A History of the US Movement for World Peace and Women's Rights*. New York: Syracuse University Press.

Alonso, H. (1997) *The Women's Peace Union and the Outlawry of War 1921–1942*. New York: Syracuse University Press.

Andersson, I. (2003) 'Women's Unarmed Uprising Against War: A Swedish Peace Protest in 1935', *Journal of Peace Research*, 40:4, 395–412.

Annan, K. (2002) Speech to the UN Security Council, 28 October 2002, Press Release SG/SM/8461, SC/7551, WOM/1366.

Aristotle (1991) *The Politics*. London: Guild.

Baker, B. (1999) 'African anarchy: Is it States, Regimes or Societies that are Collapsing?', *Politics*, 19:3, 131–8.

Briquet, J-L. (1997) *La Tradition en Mouvement: Clientélism et Politique en Corse*. Paris: Bélin.

Brock-Utne, B. (1989) *Educating for Peace: A Feminist Perspective*. New York: Pergamon.

Caprioli, M and M. Boyer (2001) 'Gender, Violence and International Crisis', *Journal of Conflict Resolution*, 45:4, 503–18.

Carroll, S and L. Zerilli (1993). 'Feminist Challenges to Political Science', in A. Finifter (ed.), *Political Science: The State of the Discipline II*. Washington, DC: American Political Science Association.

Clemens, E. (1999) 'Securing Political Returns to Social Capital: Women's Associations in the United States 1880s–1920s', *Journal of Interdisciplinary History*, 29:4, 613–38.

Department of Enterprise, Trade and Investment. (2006) *Women in Northern Ireland*. Belfast: DETI.

European Commission (1996) *Special Support Programme for Peace and Reconciliation in Northern Ireland and the Border Counties of Ireland 1995–1999: European Structural Funds* .

Fearon, K. (1999) *Women's Work: The Story of the Northern Ireland Women's Coalition.* Belfast: Blackstaff.

Finer, S. (1970) *Comparative Government.* Harmondsworth: Penguin.

Foster, M. (1958) *Masters of Political Thought Volume 1: Plato to Macchiavelli.* London: Harrap.

Galtung, J. (1996) *Peace by Peaceful Means: Peace, Conflict Development and Civilisation.* London: Sage.

Gierycz, D. (2001) 'Women, Peace and the UN', in I. Skjelsback and D. Smyth (eds), *Gender, Peace and Conflict.* London: Sage.

Hammond, M. (2002) 'Surveying Politics of Peace, Gender, Conflict and Identity in Northern Ireland: The Case of the Derry Peace Women in 1972', *Women's Studies International Forum,* 25:1, 33–49.

Harford, B. (1984) *Greenham Common: Women at the Wire.* London: Women's Press.

Henderson, M. (1994) *All Her Paths Are Peace: Women Pioneers in Peacemaking.* West Hartford: Kumarian.

Huntington, S. (2002) *The Clash of Civilisations and the Remaking of World Order.* London: Free Press.

International Labour Organisation (1998) *Guidelines for Skills Training and Employment in Conflict-Affected Countries.* Geneva: ILO.

Jacoby, T. (1999) 'Gendered Nation: A History of the Interface of Women's Protest and Jewish Nationalism in Israel', *International Feminist Journal of Politics,* 1:3, 382–402.

Jones, J. and A. Jonasdottir (1988) *The Political Interests of Gender: Developing Theory and Research with a Feminist Face.* London: Sage.

Karam, A. (2001) 'Women in War and Peacebuilding: The Roads Traversed, The Challenges Ahead', *International Feminist Journal of Politics,* 3:1, 2–25.

Keen, S. (1999) 'Associations in Australian History: Their Contribution to Social Capital', *Journal of Interdisciplinary History,* 29:4, 639–59.

Kumar, K. (ed.) (1997) *Rebuilding Societies after Civil War: Critical Roles for International Assistance.* Boulder: Lynne Rienner.

Laski, H. (1973) *A Grammar of Politics.* London: George Allan and Unwin.

Lederach, J. (1999) *Building Peace: Sustainable Reconciliation in Divided Societies.* Washington, DC: US Institute of Peace Research.

Midgley, J. (1986) *Community Participation, Social Development and the State.* London: Methuen.

Miller, R., R. Wilford and F. Donoghue (1996) *Women and Political Participation in Northern Ireland.* Aldershot: Avebury.

Montesquieu (1970) *L'Esprit des Lois: Les Grands Thèmes.* Gallimard: Paris.

Morgan, V. (1995) 'Peacemakers? Peacekeepers? – Women in Northern Ireland 1969-1995'. Paper delivered at the University of Ulster, 25 October 1995, Available at http://www.cain.ulst.ac.uk.

Moser, C. and F. Clark (eds) (2001) *Victims, Perpetrators or Actors? Gender, Armed Conflict and Political Violence.* London: Zed.

Naidoo, K. (2003) Speech at the 'Divided Societies' Conference, Armagh, 14 October 2003.

Northern Ireland Council for Voluntary Action (2006) *State of the Sector IV*. Belfast: NICVA.

Oldfield, S. (1989) *Women against the Iron Fist: Alternatives to Militarism 1900–1989*. Oxford: Basil Blackwell.

Onyx, J. and P. Bullen (2000) 'Measuring Social Capital in Five Communities', *Journal of Applied Behavioural Science*, 36:1, 23–42.

Pateman, C. (1989) *The Disorder of Woman: Democracy, Feminism and Political Theory*. Cambridge: Polity Press.

Phillips, A. (1993) *Democracy and Difference*. Cambridge: Polity Press.

Phillips, A. (2002) 'Does Feminism Need a Concept of Civil Society?', in S. Chambers and W. Kymlicka (eds), *Alternative Conceptions of Civil Society*. Princeton: University Press.

Pitkin, H. (1984) *Fortune Is a Woman: Gender and Politics in the Thought of Niccolò Macchiavelli*. Berkley: University of California Press.

Putnam, R. (1993) *Making Democracy Work: Civil Traditions in Modern Italy*. Princeton: University Press.

Putnam, R. (2000) *Bowling Alone: The Collapse and Revival of American Community*. New York: Simon and Schuster.

Reardon, B. (1993) *Women and Peace: Feminist Visions of Global Society*. Albany: State University of New York Press.

Regan, P. and A. Paskeviciute (2003) 'Women's Access to Politics and Peaceful States', *Journal of Peace Research*, 40:3, 287–302.

Rotberg, I. (1999) 'Social Capital in Africa, America, Australia and Europe', *Journal of Interdisciplinary History*, 29:3, 339–56.

Rousseau, J-J. (1963) *The Social Contract and Discourses*. London: Everyman.

Ruddick, S. (1990) *Maternal Thinking: Towards a Politics of Peace*. London: Women's Press.

Russell, B. (1985) *A History of Western Philosophy*. London: Unwin.

Skjelsback, I. (2001) 'Is Femininity Inherently Peaceful? The Construction of Femininity in War', in I. Skjelsback and D. Smyth (eds), *Gender, Peace and Conflict*. London: Sage.

Skjelsback, I. and D. Smyth (eds) (2001) *Gender, Peace and Conflict*. London: Sage.

Special European Union Programmes Body (2000) *EU Programme for Peace and Reconciliation in Northern Ireland and the Border Region of Ireland 2000–2004: Operational Programme*. Belfast: SEUPB.

Training for Women Network (1998) *An Interim Evaluation of the Impact of the Peace and Reconciliation Programme on Women's Training, Development and Subsequent Employability in Northern Ireland*. Belfast: TWN.

Trentmann, F. (2000) *Paradoxes of Civil Society*. Oxford: Berghahn.

United Nations Resolution 1325 (2000) adopted by the Security Council at its 4213th meeting on 31 October 2000 S/RES/1325 (2000).

Vogel, U. (1995) 'Guarding the Boundaries of Liberty', in R. Wokler (ed.), *Rousseau and Liberty*. Manchester: University Press.

Voutat, B. (2000) 'Territorial Identity in Europe: The Political Processes of the Construction of Identities in Corsica, the Basque Country, Italy, Macedonia and the Swiss Jura', *Contemporary European History*, 9:2, 285–94.

Woroniuk, B. and J. Schalkwyk (1998) *Conflict, Peace-Building, Disarmament, Security: Post-Conflict Initiatives and Equality Between Women and Men*. Stockholm: Swedish International Co-operation Agency.

# 7
# A Framework for Understanding Religion in Northern Irish Civil Society[1]

*Gladys Ganiel*

The churches are the largest voluntary associations in Northern Irish civil society (Morrow *et al.*, 1991), but they have rarely been included in broader analyses of it. In particular, churches and religious organisations have been overlooked when it comes to analyses of how civil society has contributed to the Northern Irish peace process (Ganiel and Dixon, 2008). Apart from the work of Brewer (2003) and Appleby (2000), which highlights significant contributions of religious peace-builders,[2] much of the scholarship on religion in Northern Ireland has focused on its contribution to the conflict or, at the very least, its role in maintaining boundaries between the Catholic and Protestant communities (Brewer and Higgins, 1998; Bruce, 1986; Fulton, 1991; Liechty and Clegg, 2001; Mitchell, 2003, 2006). Others have downplayed the religious dimensions of the conflict (McGarry and O'Leary, 1995), or argued that it matters only for a few fundamentalists or evangelicals. In this area, the Rev. Ian Paisley and his followers have been stereotyped as religious fanatics, providing ammunition for those who would exclude religion from the public sphere on the grounds that it is dangerous.[3]

This has led to a truncated understanding of religion's role in contemporary Northern Ireland. The purpose of this chapter is to move beyond the unimportant-dangerous dichotomy that has been imposed on religion, outlining a framework for understanding its role in Northern Irish civil society and its potential to contribute to the peace process. This does not imply that the conflict has been primarily or essentially about religion, or that its resolution must be solely a religious one. It is, however, a call for policy makers and practitioners to take religion seriously. Accordingly, the framework consists of understanding how

religion matters in Northern Ireland, understanding how religion interacts with the structure of civil society, and understanding how religious
beliefs may impact on conflict and reconciliation.

Below, I elaborate on each aspect of the framework as it applies in
Northern Ireland. First, I explore how religion matters, emphasising the
historical importance of Protestant evangelicalism and how its Calvinist
theology has been used to justify division and conflict. Next, I analyse how the structure of civil society has changed since the Troubles,
explaining how the British Government and other civil society actors
have created what amounts to an officially sanctioned public sphere
in which cross-community contact, dialogue, and parity of esteem for
Catholic and Protestant identities are funded and promoted. Then, I
draw on my own ethnographic research to evaluate how evangelicals
have responded to the changing structure of civil society. I focus on
the development of an Anabaptist-influenced theology that has been
used to justify pluralism and dialogue, drawing out aspects that may
contribute to conflict resolution. I also explore how both Calvinist and
Anabaptist-informed evangelicals have been interacting in civil society,
and argue that evangelicals have contributed to conflict resolution in
ways that are not usually expected. Even evangelicals who oppose the
Belfast Agreement are participating in civil society in surprising ways.
I conclude with reflections on the policy implications that flow from
this framework, in Northern Ireland and in other conflicts with religious
dimensions. This includes taking religion seriously as a contributor both
to conflict and reconciliation, carefully considering how religion can and
should be included in the public sphere, and providing encouragement
and practical support to religious peace-builders.

## How religion matters in Northern Ireland

### For whom does religion matter?

Evangelicals are numerous (25–33 per cent of the Protestant population)
and socially significant in Northern Ireland (Bruce, 1986; Boal *et al.*, 1997;
Mitchell and Tilley, 2004; Thomson, 2002). Evangelicalism is a diverse
movement, with its origins in the North Atlantic revivals of the 1740s
(Noll, 2001a,b). It encompasses Christians in a variety of denominations.
Bebbington (1989) has provided a classic four-fold definition of the term:
evangelicals believe that one must be converted or 'born again;' that the
Bible is the inspired word of God; that Christ's death on the cross was a
historical event necessary for salvation; and that a Christian must express
their faith through social action/evangelism.

Evangelicalism's prominence in the Protestant/Unionist community has not been matched by Catholicism in the Nationalist community.[4] Evangelicalism contributed to the hardening of (already-existing) boundaries between Protestants and Catholics (Liechty and Clegg, 2001). It also came to hold a privileged relationship with socio-political power, especially during the Stormont era (1921–72) (Mitchel, 2003). Addressing the religious dimension of the Northern Ireland conflict requires recognising the importance of evangelicalism.

A comprehensive account of evangelicalism's historical importance is beyond the scope of this chapter.[5] But by the late nineteenth century, evangelicalism informed Protestants' social mores and political discourses, and evangelical assumptions were articulated at both elite and populist levels. This was reflected in the Ulster Solemn League and Covenant of 1912, the purpose of which was to proclaim Protestant determination to resist home rule. It drew Scottish Calvinist traditions under the 'sacred canopy' of evangelicalism (Brewer and Higgins, 1998). The Solemn League and Covenant also identified evangelicalism with the socio-political power of the Protestants of Ulster. After the Irish War for Independence (1919–21), Ireland was partitioned: the 26 counties of the south became the Irish Free State, while six of the Ulster counties remained within the United Kingdom. With Protestants in a clear numerical majority in Northern Ireland, Unionists set about building a Protestant parliament for a Protestant people.[6] Mitchel (2003) calls this period, which stretched from 1921 until the imposition of direct rule in 1972, the 'golden era' of Ulster Unionism (86). During this time, the Orange Order understood itself as a bulwark against 'absorption within an all-Ireland Catholic state, a fate contrary to God's will' (159–60), and dismissed Catholic grievances, arguing that good citizenship meant supporting the Union and Protestantism.

## What mattered for evangelicals?

In societies divided along religious lines, the content of people's religious beliefs may be points of contention. Where there is potential for conflict amongst competing groups with different religious beliefs, the beliefs that matter most are those about the relationship between church and state; about religious or cultural pluralism; and about violence and peace. These beliefs shape the way people perceive their relationship with the state and with other groups. Evangelicalism does not have a unified theology or an agreed position on the beliefs outlined above. Rather, evangelicals tend to 'borrow' the beliefs that are dominant in the Christian denominations in their host culture. In Ulster, evangelicals borrowed from the covenantal Calvinism that was dominant from the eighteenth century onwards. The concepts and symbols of Calvinism infused the Ulster evangelical ethos and provided the resources for a 'Protestant ideology' (Wright, 1973).

Calvinism's conception of a covenantal relationship between church and state shaped evangelical attitudes about the Catholic religion and the ability of Catholics to be 'good' citizens. Covenantal Calvinism requires ordering church-state covenants to reflect God's laws. It is believed that if the state follows God's laws, God will bless it. If it disobeys God's laws, God will curse it.[7] For Calvin himself, that meant establishing the 'Christian Commonwealth' of Geneva, where all citizens covenanted to uphold the Ten Commandments. For Cromwell's English Puritans or the Puritans of New England, that meant a coercive Christian commonwealth. For the Scots who established the Solemn League and Covenant of 1643 with the English Parliament, that meant eliminating Catholicism in Scotland and extending Presbyterianism to England and Ireland. It follows that some religions are simply wrong, and allowing them free reign can wreck havoc in the body politic. In evangelical Ulster, this provided a powerful theological justification for socio-political power. Protestants – who had the right religion – must maintain their socio-political power in order to ensure God's blessing.

The covenant also shaped evangelical attitudes about religious and cultural pluralism. Catholics, because their religion was wrong, simply could not uphold the covenant. This created a sharp contrast between Protestants and Catholics. Protestants were a 'chosen people', dutifully upholding God's laws and bringing order and civilisation to the land. Catholics were outside the pale, barbaric, and uncivilised. In evangelical Ulster, this provided a powerful theological justification for resisting integration with the Catholic Irish.

Finally, the covenant provided justification for violence. The covenant required faithful citizens to monitor the state. It followed from the covenant that if the state was not fulfilling its part of the covenant, then the Christian citizens living within it could resort to legal (or constitutional) agitation. If that failed, violent revolution could be justified. In evangelical Ulster, this has provided a powerful theological justification for resistance to the policies of the British crown or the British state. When Protestants threatened to resort to armed insurrection if their opposition to Home Rule was not heeded, they followed the logic of covenantal Calvinist thinking.

These ideas shaped evangelicals' perceptions of what the socio-political order should be like. They justified Protestants' privileged relationship with power; and they legitimated their (divine) right to rule. They underpinned Protestants' resistance to integration with Catholics, contributing to an uneasy religious and cultural 'pluralism' on the island. And they provided Protestants with a justification for violence or to threaten violence, even if it was as a last resort.[8]

## The changing structure of civil society

### A civil society approach to conflict resolution

The Civil Rights movement (1964–69) and the Troubles marked the beginning of massive social and political change in Northern Ireland. There would be no going back to a Protestant parliament for a Protestant people. The social, economic, cultural and political gaps between Protestants and Catholics would narrow; and Protestants would no longer retain a privileged position with the British state. Indeed, Protestants usually felt abandoned by the British state and viewed it as a dubious ally. Evangelicalism could not legitimate and underwrite a form of Protestant power that no longer existed. One evangelical response to these changes was the 'revival' associated with Paisley's street politics and the rapid growth of the Free Presbyterian Church.[9] Paisley's Democratic Unionist Party (DUP) was also a child of the Troubles and was originally called the Protestant Unionist Party (Bruce, 1986). Another response was the formation of the political action group Evangelical Contribution on Northern Ireland (ECONI) in 1985.[10] The founders of ECONI were reacting in part to distaste at what they perceived as Paisley's inappropriate mixing of religion and politics. They rejected covenantal Calvinism and attempted to construct an alternative evangelical theology that drew largely on concepts from Anabaptism. These two broad responses were very different in style and content. They challenged the way things were and the way things were going. They said very different things about the Troubles, about the negotiation of the 1998 Belfast Agreement, and about the campaign for the Belfast Agreement referendum (Bruce, 1986; Cooke, 1996; Mitchel, 2003; Moloney and Pollak, 1986; Smyth, 1987; Thomson, 2002). The negotiation (and attempted implementation) of the Belfast Agreement reflected the widespread changes in power relationships and socio-political structures. Ruane and Todd (forthcoming) have provided a comprehensive analysis of the changing structure of the Northern Ireland conflict, examining changes in the power relationships between the British and Irish states and Catholics and Protestants in Northern Ireland. Here, I narrow my focus to the changing structure of civil society, and on how that is impacting on evangelicals' participation in it.

The changing structure of civil society can be traced to the efforts of grassroots groups to influence government policy, especially peace negotiations (Cochrane and Dunn, 2002; Wilson and Tyrrell, 1995). Change can also be traced to the British Government's 'civil society approach' to conflict resolution, which has been part of British policy since the 1970s (Dixon, 1997). This approach has been implemented concurrently with political negotiations and changes in governmental institutions; and is complementary to that process (Bloomfield, 1996; Dixon, 2005; Farrington, 2004, 2006).[11] It should be understood in two ways: as part of an overall strategy to equalise social, cultural, and political conditions between Catholics and Protestants; and as a reflection of changes and emphases in the wider UK approach to civil society. For example, throughout the Troubles, the British Government introduced a series of fair employment legislation that has gone some way towards redressing economic discrimination.[12] It also introduced a number of reforms designed to manage civil society by encouraging good community relations through cross-community contact (Dixon, 1997, 2001; Fitzduff, 2002). Although these broad reforms have been important in preparing the ground for political initiatives and in redefining interests, alliances, and identities, this chapter will not discuss them in depth.[13] Rather, the narrower aspects of the government's approach are most relevant here, as they have more immediate impacts on the restructuring of civil society.

Some of these reforms have been influenced by wider UK and European trends toward partnership, governance, and the rhetoric of dialogic democracy (Acheson *et al.*, 2004; Kearney and Williamson, 2001). These trends intensified after the election of a Labour government in 1997. Prime Minister Tony Blair was an enthusiastic proponent of the 'Third Way' ideas promoted by sociologist Anthony Giddens (Bacon, 2003; Farrington, 2004; see Giddens, 1998). Giddens argued that state and civil society should work closely together, with the state supporting, funding and consulting civil society.[14] Some of the major strategies have been establishing the Community Relations Council; attempting to mainstream 'Third Way' governance through the consultation processes on the Shared Future document and regularising funding relationships; and the Belfast Agreement's (short-lived) Civic Forum (OFMDFM, 2003, 2005; Palshaugen, 2005). These initiatives have provided civil society actors (including evangelicals) with incentives to change their identities, theologies, and socio-political projects to fit in with these emerging structures. In effect, the civil society approach has created what amounts to an officially sanctioned public sphere in which cross-community contact, dialogue, and parity of esteem for identities are funded and promoted by the state.

These strategies have met with mixed results. Critics claim that the grassroots have been encouraged to develop divisive identity politics that essentialise differences, rather than developing a shared identity. They cite evidence that attitudes on core issues such as identity, attitudes about the state, and support for the Belfast Agreement remain polarised; and that housing is becoming more segregated (Hayes and McAllister, 1999; Shirlow and Murtagh, 2006). Moreover, the British Government has not been systematic or transparent in its attempts to include victims in civil society or to construct anything resembling Keane's (1998) 'public spheres of controversy' for monitoring violence. A critique of the British Government's ad hoc and failed attempts to include victims in the public sphere is beyond the scope of this chapter.[15] However, these failures must be tempered by recognising the extent to which the structure of civil society has changed; and that those changes have, in some instances, contributed to conflict resolution and peace-building.

## Evangelicals and the changing structure of civil society

However, the British Government's civil society approach has not engaged substantially with religious groups in general – and evangelical groups in particular. This is striking, especially since the Labour government has been keen to include faith-based organisations in its plans for Third Way governance in other parts of the United Kingdom (Bacon, 2003). The reluctance to include religion may reflect sentiments like those of Little (2004), who argues that religion is so divisive in Northern Ireland that it *should* be excluded from the public sphere. Evangelicals, living in the shadow of the Paisley stereotype, are especially prone to generate this wariness amongst others. This is reflected in the 'definition of the voluntary sector followed by the NI [Northern Ireland] Community and Voluntary Sector Almanac', which 'virtually excludes churches, asserting that they exist "solely for the benefit of their members" (NICVA, 2002: 13)' (Bacon, 2003, 27). Although there is some evidence of willingness to include religious actors in civil society on relatively equal footing (Kiess and Thomson, 2004), this inclusion may be limited to those that already agree with the government's civil society approach. These groups receive government funding and favour, whilst those that do not approve of the government's civil society approach face a comprehensive network of institutions that are meant to enforce these norms, such as the Community Relations Council. Groups that do not approve are excluded if they do not sign up to these norms. This creates a powerful structural incentive for these groups to protest (violently or non-violently) against these norms; or to change to fit in with them.

The pluralist, cross-community, officially sanctioned public sphere promoted by government throws up obvious problems for evangelicals who see the world through the historical, Calvinist paradigm outlined above. However, the emergence of evangelicals who self-consciously and publicly distance themselves from the Calvinist-informed paradigm is significant. It is here that changing social and political structures interact with changes in religious belief.

## Belief, conflict and reconciliation

### What matters now for some evangelicals?

ECONI saw an important part of its task as critiquing the Calvinist-informed theology that had been dominant throughout Northern Ireland's history (Thomson, 2002). Although Northern Irish evangelicalism is more diverse than Paisley and ECONI (Brewer and Higgins, 1998; Jordan, 2001; Mitchel, 2003; Porter, 2002), the most active evangelicals clustered round those poles.[16]

A significant cluster, which I call traditional evangelicals, has continued to articulate positions influenced by Calvinist modes of thought. The other cluster, which I call mediating evangelicals, has challenged traditional Calvinist beliefs about the relationship between church and state; about religious or cultural pluralism; and about violence and peace. I call them mediating because of their expressed desire to serve as facilitators of contact between evangelicals and other groups in Northern Ireland.[17] The most systematic presentation of the themes endorsed by mediating evangelicals has come through the work of ECONI. Table 7.1 summarises the beliefs of traditional and mediating evangelicals.

ECONI's critique borrowed heavily from the Anabaptist tradition (see Carter, 2001; Hauerwas, 1983; 1995; Hauerwas and Willimon, 1995; Yoder, 1994–72). The classic Anabaptist position on the relationship between church and state is that they should be totally separate. Any sort of close relationship with the state is seen to compromise the church's ability to play its 'proper' role. The proper role of the church is conceived of as an alternative socio-political order. Being an alternative

*Table 7.1*   Taxonomy of beliefs of traditional and mediating evangelicals

|  | Traditional | Mediating |
| --- | --- | --- |
| Relationship between church and state | Covenantal (Calvinist) | Separation (Anabaptist) |
| Pluralism | Privileged place for 'right religion' | Advocates pluralism |
| Attitudes about violence and peace | Violence justified as a last resort | Non-violence |

socio-political order involves rejecting political power. If the church does not reject power, its interests become bound up with the state, leading to 'idolatry' – the worship of the state along with (or instead of) God. ECONI drew on these concepts to argue that Northern Ireland's covenantal Calvinism had made evangelicals into idol-worshippers. They claimed that they had placed their allegiance to Ulster ahead of their allegiance to Christ. ECONI viewed attempts to ensure that 'right religion' has a privileged relationship with socio-political power as misguided. This would not bring about God's blessing; rather, it would inhibit the church from doing what it was intended to do.

Insistence on the separation of church and state also shapes the Anabaptist attitude about religious and cultural pluralism. The ideal Anabaptist world is one 'in which no one is forced either by the government or by societal expectations to be Christians' (Hauerwas, 1995, 73). This allows the church to maintain its distinct identity, while at the same time leaving space for the toleration of other forms of Christianity, other religions, and other cultures.[18] In Northern Ireland, this might mean that a sharp contrast between Protestantism and Catholicism remains. Some Anabaptists have been criticised for this 'sectarian' position, but ECONI has made it a point to engage with non-evangelical Protestants and Catholics. They do so from a position that their evangelical identity is not threatened by religious or cultural pluralism.

Finally, the Anabaptist emphasis on suffering and servanthood provides no justification for violence. Pacifism is a sacred principle for classic Anabaptists. It is based on the non-violent example of Jesus in the gospels; specifically his rejection of political power, his acceptance of his role as servant, and his willingness to suffer. Violence is considered illegitimate, even if it is used to achieve noble ends. This leaves scope for the use of non-violent protest as an effective technique, as practised by Martin Luther King Jr or Gandhi, for example. But effectiveness is not the point. The Anabaptist tradition includes an acute recognition that non-violence, more often than not, seems to fail. After all, Jesus' death on the cross at first seemed a failure. What is essential is a commitment to patience, not effectiveness. The church must be willing to suffer indefinitely, confident that God will maintain its survival. In the case of ECONI, it has articulated pacifist (or generally non-violent) positions.[19] This has led to an organisational focus on issues of peacemaking, such as forgiveness and reconciliation.

These Anabaptist ideas shape mediating evangelicals' perceptions of what the socio-political order should be like. Anabaptists reject a privileged relationship with political power. They conceive of pluralism as the logical result of a separation of church and state, hoping for a public sphere in which they (and others) are free to express their identities with integrity. They also offer a strong critique of violence, leading to a focus on suffering, patience, forgiveness, and reconciliation. These beliefs provide mediating evangelicals with a theological justification for cross-community activism and peace-building projects. These beliefs fit quite comfortably with the pluralist, cross-community ethos of the British Government's civil society approach to conflict resolution.

### Evangelicals' interactions in civil society

Civil society has tended to be defined in terms of its institutions. However, it is more fruitful theoretically to define civil society in terms of its functions rather than its institutions. This avoids falling into the conceptual trap of trying to evaluate civil society in terms of the 'effectiveness' of its institutions. Rather, most of the functions of civil society can be subsumed under two broad areas: the process of socialisation/identity construction and the practice of non-governmental politics. Analysing these two areas allows for an understanding of how evangelicalism is functioning in Northern Irish civil society. Focused research allows us to see how evangelicals construct their identities through the process of socialisation (usually in the context of a congregation); and how they frame their justifications for participating in non-governmental politics (usually through organisations such as ECONI or traditional groups like the Caleb Foundation). Below, I provide examples from my own research of how evangelicals are constructing their identities and justifying their socio-political activism.[20] This research cannot demonstrate that changes in the structure of civil society 'caused' changes within evangelicalism. Indeed, mediating evangelicals tend to perceive changes in their identity – especially if it is from a traditional to a mediating identity – as the result of relationships with others and/or theological reflection (Ganiel, 2006a; Thomson, 1996). However, it is clear that the structural changes that have taken place now impact on both traditional and mediating evangelicals' ability to interact in civil society. This allows us to understand how evangelicals experience and adjust to socio-political changes, both at the individual, cognitive level and an institutional level.

## Traditional evangelicals in civil society

Evangelical identities, constructed by people over lifetimes of socialisation and experiences, provide a starting point for an analysis of adjustment and change. Adam[21] is a 33-year-old manual labourer who belongs to a rural Presbyterian congregation. His views about why the political process in Northern Ireland would fail were based on traditional evangelical beliefs. He said that the laws of the land should be based on the Bible, and that politics would fail because evil, immoral men from Sinn Féin were in government. This reflects the traditional covenantal theology that says that God will curse a land where immorality is rife:

> Sinn Féin are the evilest men on this planet. I mean that genuine. I do believe that cause they sit around a table, nicey-nicey, nicey-nicey, go out the door, take off the suit, on with the balaclava and shoot somebody cold dead. Then they come in the next day, put on the suit . . . and that's basically Sinn Féin. . . . There's no way any government, or any country . . . can from my point of view and I'm sure from God's teachings and from the Bible – you can't have a government where you have that. If you have a government . . . it's supposed to be Godly men and to take their morals and their standards from the Bible. . . . . [And] Tony Blair – he's the biggest lying, two-faced – he really is! He comes over here and tells us all we're going to do this and we're going to do that and we'll stand by you and then he goes away and does the complete opposite. . . . He tells lies and . . . the Bible tells you [that leaders should be] upright men. And whatever they say, they stand by it. There's no way any country will prosper [with leaders like that].
>
> (Interview on 18 May 2004)

This narrative is representative of other traditional evangelicals who participated in my research. It demonstrates how covenantal Calvinist ideas about the relationship between church and state, and a privileged place for 'right religion' continue to inform the beliefs and identities of some evangelicals in Northern Ireland. However, in my study of a network of traditional evangelical organisations (Caleb, the Evangelical Protestant Society, and the Independent Orange Order), activists were willing to admit that it was no longer possible for their traditional, Calvinist-informed beliefs to impact society in the way that they would like (Ganiel, 2006b). They still expressed sentiments, in interviews and publicly, that indicated they would prefer society to be constructed along Calvinist lines, but they were willing to compromise that goal and participate in the new structures of civil society. Although they had scathing criticism for the Community Relations Council and various fair employment or 'parity of esteem' measures, they tried to secure Community Relations Council funding and claimed they were attempting to initiate cross-community dialogue with ecumenical churches. They also had begun to focus their activism on moral issues such as abortion and homosexuality legislation, at the expense of issues with which they previously might have been more concerned, such as preventing a united Ireland. Although they were engaging in civil society selectively, and perceived themselves as facing discrimination from the government and other civil society groups, they had adjusted their beliefs and goals and were participating in the new structures – not trying to smash them.

## Mediating evangelicals in civil society

By way of contrast, Kelly is a 48-year-old scientist who attends an urban Presbyterian church. Her description of the process whereby she turned away from the theology and politics associated with traditional evangelicalism marked her out as a mediating evangelical. She said that process involved participating in cross-community activities; as well as trying to understand and 'reconnect' with traditional identity:

I grew up with the Orange Order as being part of life, along with the Black Perceptory. My father was a notional member of the Orange Order, had a sash and a bowler hat and on the 12th of July we went to the parade.... But I actively would have disassociated myself from it when I left Northern Ireland and when I came back here I didn't have anything to do with it. Didn't want to have anything to do with the 12th of July. For me that was part of deliberately moving away from my background.... And actually it took being involved in a Moving Beyond Sectarianism project[22] weekend... where I actually decided to reconnect with that background of mine. And say that the Orange Order *is* a part of my background. It is an organization that has a chequered history. And there are some good things about it, there are some really bad things about it... [But] I think like everything else...it's possible for it to be redeemed. ...Being at the General Assembly [of the Presbyterian Church in Ireland] last night...David Livingstone said: God transforms our human perversity. And I think that's very important. I think we need to take that position more and see that it's possible and instead of denouncing...organisations that we see not being good...To see actually, well, what way might God want to transform it. So that's how I want to start to think about the Orange Order. So any changes that I see in them where they are actually reaching out and not holding such an entrenched position, and willing to engage with others who look at them negatively, I would want to support and encourage them in that.

(Interview on 10 June 2004)

This text is representative of other mediating evangelicals. It stresses her distancing from and tension with traditional evangelical identity as she experiences changes in her beliefs. In addition, it highlights mediating evangelicals' enthusiasm about pluralism. In my study of a network of mediating evangelical organisations (ECONI, Evangelical Alliance and the 'post-evangelical' groups Zero28 and ikon[23]), activists expressed similar sentiments. As this ECONI activist said:

Part of our strategy through churches is about getting churches to look at the nature of their relationships with others in the community, whether it's people from other Protestant traditions or whether it's people from the Catholic tradition. And [to look at] how they can actually begin to make contacts based on these relationships. Through some of the public meetings we've done, like bringing in Sinn Féin and the SDLP, it's about setting up a conversation that moves beyond simply accepting that some people vote for them. [It's about accepting that] they have to have some role. One thing we've never agreed with is the position among some people in the ecumenically inclined churches that you need to create some kind of ecumenical reconciliation between churches before you can create reconciliation in society....Partly because it's wrong, partly because...it gives churches greater significance than they actually have....One of the things we need to learn in this community is not to sink our differences but to find ways to have our differences constructively and in a way that has some measure of relationship, where there is still difference. And actually churches instead of pretending those things aren't there can actually do a good job of modelling how you can relate them constructively in relationships within that. And that's a more useful role the church can play as a model.

(Interview on 29 November 2002)

Mediating evangelicals' view of their role in civil society represents a decisive break with traditional evangelicalism. They critique traditional evangelicalism and its historical relationship with power and justify it in theological terms, creating an Anabaptist-informed discourse that embraces pluralism and difference. They have constructed an evangelical socio-political project that legitimates aspects of the new order, including the British Government's civil society approach. For instance, mediating evangelicals believe that cross-community activities are achieving their ends, but that it is a very slow process. They are focusing their attention on the social justice issues that they believe most churches have ignored, such as support for the poor in Northern Ireland and abroad. Because their agenda fits quite snugly with government's civil society approach, they are accepted and even promoted by the state, participating fully in the officially sanctioned public sphere. This is ironic, given that Anabaptist theology rejects political power. Mediating activists must deal with the tensions between their theological beliefs and the practical ways they are interacting with the government. They say they must remain vigilant lest their work be co-opted or restrained for state purposes. But the extent that they are dependent on government funds (especially ECONI) forces them to maintain a delicate balance. Socio-political structures and religious beliefs do not exist in isolation; they interact and impact on each other. The re-structuring of Northern Irish civil society has placed considerable constraints upon what evangelicals can accomplish in the public sphere, and has impacted how they conceive of their identities. Traditional and mediating evangelicals have responded to these changes in different ways. However, neither of their responses seems destined to derail the peace process. The mediating response positively reinforces it, whilst the traditional response accepts it grudgingly.

## Conclusions: religion, civil society and peace processes

In conflicts with religious dimensions, religion is neither unimportant nor unavoidably dangerous. Conflicts with a religious dimension require conflict resolution policies that recognise and address the religious dimension. This is becoming increasingly recognised internationally, with religious peace-builders playing prominent roles in contexts as diverse as Guatemala, the Phillipines, Rwanda, Sri Lanka, Bosnia and South Africa (Appleby, 2000; Cejka and Bamat, 2003; Herbert, 2003; Johnston, 2003; Tombs and Leichty, 2006). This chapter has explored why addressing the evangelical dimension of the Northern Ireland conflict is vital to the wider peace process. Accordingly, it is possible to summarise a framework for understanding religion in Northern Irish civil society – and to draw out policy implications that can be applied in Northern Ireland and other conflict situations. The framework includes understanding how religion matters in each context, how religion interacts with the structure of civil society, and how religious beliefs may impact on conflict and reconciliation.

Policy implications flow from each of these three aspects of the framework. First, understanding how religion matters requires that policy makers take religion seriously, rather than dismissing it as unimportant or dangerous. This means identifying key religious actors, and supporting religious groups that are actively reconceptualising religion's relationship with conflict, including devising peace-building alternatives. Second, understanding how religion interacts with the structure of civil society means recognising which religious groups are included and excluded as a result of government approaches to civil society. Without this consideration, excluded religious groups (which may enjoy widespread public support) could become alienated and resort to violence. Some of their criticisms of specific policies and conflict resolution approaches may have merit. An effort should be made to include the viewpoints of religious actors that both agree and disagree with ongoing reforms. Finally, understanding the impact of religious beliefs means that religious contributions to conflict resolution must have a viable theological basis that appeals to the grassroots. In some cases, this may mean that aspects of religious belief that have been used to justify conflict must change. This process is most effective if indigenous religious actors critique aspects of their theology that have contributed to conflict, and articulate theological alternatives that focus on concepts like forgiveness, reconciliation, or peace-building. Secular peace-builders who dismiss the importance of theological justifications for change or peace-building do a disservice to potential allies. If they aggressively attempt to exclude religion from the public sphere, they undercut the work of religious peace-builders and risk alienating potentially large swathes of the population. In conflicts with religious dimensions, excluding religious language from the public sphere may unnecessarily eliminate the construction of a potentially transformative new vocabulary. A *re-emphasis* on religious aspects of difference – but from a pluralist rather than ethno-nationalist perspective – could contribute to conflict resolution in Northern Ireland and further afield.

## Notes

1. This research was funded by the Royal Irish Academy's Third Sector Research Programme. I wish to thank the research participants who gave so generously of their time and insights.
2. Some studies have recognised the work of religiously based peace groups or prominent clergy. See Power (2005), Wells (1999, 2005), Ericson (2003), and Love (1995).
3. See Cooke (1996) and Moloney and Pollak (1986) for highly critical accounts of Paisley's evangelicalism/fundamentalism.
4. On the role of Catholicism in the conflict, see Mitchell (2005, 2006) and Fulton (1991).
5. For more detailed analyses, see Hempton and Hill (1992), Akenson (1992), McBride (1998), Leichty and Clegg (2001), Thomson (2002) and Mitchel (2003).
6. In the words of James Craig, Prime Minister of Northern Ireland from 1921 to 1940: 'In the South they boasted of a Catholic State. All I boast of is that we are a Protestant Parliament and a Protestant State' (quoted in Dixon, 2001, 50).
7. The logic behind this mindset does not require any public or formal covenant between church and state; it works something like an immutable universal law (Akenson, 1992).
8. Evangelicalism was not as unified as it may appear in this account. On occasion, evangelicals and other Protestants 'dissented' from the dominant Calvinist-inspired position (Ganiel, 2003; McBride, 1998).
9. Paisley founded the Free Presbyterian Church in 1951, but it experienced its most rapid growth shortly after the beginning of the Troubles.
10. ECONI changed its name to the Centre for Contemporary Christianity in Ireland in 2005.
11. Bloomfield's (1996) term for it is a 'cultural approach.'
12. The British Government introduced Fair Employment Acts in 1976 and 1989, including a Fair Employment Agency. After the Belfast Agreement, an Equality Commission was introduced (http://www.equalityni.org). The Equality Commission replaced the Fair Employment Commission, the Equal Opportunities Commission, the Commission for Racial Equality, and the Northern Ireland Disability Council. See McCrudden in Ruane and Todd (1999).
13. The British Government's broader project has attempted to narrow the economic, social, and culture gap between Catholics and Protestants, through measures such as Fair Employment and public recognition/'parity of esteem' for identities (Thompson, 2002). These include provisions of the Belfast Agreement such as the Equality Commission and the Northern Ireland Human Rights Commission (NIHRC), as well

as Section 75 of the Northern Ireland Act. There is evidence that fair employment and equality measures have contributed to the narrowing of the gap (McCrudden, 1999; Osborne and Shuttleworth, 2004). However, the NIHRC has come under severe criticism for failing to meet its objectives, which included reviewing the effectiveness of laws and practices, making recommendations to government, and promoting awareness of human rights. For instance, it was charged with drawing up a bill of rights for Northern Ireland, but this project collapsed due to internal divisions and lack of support from the British Government (Livingstone and Murray, 2005). Section 75 of the Northern Ireland Act required public authorities 'to promote equality of opportunity' and 'good relations' between people of different religious belief, political opinion, racial group, age, marital status, sexual orientation, gender, and disability.

14. As Farrington (2004) has pointed out, devolution in the United Kingdom has altered the framework in which public policy is formulated. Now, government is 'legally obliged to consult with all relevant groups when it is making legislation (10).'

15. Some attempts to cultivate 'public spheres of controversy' have originated at the grassroots, including the Healing Through Remembering project and the 'long march' from Londonderry to Portadown to publicise victims' rights. The sisters of Belfast man Robert McCartney, who was murdered by members of the IRA in February 2005, could be said to have created a public sphere of controversy through their high-profile efforts to have his accused killers process through the court system.

16. Mitchel (2003) makes a similar distinction between 'closed' and 'open' evangelicalism.

17. The term mediating is borrowed from Noll's (2001a,b) characterisation of Canadian evangelicals as a group that have 'moderated extremes' in Canadian politics, interacting with government and non-evangelical groups with an 'accommodating spirit' (2001b, 253).

18. Historically, some groups in the Anabaptist tradition have tended to withdraw from society, setting up alternative religious communities such as the Amish. Some contemporary Anabaptists have rethought this position and argued for a more focused engagement with the society (Appleby, 2000, chapter four). Yoder's (1994–72) *Politics of Jesus* might be considered a call to engagement as well.

19. It is not clear if ECONI is purely pacifist in the Anabaptist sense or if some evangelicals within it would adhere to some versions of just war theory.

20. This research was carried out from 2002 to 2005 and involved 61 interviews with 57 evangelicals. Participants were drawn from traditional organisations (the Caleb Foundation, the Evangelical Protestant Society, and the Independent Orange Order), mediating organisations (ECONI, Evangelical Alliance, Zero28, and ikon), and congregations (rural Church of Ireland, rural Presbyterian, urban Free Presbyterian, and urban Presbyterian).

21. Names have been changed to protect confidentiality.

22. The Moving Beyond Sectarianism project was facilitated by the Irish School of Ecumenics, Trinity College Dublin.
23. Zero28 and ikon are more accurately described as 'post-evangelical', because they perceive themselves as having moved beyond evangelicalism (Ganiel, 2006a). Post-evangelicals share the beliefs of mediating evangelicals about the relationship between church and state, pluralism, and violence and peace. Since they still cooperate with a number of mediating organisations, I included them in this analysis.

# References

Acheson, N., B. Harvey, J. Kearney and A. Williamson (2004) *Two Paths, One Purpose: Voluntary Action in Ireland – North and South*. Dublin: Institute of Public Administration.

Akenson, D. (1992) *God's People: Covenant and Land in South Africa, Israel and Ulster*. Ithaca and London: Cornell University Press.

Appleby, S. (2000) *The Ambivalence of the Sacred: Religion, Violence and Reconciliation*. New York: Rowman & Littlefield.

Bacon, D. (2003) *Communities, Churches and Social Capital in Northern Ireland*. Coleraine: Centre for Voluntary Action Studies, University of Ulster.

Bebbington, D. (1989) *Evangelicalism in Modern Britain: A History from the 1730s to the 1980s*. Boston: Allen & Unwin.

Bloomfield, D. (1996) *Peacemaking Strategies in Northern Ireland: Building Complementarity in Conflict Management Theory*. Basingstoke: Palgrave Macmillan.

Boal, F., M. Keane and D. Livingstone (1997) *Them and Us: Attitudinal Variation among Churchgoers in Belfast*. Belfast: Institute of Irish Studies, Queen's University Belfast.

Brewer, J. (2003) 'Northern Ireland: Peacemaking among Protestants and Catholics', in M.A. Cejka and T. Bamat (eds), *Artisans of Peace*. Maryknoll, NY: Orbis Books.

Brewer, J. and G. Higgins (1998) *The Mote and the Beam: Anti-Catholicism in Northern Ireland, 1600–1998*. Basingstoke: Macmillan Press.

Bruce, S. (1986) *God Save Ulster! The Religion and Politics of Paisleyism*. Oxford: Clarendon Press.

Carter, C. (2001) *The Politics of the Cross: The Theology and Social Ethics of John Howard Yoder*. Grand Rapids: Brazos Press.

Cejka, M.A. and T. Bamat (eds) (2003) *Artisans of Peace: Grassroots Peacemaking among Christian Communities*. Maryknoll, NY: Orbis Books.

Cochrane, F. and S. Dunn (2002) *People Power? The Role of the Voluntary and Community Sector in the Northern Ireland Conflict*. Cork: Cork University Press.

Cooke, D. (1996) *Persecuting Zeal: A Portrait of Ian Paisley*. Dingle: Brandon.

Dixon, P. (1997) 'Paths to Peace in Northern Ireland (I) Civil Society and Consociational Approaches', *Democratization*, 4:2, 1–27.

Dixon, P. (2001) *Northern Ireland: The Politics of War and Peace*. Basingstoke: Palgrave Macmillan.

Dixon, P. (2005) 'Why the Good Friday Agreement in Northern Ireland is Not Consociational', *Political Quarterly*, 76:2, 357–67.

Ericson, M. (2003) 'Reconciliation and the Search for a Shared Moral Landscape: Insights and Challenges from Northern Ireland and South Africa', *Journal of Theology for Southern Africa*, 115, 19–42.

Farrington, C. (2004) 'Models of Civil Society and Their Implications for the Northern Ireland Peace Process'. IBIS Working Paper No. 43. Dublin: Institute for British Irish Studies.

Farrington, C. (2006) *Ulster Unionism and the Peace Process in Northern Ireland*. Basingstoke: Palgrave Macmillan.

Fitzduff, M. (2002) *Beyond Violence: Conflict Resolution Process in Northern Ireland*. New York: United Nations University Press.

Fulton, J. (1991) *The Tragedy of Belief: Division, Politics and Religion in Ireland*. Oxford: Clarendon Press.

Ganiel, G. (2003) 'The Politics of Religious Dissent in Northern Ireland'. IBIS Working Paper No. 32. Dublin: Institute for British-Irish Studies.

Ganiel, G. (2006a) 'Emerging from the Evangelical Subculture in Northern Ireland: A Case Study of the Zero28 and ikon Community', *International Journal for the Study of the Christian Church*, 6:1, 38–48.

Ganiel, G. (2006b) 'Ulster Says Maybe: The Restructuring of Evangelical Politics in Northern Ireland', *Irish Political Studies*, 21:2, 137–55.

Ganiel, G. and P. Dixon (2008) 'Religion and Conflict Transformation: Lessons from Northern Ireland', *Journal of Peace Research*.

Giddens, A. (1998) *The Third Way*. Cambridge: Polity Press.

Hauerwas, S. (1983) *The Peaceable Kingdom: A Primer in Christian Ethics*. Indiana: University of Notre Dame Press.

Hauerwas, S. (1995) *In Good Company: The Church as Polis*. Indiana: University of Notre Dame Press.

Hauerwas S. and W.H. Willimon (1995) 'Why Resident Aliens Struck a Chord', in S. Hauerwas (ed.), *In Good Company: The Church As Polis*. Indiana: University of Notre Dame Press.

Hayes, B.C. and I. McAllister (1999) 'Ethnonationalism, Public Opinion and the Good Friday Agreement', in J. Ruane and J. Todd (eds), *After the Good Friday Agreement*. Dublin: UCD Press.

Hempton, D. and M. Hill (1992) *Evangelical Protestantism in Ulster Society 1740–1890*. London and New York: Routledge.

Herbert, D. (2003) *Religion and Civil Society: Rethinking Religion in the Contemporary World*. Aldershot: Ashgate.

Johnston, D. (ed.) (2003) *Trumping Realpolitik: Faith-Based Diplomacy*. Oxford: Oxford University Press.

Jordan, G. (2001) *Not of This World: The Evangelical Protestants of Northern Ireland*. Belfast: Blackstaff Press.

Keane, J. (1998) *Civil Society: Old Images, New Visions*. Cambridge: Polity Press.

Kearney, J.R. and A.P. Williamson (2001) 'The Voluntary and Community Sector in Northern Ireland: Developments Since 1995–96', in *Next Steps in Voluntary Action: An Analysis of Five Years of Development in the Voluntary Sector in England, Northern Ireland, Scotland and Wales*. London: Centre for Civil Society, London School of Economics and National Council of Voluntary Organisations.

Kiess, J. and A. Thomson (2004) *The Future of the Church in the Public Sphere: Final Report*. Belfast: ECONI.

Liechty, J. and C. Clegg (2001) *Moving Beyond Sectarianism: Religion, Conflict and Reconciliation in Northern Ireland*. Dublin: Columba Press.

Little, A. (2004) *Democracy and Northern Ireland: Beyond the Liberal Paradigm?* Basingstoke: Palgrave Macmillan.

Livingstone, S. and R. Murray (2005) *Evaluating the Effectiveness of National Human Rights Institutions: The Northern Ireland Human Rights Commission with Comparisons from South Africa*. London: Nuffield Foundation.

Love, M.T. (1995) *Peace Building Through Reconciliation in Northern Ireland*. Aldershot: Avebury.

McBride, I. (1998) *Scripture Politics: Ulster Presbyterians and Irish Radicalism in the Late Eighteenth Century*. Oxford: Clarendon Press.

McCrudden, C. (1999) 'Equality and the Good Friday Agreement', in J. Ruane and J. Todd (eds), *After the Good Friday Agreement*. Dublin: UCD Press.

McGarry, J. and B. O'Leary (1995) *Explaining Northern Ireland*. Oxford: Blackwell.

Mitchel, P. (2003) *Evangelicalism and National Identity in Ulster, 1921–1998*.Oxford: Oxford University Press.

Mitchell, C. (2005) 'Behind the Ethnic Marker: Religion and Social Identification in Northern Ireland', *Sociology of Religion*, 66:1, 1–22.

Mitchell, C. (2006) *Religion, Identity and Politics in Northern Ireland*. Aldershot: Ashgate.

Mitchell, C. and J. Tilley (2004) 'The Moral Minority: Evangelical Protestants in Northern Ireland and Their Political Behaviour', *Political Studies*, 52:4, 585–602.

Moloney, E. and A. Pollak (1986) *Paisley*. Swords: Poolbeg.

Morrow, D., D. Birrell, J. Greer and T. O'Keefe (1991) *The Churches and Inter-Community Relationships*. Coleraine: Centre for the Study of Conflict.

Noll, M. (2001a) *American Evangelical Christianity: An Introduction*. Oxford: Blackwell.

Noll, M. (2001b) *A History of Christianity in the United States and Canada*. Grand Rapids: Eerdmans.

OFMDFM (Office of the First Minister and Deputy First Minister) (2003) *A Shared Future: Improving Relations in Northern Ireland*. Belfast: HMSO.

OFMDFM. (2005) *A Shared Future: Policy and Strategic Framework for Good Relations in Northern Ireland*. Belfast: HMSO.

Osborne, B. and I. Shuttleworth (eds). (2004) *Fair Employment in Northern Ireland: A Generation On*. Belfast: Blackstaff.

Palshaugen, L. (2005) 'The Northern Ireland Civic Forum and the Politics of Recognition', *Irish Political Studies*, 20:2, 147–69.

Porter, F. (2002) *Changing Women, Changing Worlds: Evangelical Women in Church, Community, and Politics*. Belfast: Blackstaff.

Power, M. (2005) 'Building Communities in a Post-Conflict Society: Churches and Peace-Building Initiatives in Northern Ireland since 1994', *The European Legacy*, 10:1, 55–68.

Shirlow, P. and B. Murtagh (2006) *Belfast: Segregation, Violence and the City*. London: Pluto Press.

Smyth, C. (1987) *Ian Paisley: Voice of Protestant Ulster*. Edinburgh: Scottish Academic Press.

Thomson, A. (ed.) (1996) *Faith in Ulster*. ECONI: Belfast.

Thompson, S. (2002) 'Parity of Esteem and the Politics of Recognition', *Contemporary Political Theory*, 1:2, 203–20.

Thomson, A. (2002) *Fields of Vision: Faith and Identity in Protestant Ireland*. Belfast: Centre for Contemporary Christianity in Ireland.

Tombs, D. and J. Leichty (eds) (2006) *Explorations in Reconciliation: New Directions in Theology*. Aldershot: Ashgate.

Wells, R. (1999) *People Behind the Peace*. Grand Rapids: Eerdmans.

Wells, R. (2005) *Friendship Towards Peace: The Journey of Ken Newell and Gerry Reynolds*. Dublin: Columba Press.

Wilson, D. and J. Tyrrell (1995) 'Institutions for Conciliation and Mediation', in S. Dunn (ed.), *Facets of the Conflict in Northern Ireland*. London: Macmillan Press.

Wright, F. (1973) 'Protestant Ideology and Politics in Ulster', *European Journal of Sociology*, 14:2, 213–80.

Yoder, J. H. (1994–72) *The Politics of Jesus*. Grand Rapids: Eerdmans.

# Part III

# Consociationalism and Civil Society

Part III

Consociationalism and Civil Society

# 8
# The Belfast Agreement and the Limits of Consociationalism

*Rupert Taylor*

The previous two sections have examined issues of political, identity, and attitudinal change among all levels of Northern Irish society. However, these changes occur in the context of the institutional framework of the Belfast Agreement as a consociational conflict regulation device. To date, as Adrian Guelke has written, 'too little attention has been paid to the drawbacks of consociational settlements' (Guelke, 2003, 75); and, as Rudy Andeweg has acknowledged in a recent scholarly overview of consociational democracy, 'the level of abstraction of many...critiques of...consociationalism is rather low' (Andeweg, 2000, 531). This chapter directly addresses the state of debate by contending that the Belfast Agreement (1998), as a consociational settlement, rests on and promotes an ethno-national group-based understanding of politics that is inherently illiberal – with the result that, in spite of recent seemingly positive developments, the space for a more deliberative form of democracy around a common citizenship agenda is foreclosed.

## A consociational settlement

There are two core mutually reinforcing ideas behind the Belfast Agreement: one, that in the 'nature of things' Northern Ireland is deeply, indeed irrefutably, divided between two competing ethno-national communities; and two, that consociationalism as advocated by a number of highly regarded and influential political scientists – notably Arend Lijphart (1982), John McGarry and Brendan O'Leary (2004a) – provides the only democratic form of governance that can accommodate such ethno-national antagonism.

The received wisdom in interpreting the Northern Ireland conflict is to see it as primarily being between two communities: Protestants and Catholics. Indeed, in *Interpreting Northern Ireland* (1990), John Whyte concluded that this view has been 'supported by more writers than all alternatives put together' (Whyte, 1990, 244), and certainly within academia, as Bernadette Hayes and Ian McAllister acknowledge, ethno-nationalism is seen to be 'the most promising theoretical explanation for the Northern Ireland conflict' (Hayes and McAllister, 1999, 35). Generally, Protestants and Catholics are seen to constitute intractable ethno-national groups with distinctive and different cultural traditions, values, and needs. The categories of 'Protestant' and 'Catholic' are taken to be synonymous with Ulster Unionist and Irish Nationalist politics in which on the one hand the Ulster Unionist Party and Democratic Unionist Party, and on the other hand the Social Democratic and Labour Party and Sinn Féin constitute the main parties locked into a power struggle to maximize group interests.

In such a context, it is accepted as axiomatic amongst political scientists and elite level policy-makers that to pursue a common rights-based resolution of the conflict is unrealistic. It is further maintained that democratic prospects are bleak unless institutional structures are strategically crafted in such a way as to recognize and accommodate competing ethno-national identities and interests through power-sharing that ensures group autonomy and equality – that is, through consociationalism (Lijphart, 1977). The argument, stated by McGarry and O'Leary (1995, 286), is that 'conventional' liberalism cannot come to terms with the importance of ethno-nationalism and as such 'fails to grasp what is at stake.' Specifically, following Lijphart's (1977) *Democracy in Plural Societies*, consociationalism holds that 'deeply divided' societies can become democratic through pragmatically driven elite-level bargaining for a form of executive power-sharing in which the autonomy of contending groups is constitutionally guaranteed and protected through mutual veto rights, and where there is strong respect for principles of proportionality in elections, civil service appointments, and government subsidies.

In line with this, the Belfast Agreement accepts and legitimates the two ethno-national communities – Unionist and Nationalist – reading of the conflict and seeks to promote a form of politics that treats them as fixed, autonomous, and equally valid. Notably, in terms of the workings of the Northern Ireland Assembly, the party politicians (elected via proportional representation) *must* identify and function as 'nationalist, unionist or other', and it is accepted that mutual veto power be held on matters of key concern (*The Belfast Agreement*, Strand One, para. 6). Key decisions – such as the election of the First Minister and Deputy First Minister, standing orders, and budget allocations – require cross-community support either by parallel consent or by a weighted majority (ibid, para. 5[d]). Moreover, ministerial positions are 'allocated to parties on the basis of the d'Hondt system by reference to the number of seats each party has in the Assembly' (ibid, para. 16). In addition, so as to advance respect and equality for communal difference, the Agreement provided for a new Equality Commission and a Bill of Rights for Northern Ireland (ibid, para. 5[b][e]).

There can, then, be little doubt that the Belfast Agreement is a consociational settlement, that it can 'safely be identified as consociational' (Wagner, 2004, 19). There is also little doubt that the Agreement is widely accepted and endorsed by elite decision-makers and establishment politicians in Britain, Ireland, and around the globe. The question, however, is: Has it led to democratic advance?

## 'A liberal consociation?'

Lijphart maintains that: 'There is nothing in consociational democracy that people who are both consociationalists and democrats have to be apologetic about' (Lijphart, 1985, 112). And with respect to the Belfast Agreement, McGarry and O'Leary have proclaimed that the 'consociational arrangements are liberal and consistent with democracy', that it is a 'liberal consociation' (McGarry and O'Leary, 2006, 277; also see, McGarry and O'Leary, 2004b). But this is not self-evidently true. For, the Belfast Agreement has not appeared to readily mark the birth of a new era of democratic politics in Northern Ireland – sustainable peace is not in sight (Wolff, 2003).

The Assembly that came into effect on 3 December 1999 lasted a mere 72 days before being suspended by the British Government on 11 February 2000 – at an estimated cost of £33.4 million – 'that is almost £500,000 per day' (Morison, 2001, 292). In fact, over a period of seven years the Assembly was suspended four times, only recently being reinvigorated in March 2007 under increasing political pressure from the British and Irish Governments. The real cause for concern, however, is not so much that the Agreement has proved hard – practically speaking – to put on track, but rather that there are processes integral to consociational politics that are inimical to liberal democracy.

There are a number of ways in which the Agreement can be shown to have worked to encourage and reward those who pursue strategic ethno-national group calculations and interests – and to have thereby reinforced and politicized ethno-national group divisions – in ways that run counter to promoting liberal politics. This can be most clearly shown with respect to the key aggregation mechanisms within the ambit of the Agreement, namely: group designation in the Assembly; Executive formation; and the electoral system.

The requirement that the 108 elected members of the Assembly must accept communal registration as 'nationalist, unionist, or other' – that then underpins group veto powers – locks individual politicians into group-thinking and unequal rights. For, when it comes to decisions requiring cross-community support, the designation of 'others' does not carry meaningful weight. As Ian O'Flynn observes, 'By effectively discounting the votes of the "others" on certain important issues, the agreement privileges national over individual identities' (O'Flynn, 2003, 144). The unfair nature of all this was most clearly shown when the election of the First and Deputy First Ministers in late 2001 saw the temporary re-designation of three Alliance Party members of the Assembly – from 'other' to 'unionist' – so as to shore up the institution. This went against the beliefs of most Alliance party members who favour a non-sectarian approach, and it also dictated that these Assembly members 'lie' about their self-identity (Evans and Tonge, 2003, 27).

With respect to Executive formation, the form of power-sharing encapsulated in the Agreement is one of an 'involuntary' coalition that has been – in the words of a former Lord Mayor of Belfast – 'less than successful in achieving a collective character akin to any recognizable government or executive body elsewhere' (Maginness, 2002, 37). The Executive functions by sharing out power without collective cabinet responsibility: the ten ministerial portfolios are allocated to political parties in proportion to their representation in the Assembly following the D'Hondt electoral formula, such that the cabinet so formed is insulated from any effective opposition or censure. In a situation in which party elites assign their own spheres of ministerial control, the Executive assumes the form of 'a series of political silos loosely connected by weekly meetings', where questions of ministerial accountability become especially contentious (ibid). For example, Unionist politician Robert McCartney (2004) writing in *The Belfast Telegraph* at a time when the Assembly was running, openly accused Sinn Féin ministers of accepting 'responsibility to no one but their own party.' It transpires, then, that Executive level politics is not so much about sharing power, but is more a contest for ministerial power and influence 'in order to assert the rights of [the] respective communities' (Maginness, 2002, 37).

This state of affairs is compounded by the mandated electoral system– PR-STV (Proportional Representation with Single Transferable Vote) in six member constituencies – to elect members of the Assembly. Contrary to optimistic expectations of scholars such as Benjamin Reilly (2001, 134–41), PR-STV has not, over time, had an effective moderating influence. The choice of this electoral system has not worked to significantly encourage tactical voting across communal lines. In the 1998 Assembly election, survey evidence suggests that only about 9 per cent of lower preference votes were transferred across the community divide (Evans and O'Leary, 2000). And the results of the 26 November 2003 Assembly election revealed that the single transferable vote has actually served, through strategic voting, to strengthen communal bloc voting (Hazleton, 2004, 229). Indeed, leading psephologist Sydney Elliott (2003) noted in *The Irish Times*, 'It was all too evident that the political parties were familiar with vote management tricks to combat the voting power of the elector under the single transferable vote.'

In fact, the results of the 2003 election marked a dramatic shift to more polarized communal politics – witnessing the strengthening of the more hard line parties at the expense of the moderate centre. The Democratic Unionist Party, which was opposed to the Agreement, received the largest percentage of first-preference votes (displacing the pro-Agreement Ulster Unionist Party as the largest Unionist party in the Assembly), followed by Sinn Féin (displacing the Social Democratic and Labour Party as the largest Nationalist party in the Assembly). Support for the Alliance Party dropped dramatically to under 4 per cent, its lowest level in 30 years, and the Northern Ireland Women's Coalition lost their two Assembly seats. Clear evidence of increasing ethno-nationalist solidarity is that, 'the DUP and UUP accounted for 95% of unionist first preference votes, a significant advance over their combined total of 78% in 1998' (Hazleton, 2004, 232). Within the Unionist bloc the anti-Agreement members of the Assembly came to outnumber pro-Agreement members by over one-third; and following the 5 May 2005 Westminster election, the party leader of the Ulster Unionists – Nobel Peace Prize laureate, David Trimble – lost his Upper Bann seat and subsequently resigned from his leadership role. The rise in electoral support for the 'hardliners' undoubtedly worked to forestall the re-institution of Executive level power-sharing.

In these ways – group designation, Executive formation, and the electoral system – the Agreement, as a consociational settlement, privileges 'natural' pre-given ethno-national group categories and promotes the pursuit of a group-differentiated politics that is reduced to the 'positional logic' of winning and losing, of promoting and maximizing communal advantage (also consider, Aughey, 2005). In this regard, though, if it is accepted, following Alain Touraine's argument in *What is Democracy?* (1997, 67), that 'all democracies' must 'privilege freedom of political choice over the "natural" categories of social life', then consociation-alism is fundamentally and systematically mistaken in believing it can advance liberal democracy. Consociationalism and liberal democracy pull in different directions.

Consociationalists themselves contest that consociationalism is illiberal (O'Leary, 2005). O'Leary holds that the Agreement is 'a liberal consociational agreement because it did not mandate that individuals must have group identities – citizens are free to exit from, and to adopt other, recognized group identities, but are also free to insist that they belong to none (to "others")' (O'Leary, 2001, 354). This, however, is mis-leadingly put: as individuals do not have the autonomy of exiting from group designation *per se*, 'others' *is* a group designation. In this respect, the Agreement does stand in direct violation of the individual right to freedom of association.

O'Leary further claims that, 'a liberal consociation, is an association of communities based on recognition of the mutual equality of groups *and* individuals' (ibid, 353). This, though, is to beg the question as to what has to be granted to groups that cannot be given to individuals (consider, Barry, 2001)? Can separate ethno-national group rights be intellectually justified against universalistic rights? If so, how? In this regard, pursuance of the equality agenda and a Bill of Rights for Northern Ireland – as conceived by the Agreement – has to answer why groups should be given rights over and above those of the individual, and how this could be done equally.

The equality agenda is unambiguously couched in the language of 'two communities'; as Katy Hayward and Claire Mitchell state (2003, 296), 'the clauses of the Agreement connected to equality are clearly intended to adjust the relationship between Catholics and Protestants, nationalists and unionists.' In terms of the Agreement, anti-discrimination legisla-tion and public policies that advance 'mutual respect' (such as governing the use of symbols and emblems) as well as 'parity of esteem' for cultural difference (such as support for the Irish language) tie equality to group membership. The problem with all this is not only that here, as else-where, do gains and losses assume zero-sum form amongst Unionists and Nationalists, but that the idea that the 'two communities' can be treated equally flies in the face of prior acceptance of the conflict as being intract-able – for equal recognition requires one to adopt a universal standard of value against which groups can be equally judged (Benhabib, 2002). In any case, it is not even established as to *why* ethno-national groups should be treated equally – after all, and the history of Northern Ireland bears this out, some might be oppressive.

The issue of a Bill of Rights for Northern Ireland confronts the same set of problems. In a paper published in *The Political Quarterly* (2001) on 'The Protection of Human Rights under the Belfast Agreement', O'Leary asserts that any 'Bill of Rights should, so far as is possible, guarantee the power-sharing logic of the Agreement' (355). In particular, the Agreement stipulates that in drawing up a Bill of Rights the Northern Ireland Human Rights Commission has to 'reflect the principles of mutual respect for the identity and ethos of both communities and parity of esteem' (*The Belfast Agreement*, Rights, Safeguards and Equality of Opportunity, para. 4). Just how, though, can this be done?

If notions of 'separate but equal' could not be intellectually upheld through any appeal to reason or developed through any accepted principles of social organization in the American South or in apartheid South Africa, why should it be any different for Northern Ireland? In fact, there is no clarity as to the way forward; for as Michael Meehan acknowledges (2001, 46), 'international rights instruments relating to minorities offer no concrete guidance on how to develop this . . . and formulate rights relative to the Irish context.' When it comes down to it, McGarry and O'Leary's argument (2004a, 286) that 'Authentic collective equality requires that both groups' (national) identities be accepted as equally valid and legitimate', is one that is theoretically – and therefore practically – impossible to establish.

## Consociation and deliberation

The consociational position does, however, have recourse to a further line of defence. For, scholars such as John Dryzek (2000) and Jürg Steiner *et al.* (2004) have argued that, in general, consociationalism is open to deliberative politics, whereby citizens are 'amenable to reflecting upon and changing their preferences and views' (Dryzek, 2000, 170; also consider, O'Flynn, 2006). However, the nature of the Belfast Agreement suggests otherwise. As consociational settlements are driven by bargaining based on fixed ethno-national group interests, cost/benefit calculations trump deliberative politics time and again. This can most clearly be shown with respect to the crafting of the Agreement and the manner in which it faces the future.

In his book *Liberal Virtues* (1991), Stephen Macedo writes 'Public justification must . . . be *critical* in that objections have been sought out and reasonable alternatives confronted or anticipated' (46). Does this hold for the Belfast Agreement? In essence, the Agreement was grounded in prior decisions of the British and Irish Governments, supported by US diplomacy, and brokered through ethno-national elite-level group-interested bargaining between party leaderships in which the ethno-national 'nature' of the conflict was taken as a given background condition. True, the Agreement was supported through the 22 May 1998 public Referendum in which the 'Yes' campaign engaged people outside formal institutional politics (Irwin, 2002). The Referendum was passed with a 71.1 per cent 'Yes' vote in Northern Ireland and a 94.4 per cent vote in the Irish Republic, but there was a clear sense in which the Agreement was 'sold' through spin-doctoring and obstructionism. As Paul Dixon has argued (2002, 739), 'little attempt' was 'made by Northern Irish politicians and the two governments to *persuade* rather than *manipulate*.' And in this latter regard, Dixon points to the use of such tactics as creating 'constructive ambiguity' and 'necessary fictions'.

The point, here, is that the Agreement was bargained at elite level, *tête-à-tête* (Horowitz, 2002), not defended in wide-ranging deliberation in the civic public sphere – people were not motivated to think through the issues or discuss them with others. In fact, even the 'Northern Ireland political parties bargained little with one another face to face' (Oberschall and Palmer, 2005, 81–2). Hence, here again, the Agreement represents a form of politics that runs counter to virtuous practice; whereby, following Cicero (1991, 33), one might expect elite interests to 'care for the whole body' politic.

Nowhere, though, has deliberative politics been more foreclosed than with regard to the unresolved overarching constitutional question: Will Northern Ireland remain part of the United Kingdom or become part of a new Ireland? To a large extent the Agreement is seen by Unionists as safeguarding the Union and by Nationalists as signalling a united Ireland – a state of affairs that results in the present remaining inherently conflictual as it feeds uncertainty and anxiety about the future. The Agreement makes provision for a poll for the people of Northern Ireland to determine by simple majoritarianism whether Britain or the Irish Republic holds ultimate sovereignty over Northern Ireland (*The Belfast Agreement*, Constitutional Issues). By proposing, however, 'to settle the dispute over democratic sovereignty by means of the principle of majority decision', the Agreement postpones the question and reverts 'to the problematic principle which provoked the original crisis in Northern Ireland' (Bourke, 2003, 3).

The standpoint of the Agreement rests on the grounds that there are irreconcilable claims at stake here, but the counterpoint is that this has not been incontrovertibly established. Rather than adhering to the majority principle, it can be maintained that a common citizenship agenda be sought through democratic deliberation, that democratic deliberation 'is best suited to those decisions which are important, or otherwise intractable, or both' (Dryzek, 2000, 174). Besides, why should the constitutional question be so starkly posed as a single-choice option divorced from wider transformative trends? – especially when increasing global interconnectedness (economically, culturally, and politically) has resulted in a declining significance of national sovereignty and state borders, and led Britain and Ireland to become two of the world's most globalized countries (*Foreign Policy*, Globalization Index, 2003). As Seyla Benhabib argues (2002, 180), 'territoriality is fast becoming an anachronistic delimitation of material functions and cultural identities.' There has been a dispersal of power to subnational, transnational, and global levels such that beneath and beyond the level of formal institutionalized politics attached to the state, issues of governance and civil society have assumed new import.

Indeed, in Northern Ireland, more and more the importance and capacity of central government involvement is being put into question, with governance becoming multilevel and multi-form (Morison, 2001). Under the sway of Third Way social policies and special European Union programmes (supported through the Peace Fund), governance has increasingly become tied to the active participation of voluntary and community organizations, and ideas of 'joined-up' government and multilevel partnership structures have proliferated – notably involving cross-border groups, Belfast City Council, and district partnerships that pursue social inclusion projects (Hayward, 2004; Knox and Quirk, 2000, chapter 3). Today, the Northern Ireland Council for Voluntary Action (NICVA) has over 5,000 organizations on their database (with total assets exceeding £750 million) and it is estimated that 'three out of every five adults in Northern Ireland have an association with some form of voluntary or community organization' (NICVA, 2002). And yet, here, the potential for civil society to advance democracy – through, for example, promoting social integration or encouraging active civic involvement – has again not been well served by the Belfast Agreement. If anything, the post-Agreement period has witnessed the depoliticization of civil society – as the fate of the Civic Forum well illustrates.

The Belfast Agreement incorporated a 60-member Civic Forum, with significant voluntary and community sector membership, to 'act as a consultative mechanism on social, economic and cultural issues' (*The Belfast Agreement*, Strand One, para. 34), but rather than – as hoped – promote deliberative politics (McCall and Williamson, 2001), it has lacked influence. This is true in a number of important respects: the composition of the Civic Forum is beholden to powers held by the First and Deputy First Ministers; it has struggled over how to position itself 'between the legislative Assembly and society in general' (Bell, 2004, 570); is guided by a chair that sees the Civic Forum as being '*in* politics but not *of* politics' (ibid, 574); and has been sidelined by suspicious and hostile power-brokers (especially 'hardliners') in the Assembly and civil service (McCall and Williamson, 2001, 378). In sum, the Civic Forum is widely seen to have failed, having come to constitute a space which civil society does 'not control' (see Farrington in Chapter 5 of this volume).

Altogether then, consociationalism proves hostile to deliberative politics: the constitutional question has been postponed and civil society has been depoliticized. In such ways, the Agreement turns its back on, rather than faces the future. If, following Benjamin Barber's argument in *Strong Democracy* (1984), politics 'is the art of inventing a common destiny for women and men in conflict' (53), the Agreement has little to commend it. The Agreement has hardly encouraged the kind of virtuous citizenship propounded by such political theorists as Niccolò Machiavelli (1974 [1532]) and James Harrington (1992 [1656]). Consociational politics has worked to systematically close down the space for people to question conventional understandings, to collectively think through the issues, and extend political imaginings. In too many ways, the Belfast Agreement represents a troublesome case of an 'incompletely theorized agreement' (Sunstein, 2001, chapter 2); it certainly does not 'combine political accountability with a high degree of reflectiveness and a general commitment to reason-giving' (ibid, 6–7).

## From consociation to deliberation

As made evident from the above, the Agreement, as a consociational settlement, is hardly 'the product of an imaginative consensus of the citizen's autonomous wills' (Barber, 1984, 168) – but why should this not be the standard by which the future of Northern Ireland be justified? Particularly when, in terms of political theory, the premises of the Agreement are not justified. To view the conflict as being in 'the nature of things' driven by irreconcilable ethno-national group interest is presumptive, inscriptive, and far from progressive (also see, Taylor, 2001). McGarry and O'Leary begin their collected volume *The Northern Ireland Conflict: Consociational Engagements* (2004a, 1) with a telling quote from Montesquieu: 'I did not draw my principles from my prejudices, but from the nature of things' (Montesquieu, 1989 [1748], xliii). Surely, though, as construct-ivists recognize, the social world is created by the debates that we have about it – it is not unproblematically tied to the 'nature of things'.

Already, contrary to the presumed 'nature of things', there is an increasing disengagement from, and decreasing respect for, consoci-ational politics. Around 35 per cent of people in Northern Ireland claim to be 'neither unionist nor nationalist' (*The 2001 Northern Ireland Life and Times Survey*, cited in Tonge, 2005, 82). In the 2001 census, 14 per cent of respondents ($N = 233,853$) did not describe themselves as either 'Prot-estant' or 'Catholic'. Alongside this, more and more people have become disengaged from conventional politics, as – for example – reflected in the fact that a recent survey found that only 17 per cent of Protestants and 34 per cent of Catholics 'trusted the parties and governments "a lot" or "a little"'' (Gilligan, 2003, 33). Both the Social Democratic and Labour Party (SDLP) and the Ulster Unionist Party have rapidly ageing member-ship profiles: notably, '30.1 percent of SDLP membership is above the age of 65' (Murray, 2003, 57).

The nature of Unionist and Nationalist identities have been changing over time, such that secularists and liberal Catholics and liberal Protest-ants are now closer to each other theologically than they are to conser-vatives of their own faith, and indeed, the fluidity of Unionist politics is such that preferred constitutional solutions no longer readily corres-pond to discrete party divisions (Tonge, 2005). Moreover, there are clear signs of deliberation amongst 'hardliners', with a 'new loyalism' con-cerned to 'create real alignment in politics on economic and social issues' (David Ervine quoted in McAuley, 2002, 111), and a new respect within Republicanism towards legalism and inclusive dialogue (McEvoy, 2000).

Beyond the formal political arena, the number of religiously mixed marriages is on the rise, and there is increasing evidence of mixed housing and schooling. In fact, *prior* to the Agreement, the willing-ness of Catholics and Protestants to live, work, and be educated in mixed communities had been consistently increasing to well over 50 per cent (Curtice and Dowds, 1999, 19). Despite the pall cast over civil society, there is – as suggested above – reason to believe that the non-governmental organizational sector is a growing and vibrant force for social integration and homogenization, that can provide, as Michael Edwards puts it, 'a framework for engaging with each other about ends and means' (Edwards, 2004, viii–ix).

A turn away from consociational politics towards a deliberative app-roach to politics would, it can be argued, do much to 'broaden per-spectives, promote toleration and understanding between groups, and generally encourage a public-spirited attitude' (Chambers, 2003, 318). For crucially, as Dryzek argues (2000, 169), 'there are mechanisms endogenous to deliberation which promote the expression of interests in public interest terms.' To this end, enlightened leadership, political will, and institutional creativity would best be directed to rooting legitimacy in civil society and the pursuit of such initiatives as deliberative opinion polling, online deliberation systems, citizens' panels and juries, public issue forums, vouchers for funding organizations in civil society, and multi-option electronic referendums (Giddens, 1998; Schmitter, 2003); some of which could be developed on cross-border lines.

New moves to encourage deliberative democracy – to promote a civic activism that widens people's political and social horizons – represent the best path to sustainable peace: as it would create 'space in which a new, more transcendent logic might begin to emerge' (Morrow, 2005, 54). A turn from consociational democracy to deliberative democracy, in which outcomes are justified by reasons rather than voting numbers, would mark a 'genuine *constitutive* change' – for as Morison argues (2001, 309), 'a real constitutional agreement cannot be imposed' through a formal constitutionalism emphasizing state and structure.

In January 2007 social scientists from Newcastle University, Queen's University Belfast, and Stanford University conducted Northern Ireland's first deliberative poll amongst 127 randomly selected parents in Omagh, focusing on the public policy issue of community perceptions on shared education. Post-opinion deliberations revealed that changes in community perceptions had indeed occurred: 'The percentage believing Protestants "open to reason" increased from 36% to 52%, and the percentage believing Catholics "open to reason" increased from 40% to 56%' (Newcastle University, 2007). As James Fishkin, one of those involved in framing the poll, noted: 'They [the participants] became more informed, they changed their views and they found a greater basis for mutual understanding' (ibid). Similarly, another scholar who participated in this project has more broadly maintained that 'deliberative democracy has a crucial normative contribution to make with respect to the larger purposes and goals towards which a divided society might aspire' (O'Flynn, 2006, 161).

This suggests, more substantively, that much can be gained if the Belfast Agreement be succeeded (or at least supplemented) by some form of National Issues Convention or 'Deliberation Day'. As proposed by Bruce Ackerman and James Fishkin (2004) in the context of American presidential elections, a 'Deliberation Day' would constitute a civic holiday on which people meet in a series of small- and large-group sessions to engage in deliberative debate on matters of pressing concern. In the Northern Ireland context, such an initiative could be held, with the support of philanthropic foundations prepared to engage in creative philanthropy for social justice (Anheier and Leat, 2002), such as the well-funded Community Foundation for Northern Ireland (Garrill and Knight, 2004). This would enable citizens to forge a common destiny and to creatively consider the political design for a constitutional convention, at which – as with the creation of the American Republic in Philadelphia in 1787 – elected delegates would meet face-to-face to determine the future form of government (Fishkin, 1997). After 40 years of conflict, it is perhaps about time to encourage all citizens to freely deliberate, to generalize outside the frame of maximizing ethno-national group bargaining, and to ask the question: 'What is good for the political future of us all?'

## Acknowledgments

An earlier, less extensive, version of this article was published in *The Political Quarterly* (April–June 2006, 77:2, 217–26) under the title 'The Belfast Agreement and the Politics of Consociationalism: A Critique.' The author is grateful for the comments of James Anderson, Guy Ben-Porat, Paul Dixon, Christopher Farrington, Adrian Guelke, Cathal McCall, John McGarry, Ronaldo Munck, Ian O'Flynn, and Robin Wilson.

## Bibliography

Ackerman, B. and J.S. Fishkin (2004) *Deliberation Day*. New Haven: Yale University Press.

Andeweg, R.B. (2000) 'Consociational Democracy', *Annual Review of Political Science*, 3, 509–36.

Anheier, H.K. and D. Leat (2002) *From Charity to Creativity: Philanthropic Foundations in the 21st Century*. Near Stroud, UK: Comedia.

Aughey, A. (2005) *The Politics of Northern Ireland: Beyond the Belfast Agreement*. London: Routledge.

Barber, B.R. (1984) *Strong Democracy: Participatory Politics for a New Age*. Berkeley: University of California Press.

Barry, B. (2001) *Culture and Equality: An Egalitarian Critique of Multiculturalism*. Cambridge: Polity Press.

*The Belfast Agreement: An Agreement Reached at the Multi-Party Talks on Northern Ireland*, April 1998. Cm 3883. Available at http://cain.ulst.ac.uk/events/peace/docs/agreement.htm.

Bell, V. (2004) 'In Pursuit of Civic Participation: The Early Experiences of the Northern Ireland Civic Forum, 2000–2002', *Political Studies*, 52, 565–84.

Benhabib, S. (2002) *The Claims of Culture: Equality and Diversity in the Global Era*. Princeton, New Jersey: Princeton University Press.

Bourke, R. (2003) *Peace in Ireland: The War of Ideas*. London: Pimlico.

Chambers, S. (2003) 'Deliberative Democratic Theory'. *Annual Review of Political Science*, 6, 307–26.

Cicero (1991) *On Duties*. Cambridge: Cambridge University Press.

Curtice, J. and L. Dowds (1999) 'Has Northern Ireland Really Changed?'. Centre for Research into Elections and Social Trends. Working Paper No. 74. Available at http://www.crest.ox.ac.uk/papers.htm.

Dixon, P. (2002) 'Political Skills or Lying and Manipulation? The Choreography of the Northern Ireland Peace Process', *Political Studies*, 50, 725–41.

Dryzek, J.S. (2000) *Deliberative Democracy and Beyond: Liberals, Critics, Contestations*. Oxford: Oxford University Press.

Edwards, M. (2004) *Civil Society*. Cambridge: Polity Press.

Elliott, S. (2003) 'Northern Vote Sees over 80 per cent of Transfers Stay Within Main Parties', *The Irish Times*, 1 December.

Evans, G. and B. O'Leary (2000) 'Northern Irish Voters and the British-Irish Agreement: Foundations of a Stable Consociational Settlement?', *The Political Quarterly*, 71:1, 78–101.

Evans, J.A.J. and J. Tonge (2003) 'The Future of the "Radical Centre" in Northern Ireland after the Good Friday Agreement', *Political Studies*, 51:1, 26–50.

Fishkin, J.S. (1997) *The Voice of the People: Public Opinion and Democracy*. New Haven: Yale University Press.

*Foreign Policy*. 'Globalization Index for 2003'. Available at http://www.foreignpolicy.com/wwwboard/g-index.php.

Garrill, J. and B. Knight (2004) 'Foundations for Peace'. Paper presented to Community Foundations: Symposium on a Global Movement, Berlin, 2–5 December.

Giddens, A. (1998) *The Third Way: The Renewal of Social Democracy*. Cambridge, Polity Press.

Gilligan, C. (2003) 'Constant Crisis/Permanent Process: Diminished Agency and Weak Structures in the Northern Ireland Peace Process', *The Global Review of Ethnopolitics*, 3:1, 22–37.

Guelke, A. (2003) 'Civil Society and the Northern Ireland Peace Process', *Voluntas*, 14:1, 61–78.

Harrington, J. (1992 [1656]) *The Commonwealth of Oceana and a System of Politics*. Cambridge: Cambridge University Press.

Hayes, B.C. and I. McAllister (1999) 'Ethnonationalism, Public Opinion and the Good Friday Agreement', in J. Ruane and J. Todd (eds), *After the Good Friday Agreement: Analysing Political Change in Northern Ireland*. Dublin: University College Dublin Press, pp. 30–48.

Hayward, K. (2004) 'Defusing the Conflict in Northern Ireland: Pathways of Influence for the European Union'. Working Paper Series, European Union and Border Conflicts, Queen's University Belfast. Available at http://www.euborderconf.bham.ac.uk/publications/workingpapers.htm.

Hayward, K. and C. Mitchell (2003) 'Discourses of Equality in Post-Agreement Northern Ireland', *Comparative Politics*, 9:3, 293–312.

Hazleton, W.A. (2004) 'Suspended Vote: The 2003 Northern Ireland Assembly Election', *The Political Quarterly*, 75:3, 226–37.

Horowitz, D. (2002) 'Explaining the Northern Ireland Agreement: The Sources of an Unlikely Constitutional Consensus', *British Journal of Political Science*, 32: 2, 193–220.

Irwin, C. (2002) *The People's Peace Process in Northern Ireland*. London: Palgrave Macmillan.

Knox, C. and P. Quirk (2000) *Peace Building in Northern Ireland, Israel and South Africa*. Basingstoke: Palgrave Macmillan.

Lijphart, A. (1977) *Democracy in Plural Societies: A Comparative Exploration*. New Haven: Yale University Press.

Lijphart, A. (1982) 'Consociation: The Model and its Application in Divided Societies', in D. Rea (ed.), *Political Co-Operation in Divided Societies: A Series of Papers Relevant to the Conflict in Northern Ireland*. Dublin: Gill and Macmillan, pp. 166–86.

Lijphart, A. (1985) *Power-Sharing in South Africa*. Berkeley: University of California Press.

Macedo, S. (1991) *Liberal Virtues: Citizenship, Virtue, and Community in Liberal Constitutionalism*. Oxford: Clarendon Press.

Machiavelli, N. (1974 [1532]) *The Prince*. Harmondsworth: Penguin.

Maginness, A. (2002) 'Redefining Northern Nationalism', in J. Coakley (ed.), *Changing Shades of Orange and Green: Redefining the Union and the Nation in Contemporary Ireland*. Dublin: University College Dublin Press, pp. 33–40.

McAuley, J.W. (2002) 'The Emergence of New Loyalism', in J. Coakley (ed.), *Changing Shades of Orange and Green: Redefining the Union and the Nation in Contemporary Ireland*. Dublin: University College Dublin Press, pp.106–22.

McCall, C. and A. Williamson (2001) 'Governance and Democracy in Northern Ireland: The Role of the Voluntary and Community Sector after the Agreement', *Governance*, 14:3, 363–83.

McCartney, R. (2004) 'Power Shift that Suits the Sinn Féin Agenda', *The Belfast Telegraph*, 27 September.

McEvoy, K. (2000) 'Law, Struggle, and Political Transformation in Northern Ireland', *Journal of Law and Society*, 27:4, 542–71.

McGarry, J. and B. O'Leary (1995) *Explaining Northern Ireland: Broken Images*. Oxford: Blackwell.

McGarry, J. and B. O'Leary (2004a) *The Northern Ireland Conflict: Consociational Engagements*. Oxford: Oxford University Press.

McGarry, J. and B. O'Leary (2004b) 'Stabilising Northern Ireland's Agreement', *The Political Quarterly*, 75:3, 213–25.

McGarry, J. and B. O'Leary (2006) 'Consociational Theory, Northern Ireland's Conflict, and its Agreement. Part 2: What Critics of Consociation can learn from Northern Ireland', *Government and Opposition*, 41:2, 249–77.

Meehan, M. (2001) 'Towards a Northern Ireland Bill of Rights', *Liverpool Law Review*, 23, 33–56.

Montesquieu, Charles de Secondat Baron de (1989 [1748]) 'Preface', in A.M. Cohler, B.C. Miller and H.S. Stone (eds), *The Spirit of the Laws*. Cambridge: Cambridge University Press.

Morison, J. (2001) 'Democracy, Governance and Governmentality: Civic Public Space and Constitutional Renewal in Northern Ireland', *Oxford Journal of Legal Studies*, 21:2, 287–310.

Morrow, D. (2005) 'Breaking Antagonism? Political Leadership in Divided Societies', in I. O'Flynn and D. Russell (eds), *Power Sharing: New Challenges for Divided Societies*. London: Pluto Press, pp. 45–58.

Murray, G. (2003) 'The Good Friday Agreement: An SDLP Analysis of the Northern Ireland Conflict', in J. Neuheiser and S. Wolff (eds), *Peace at Last? The Impact of the Good Friday Agreement on Northern Ireland*. New York: Berghahn Books, pp. 45–59.

Newcastle University (2007) Press Release: Northern Ireland's First 'Deliberative Poll'. Issued 31 January.

Northern Ireland Council for Voluntary Action [NICVA] (2002) *State of the Sector III: Northern Ireland Voluntary and Community Sector Almanac*. NICVA: Belfast.

Oberschall, A. and L.K. Palmer (2005) 'The Failure of Moderate Politics: The Case of Northern Ireland', in I. O'Flynn and D. Russell (eds), *Power Sharing: New Challenges for Divided Societies*. London, Pluto Press, pp. 77–91.

O'Flynn, I. (2003) 'The Problem of Recognising Individual and National Identities: A Liberal Critique of the Belfast Agreement', *Critical Review of International Social and Political Philosophy*, 6:3, 129–53.

O'Flynn, I. (2006) *Deliberative Democracy and Divided Societies*. Edinburgh: Edinburgh University Press.

O'Leary, B. (2001) 'The Protection of Human Rights under the Belfast Agreement', *The Political Quarterly*, 72:3, 353–65.

O'Leary, Brendan (2005) 'Debating Consociational Politics: Normative and Explanatory Arguments', in S. Noel (ed.), *From Power Sharing to Democracy*. Montreal and Kingston: McGill-Queen's University Press, pp. 3–43.

Reilly, B. (2001) *Democracy in Divided Societies: Electoral Engineering for Conflict Management*. Cambridge: Cambridge University Press.

Schmitter, P.C. (2003) 'A Sketch of What a "Post-Liberal" Democracy might Look Like'. Unpublished Paper. Istituto Univeristario Europeo.

Steiner, J., A. Bächtiger, M. Spörndli, and M.R. Steenbergen (2004) *Deliberative Politics in Action: Analysing Parliamentary Discourse*. Cambridge: Cambridge University Press.

Sunstein, C.R. (2001) *Designing Democracy: What Constitutions Do?* Oxford: Oxford University Press.

Taylor, R. (2001) 'Northern Ireland: Consociation or Social Transformation?', in J. McGarry (ed.), *Northern Ireland and the Divided World: Post-Agreement Northern Ireland in Comparative Perspective*. Oxford: Oxford University Press, pp. 37–52.

Tonge, J. (2005) *The New Northern Irish Politics?* London: Palgrave Macmillan.

Touraine, A. (1997) *What is Democracy?* Boulder, Colorado: Westview Press.

Wagner, P. (2004) 'Northern Ireland after the Good Friday Agreement: On the Way to Peace or Conflict Perpetuated?' Global Research & Information Network. Available at www.grin.info.

Whyte, J. (1990) *Interpreting Northern Ireland*. Oxford: Clarendon Press.

Wolff, S. (2003) 'Conclusion: The Peace Process since 1998', in J. Neuheiser and S. Wolff (eds), *Peace at Last? The Impact of the Good Friday Agreement on Northern Ireland*. New York: Berghahn Books, pp. 205–32.

# 9
# From Violence to Intolerance: Ethno-Nationalism and the Crowding Out of Civic Life

*Robin Wilson*

While Taylor, in the previous chapter, discussed consociationalism as less justifiable normatively than other modes of participative democracy, this chapter focuses on how the Northern Ireland 'peace process', as it became rather grandly described by its various participants, arguably defied the norms of international peace-making by disdaining moderation and embracing extremism, marginalised civic actors while rewarding ethnic protagonism, and widened the gulf between the political arena and civic society. Peace, of a sort, did eventuate, as the embers of paramilitary violence slowly burned themselves out, and modest economic progress continued, as a result of normalising trends and global forces. But the society which blinkingly emerged was marked by chronic political polarisation, deep-seated sectarian (and racial) intolerance, and growing disengagement from politics.

This was a scenario quite unlike (presumably) what was intended by those who saw themselves as the authors of the process – though, in fact, those intentions were rather more diverse, and in some cases more nefarious, than that unimpeachable phrase encapsulated. It was, in short, a scenario of peace without, even peace *instead of*, reconciliation. It was eerily reminiscent of the period before the 'Troubles' began, when sectarian tension was all-pervasive even if, as latterly, violence was episodic and low-level.

These disconnections between 'high politics' and facts on the ground should not really surprise us. The 'levers' of government are always rubbery, given the complexity and interlocking trajectories of contemporary societies. And for reasons ranging from ideology to ignorance, ministers mostly pull the wrong ones, or in the wrong direction or at the wrong time. So we should be wary of taking what will inevitably be their self-validating claims at face value.

## Violence in Northern Ireland

In his excellent study of the origin of the civil-rights movement,Bob Purdie (1990) stressed that, contrary to the Unionist self-image of the day, 1960s Northern Ireland was no 'great wee province' but was disfigured by frequent sectarian incidents. Interestingly, Dan Keenan recalled Purdie's point in a piece written in the run-up to the tenth anniversary of the IRA ceasefire (*Irish Times*, 26 August 2004). The article was headed: 'Where peace is a relative concept: Just below the North's seemingly calm surface, incident after incident illustrates a simmering hostility'.

It is not, it is true, simply a case, as Churchill might have said, that as the Troubles 'deluge' has receded, the same 'dreary steeples' have re-emerged in Fermanagh and Tyrone. The big change since 1968, in terms of the 'Irish question', is that Northern Ireland has moved from a relationship of inequality and domination (a vertical relationship of oppression) to one of incomprehension and polarisation (a horizontal relationship of intolerance). From a Catholic, or secular liberal-left, point of view, that is, within its limits, a huge advance.

If it is an advance, however, it is an advance that has nothing to do with the 'peace process' and everything to do with the civil-rights movement. All of the demands of the latter had been addressed by 1976 – though tougher fair-employment legislation followed in 1989. Section 75 of the 1998 Northern Ireland Act, requiring designated public authorities to have 'due regard' for equal opportunities, has created a mountain of paperwork for NGOs but has had negligible tangible effect. True, the detested Special Powers Act was replaced by the 1973 Emergency Provisions Act (the latter, in turn, subsumed into UK-wide 'anti-terrorist' provisions), but this can hardly be blamed on the civil-righters – rather, those paramilitaries who subsequently sought to claim their mantle, having disdained such 'reformist' political activity at the time.

Nor, by the same token, did the 1994 'ceasefires' by the paramilitaries install 'peace'. Leaving aside the tautological nature of the Sinn Féin claim that there would have been no 'peace process' without the IRA, there were *more* paramilitary attacks during 1995–8 than 1991–4 (the majority of them, it should be stressed, perpetrated by 'loyalists'). Neither, moreover, did the Belfast Agreement achieve that desired goal – given there were *more* attacks *again* (again, predominantly Loyalist) during 1999–2002. Indeed, as the first report of the Independent Monitoring Commission

(2004, 20) pointed out, the number of shootings and assaults was thus nearly double in the three years after the Agreement what it had been in the three years before the ceasefires.

On the ground, checkpoints have now gone and army posts have been progressively demolished, because police and soldiers are no longer threatened. But 'peace walls' and other physical barriers have proliferated at interfaces marked by sectarian tension: the Northern Ireland Office has identified 37 of them (Jarman, 2004, 26). And the malaise of intolerance has found further expression in soaring reports of racist and homophobic incidents, as well as a slower increase, from a much higher level, in reported domestic violence, as indicated by successive chief constables' reports (available at *www.psni.police.uk/*) – albeit the picture is softened by recognition that policing reform may have made some victims more willing than hitherto to report these crimes.

Conversely, should the citizenry of Northern Ireland really have had to wait until 1994 for the paramilitary penny to drop? Even taking that as the year violence ceased – and Loyalist paramilitarism, as indicated, continues, while the IRA ceasefire was breached in 1996–7 – 25 years of politically motivated violence would represent one of the longest-running violent ethno-nationalist conflicts in the advanced capitalist democracies. In modern Irish history, it would comprise the longest and bloodiest by a very clear margin. The only comparator, ETA's 'armed struggle' – a source of many fewer casualties – has finally similarly fizzled out, even if the supportive sub-culture of the bars in the Basque country had hitherto been even more immune from the real world than the drinking clubs of north and west Belfast. Nobody in touch with that reality could, however, indefinitely continue to equate democratic Spain with Francoism – any more than one could compare direct rule, for all its lack of accountability, with the one-party sectarian *régime* it replaced in 1972. The proof lay in the rapid moves after London took over towards power-sharing, allied to an 'Irish dimension', which the armed-strugglers themselves (on both sides) belatedly signed up to in 1998.

Paramilitary violence emerges in the 'security dilemma' associated with a collapsing state, where the political incentives are not towards intercommunal accommodation but getting one's retaliation in first. This was as true of Northern Ireland in 1969–72 as of the wars of succession in former Yugoslavia (Ignatieff, 1999, 45). By the same token, such violence was simply unsustainable in a society guaranteeing basic democratic freedoms – for all that legitimate human-rights criticisms of emergency legislation remained, once internment was removed – and the longer it went on, the more unsustainable it became.

A glance at the graph of deaths due to the 'security situation' and the associated table of 'terrorist incidents' in the 1995 chief constable's report (Royal Ulster Constabulary, 1995, 116–17) shows a dramatic fall from 1972. True, with the IRA's development of the car bomb – a technological innovation now tragically exported to Iraq – there was an upward turn in 1975 and 1976. But the emergence of the Peace People in that year saw a further steep decline begin.

Indeed, far from violence being sustained by a 'political vacuum' within Northern Ireland, two external political miscalculations appear to have been significant in preventing the secular decline of the graph to zero well before 1995. First was the political insensitivity shown by the British Government towards the Catholic community at the time of the first hunger strike in 1980, when generalised prison reform could have addressed the humanitarian concerns in that community about the treatment of prisoners, while undercutting the impossibilist IRA demand for 'prisoner-of-war status' (and thus avoiding the segregation which, a senior Republican once triumphantly confided, secured the mass escape from the Maze in 1983). So 1981 saw a new surge before a further decline set in.

Second was the political insensitivity shown by the Republic's government towards the Protestant community when the Anglo-Irish Agreement was introduced, when legitimate Catholic-minoritarian concerns could have been supported in a manner which did not so obviously represent to Bible-reading Presbyterians the imposition of unaccountable authority. Thus 1987 saw another surge, before another decline in the early 1990s.

When the IRA announced its 'cessation', followed by the (even more nominal) 'loyalist' equivalents, it was still well short of the decision to 'dump arms' that followed, in 1962, just six years after the launch of the failed '50s campaign'. It was not until July 2005 – spurred on by popular revulsion against the IRA robbery of the Northern Bank headquarters in Belfast in December 2004 and its murder nearby of Robert McCartney the following month – that the campaign of the IRA was formally ended (and even then not *finally* ended, as this would have required an 'army convention' of members to determine (Moloney, 2002, 506)). Though this was allied to decommissioning of at least most IRA weapons in September 2005, the refusal of the Republican movement to embrace the rule of law meant it did not turn the trick, any more than in the past, in terms of instituting stable power-sharing. The argument – at root an argument over the Weberian monopoly of legitimate violence – simply moved on to policing.

# The politics of 'peace'

Why do we talk about a Northern Ireland 'peace process' at all? In 1991 and 1992, after all, we had a 'talks process'. Two things changed the terminology: the international connotations of contemporaneous developments in South Africa and Israel/Palestine – which seemed, at the time, to offer an auspicious climate in which aspiring statespersons might bask – and the promulgation by the Republican movement, at that stage outside the talks, of what it called the 'Irish peace initiative'.

But what should a 'peace process' mean in international terms? The South African situation offered little by way of a model, since that was a 'ranked' ethnic conflict with a vengeance – and 'majority rule' was the solution, not the problem. Nor did the Middle East – and not only because it was to be a comprehensive failure post-Oslo: there, entrenched ethnic partition, the 'two-state solution', was again seen as the solution, not the problem. Fashion, not fact, dictated the comparisons. The obvious Northern Ireland parallel – the ethno-nationalist conflicts in former Yugoslavia – had little purchase by comparison, doubtless because the international community saw nationalism (on all sides) there as the problem, not the solution.

One person well placed to give a sensible answer to the question was Cedric Thornberry, originally from Northern Ireland and at the time the top civilian official with UNPROFOR in ex-Yugoslavia. Interviewed in Belfast in the wake of the ceasefires, and asked about the lessons to be learned from his UN experiences, Mr Thornberry said (*Irish News*, 31 October 1994): 'I think that the lessons are extremely clear—effective human rights and politics of consensus, isolating extremists on both sides.' And he suggested: 'It is time for another generation to take over in this country.'

Similarly, Donald Horowitz pointed out at a Democratic Dialogue/ Constitution Unit seminar at University College London in January 2004 that what made the Northern Ireland 'peace process' an outlier was its 'inclusive' aspiration. The imperative that all parties to a conflict be included in government after a peace deal, even if that were possible – and the Democratic Unionist Party did not sign up on Good Friday 1998, while the Ulster Unionist Party began to split that very day – would imply that the conflict had been at that moment magicked away. The best that one could hope for in ethnically divided societies, Horowitz contended, was to put together a coalition of the 'moderate middle' sufficient to begin a break with the past, with the hope of incremental progress in a subsequent long haul.

Ironically, the 'talks process' was more like what a 'peace process' should be in this sense, in terms of its goals if not its rather conservative methodology: its élite focus and régime of strict confidentiality militated against any complementary 'track two' effort, though this was also true of what followed. Recognising that the principal challenge in societies torn by ethnic conflict is not violence *per se* but the underlying political divisions, it focused on a political accommodation between parties eschewing violence with a view to making the latter unsustainable. It failed because the governments in London and Dublin enshrined multiple vetoes in the talks, rather than adopting a common, proactive approach, mobilising potential civic support in the region (from business, the churches, the unions and so on) behind a vision for a 'new Northern Ireland'.

It was in that light that the Opsahl Commission stepped forward in 1993 with a template for such an approach to a settlement, on the basis of wide-ranging civic participation (Pollak, 1993). (Whether, given its strongly consociationalist inflection, it was the correct template is another day's argument.) It was taken up with enthusiasm by the Irish Minister for Foreign Affairs, Dick Spring, as offering a 'menu of options' and, to a lesser extent, embraced by the then Northern Ireland secretary, Sir Patrick Mayhew. A subsequent poll (details of which are in the second edition of the report), showed cross-community support for all its principal recommendations (albeit more so from Catholics), focusing as these did on intercommunal accommodation: power-sharing, a bill of rights, a consensual approach to North–South relationships. The marked exception was its suggestion that the government explore with Sinn Féin the possibility of a Republican ceasefire, which met a sharply polarised response (Pollak, 1993, 443).

Within weeks of the report's endorsement by these two government representatives, at a high-powered private conference in Cambridge in September 2003, at which Torkel Opsahl was the keynote speaker, the 'Hume-Adams' initiative between the leaders of the SDLP and Sinn Féin had become public knowledge, and politics was driven dramatically away from the focus on intercommunal accommodation towards *intra*communal solidarity, with inevitably polarising consequences.

The secret accord between the two Nationalist leaders on Irish 'self-determination' engendered an atmosphere of great uncertainty and insecurity. It was followed in October not by peace but by the worst month of fatalities in Northern Ireland since 1976, with the horrors of Shankill and Greysteel. As in 1976, however, civic society once more came to the rescue, with the biggest peace demonstrations since that year, organised by the Irish Congress of Trade Unions, with the notion of a 'unifying peace' a key theme. The impact on the bloodletting was immediate and dramatic. In a way, the ceasefires of the subsequent autumn were only a recognition – still highly qualified at that, as the above data on paramilitary incidents indicate – of the reality that the future lay in democratic accommodation and violence had no place in it.

The IRA ceasefire was quickly followed by the famous picture of the triple handshake between now three shades of Nationalism – Albert Reynolds of Fianna Fáil (then Toiseach), John Hume of the SDLP, and Gerry Adams of Sinn Féin – on the steps of Government Buildings in Dublin. Aware of the potential comparison with Michael Collins, Mr Adams declared, with no sense of historical modesty, that Collins 'didn't bring an end to partition'. In an interview with the *Guardian* a few days later (10 September 1994), he made clear that he saw Unionist and Nationalist sovereignty claims as 'irreconcilable': 'I'm an Irish republican and I want to see British jurisdiction ended and an Irish jurisdiction begin.'

As Kevin Toolis put it (*Times*, 5 March 2003), 'Sinn Féin is a democratic party in the same way as the "democratic centralist" communist parties of the Eastern bloc were democratic. Adams and McGuinness are part of the same tiny hermetic leadership elite that has ruled the IRA since the early 1970s. They fire and call the shots.' And first the SDLP, and subsequently Fianna Fáil, were to have reason to discover that Sinn Féin's totalitarian character meant that this show of Nationalist solidarity was only to work one way. Having demanded 'inclusive' dialogue when Sinn Féin was isolated – and it is from Mr Adams that the 'inclusive' tag attached to the 'peace process' derived – there was no associated show of Republican concern when the DUP (and the smaller UK Unionist Party) felt unable to attend the talks in 1997 when Sinn Féin arrived in the room, even though in both cases the 'exclusion' was in reality self-inflicted. Worse, there was no concern whatever about what was actually the exclusion of the SDLP by Downing Street from the talks that led to the 'failed choreography' of October 2003, ahead of the assembly election a month later, or the fact that the unsuccesful 'review' of the Agreement in 2004 by the two governments revolved entirely around the Republican movement and the DUP.

In the Westminster and local elections of 2001, Sinn Féin overtook the SDLP, even as Mr Hume was denying in television interviews it could ever happen. In the European and local elections in the Republic in 2004, Sinn Féin made sufficient inroads to heighten speculation that it would be difficult for Fianna Fáil to return to government without Sinn Féin endorsement after the 2007 Dáil election (unless Labour could be persuaded to change potential coalition partners).

Enhanced political power for Sinn Féin has been what the Republican 'peace strategy' Mr Adams largely devised has been about. Not only has it not been about interethnic accommodation – though just after his comments, cited above, about outdoing Collins in ending partition, he archly suggested that the show of ethnic solidarity held 'no threat to our Protestant brothers and sisters in the North, none at all'. It took Dick Walsh, the astute late political editor of the *Irish Times* (10 September 1994), to compare the Merrion Street 'show' with the celebration by Offaly of All-Ireland victory over Limerick – with the difference that the Offaly players 'paid generous tribute to their rivals', whereas any reassurance for Protestants 'was drowned in a chorus of triumphalism'.

On the contrary, replying eight years later to the post-suspension call in Belfast by Mr Blair for 'acts of completion' by Republicans, Mr Adams told his party's first conference of elected representatives across the island (*An Phoblacht*, 31 October 2002):

> This party is on the rise. Irish republicanism is growing and increasingly popular as a political philosophy. And that my friends, all other things to one side, is what has brought us to this crisis in the peace process. The British and Irish governments' version of the peace process had a different script from the one that has been written in recent years. The rise of Sinn Féin was not part of that script. In their script, the SDLP and the Ulster Unionist Party were to coalesce to form the so-called centre ground ... But it hasn't turned out like that.

Mr Adams went on to rehearse his view of the 'peace process': 'Our strategy, and Mr Blair knows this[,] is about bringing an end to physical force republicanism, by creating an alternative way to achieve democratic and republican objectives.' He said 'Mr Blair should see Britain's strategic interest being best served by the democratic resolution of the longstanding quarrel between the people of these two islands.' As for Unionists, 'In their hearts they know the game is up.'

It is perfectly clear from this that the phrase 'peace process' obscures two quite different conceptions of what is going on – never mind the reactive, Unionist version (Guelke, 2003). For London and Dublin, rather like Bernstein, the famous nineteenth-century revisionist socialist, 'The goal is nothing, the movement is everything': it is the process of peaceful accommodation between Protestants and Catholics, as an alternative to sectarian strife, that is key – not any particular outcome that may take.

For Sinn Féin and the IRA, on the contrary, the process is an accommodation by Unionism, cajoled by Britain, *to* Nationalism; the goal, a united Ireland, remains everything; and peace is only secured by demonstrating (and again the onus is placed on the British state) to those who would otherwise espouse violent means that politics offers a more effective (rather than the only legitimate) route to that end.

Hence Mr Adams' otherwise inexplicable comment 'Before the Good Friday Agreement, the six-county state was an undemocratic, illegitimate and failed political entity and after it, it remains so' (*Irish Times,* 12 March 1999). The logic of an 'inclusive peace process' flowed in that sense from the conventional Republican conception of history as essentialised antagonism between the 'Irish nation' and 'British imperialism', as against the now widely accepted conclusion that the 'principal contradiction' in Northern Ireland (to borrow a phrase from Mao) is between the two sectarian blocs themselves. The late John Whyte (1990, 172) pointed out, in his classic survey of the literature, that this internal, intercommunal tension would be undiminished by the removal of Britain, or the Republic of Ireland, from the political equation – a conclusion that, as far as I am aware, no one has attempted to challenge.

To paraphrase Stalin, however, how many divisions did John Whyte have? And so it was that it was Mr Adams' homespun wisdom which was to prevail in defining the politics of Northern Ireland in the 1990s, despite what Roy Foster calls his 'child-like solipsism' (2001, 183). And the Sinn Féin president, it should be said, was very conscious of this. Apparently determined to mimic the cleric-cum-amateur-historian in Brian Friel's play *Making History,* he once told the *Guardian* (6 October 2001): 'There's a slogan that says the victor writes the history.'

It is for these reasons, of course, that the 'decommissioning' issue took so many years to resolve (again, with Loyalists remaining implacable). Toolis, not an unsympathetic writer on Irish Republicanism, was brutally frank (*Times,* 5 March 2003): 'No one should be fooled. The IRA might bury its guns but its fundamental aim remains the same. Like the organisation's political forefather Pearse, it doesn't want to accommodate British rule in Ireland, it wants to destroy it politically.'

But, contrary to the external focus of Republican and Unionist narratives on the conflict, the relationship between the British and Irish states is now non-antagonistic: the introductions by the two premiers to a British Council Ireland (2005) publication on British–Irish interconnections make that abundantly clear. On the one hand, both are members of the European Union since 1973, they are on the other, and paradoxically, equally removed from mainstream European perspectives – with their respective deferential claims to be 'a bridge' to the United States or 'closer to Boston than Berlin'. And in as far as the Adams' version of the 'peace process' has prevailed, this already benign relationship between London and Dublin remains so, whereas the sectarian antagonism that should have been addressed – between the Shankill and the Falls in Belfast – is as poisonous as ever.

Notably absent from the Adams model are those 'Protestant brothers and sisters', whom he accused of stealing his seat from 'the people of West Belfast' when he lost it in 1992. Protestant paramilitaries do play a role, but only as marionettes whose strings are pulled by 'securocrats' working to the designs of the British state.

But with an inexorability like Newton's third law of motion, the rise of Sinn Féin which Mr Adams identified with the 'peace process' has been matched by the aggrandisement of the DUP. The two parties have advanced in lock-step in elections since the paramilitary ceasefires, at the expense of their more moderate counterparts (Wilford and Wilson, 2006, 13). No wonder that, by 2002, the centre simply could not hold.

In that sense, the Republican movement is hoist by its own sectarian petard. Far from embodying the civic-Republican vision of the United Irishmen – the highly desirable goal to unite Catholic, Protestant, and Dissenter in the common name of Irishman – the ethnic nationalism that the modern Republican movement has always represented since it emerged from its ghetto fastnesses in 1969 prevents it realising, by arms or by politics, the 'united-Ireland' objective many of its members, and many more others, have died for.

It is true – and much to be grateful for – that however strong the DUP becomes it is caught on just the same hook as its Republican enemy. For it could not establish the form of devolution it sought because of its inability to present any scheme which is not imbued with ethnic Unionism. In the small print in the two options it presented for coalition in 2004 (DUP, 2004), it proposed that any power-sharing executive be required at any time to face, and pass, a 70 per cent vote of confidence to survive. With 30 per cent plus of MLAs following the November 2003 assembly election, this of course would give the DUP a stranglehold on any government nominally shared with Catholics on the basis of political equality. Such inability to countenance a relationship of interdependence between Catholics and Protestants ensured that neither of these DUP proposals was a runner.

# Civic society

It is no surprise that in this chapter, as in the 'peace process', the role of civic actors has diminished over time. True, there was the excellent work of the 'Yes' campaign in 1998, which if it did nothing else ensured that floating Protestant voters went to the polling booths with the positive image in their minds of the UUP and SDLP leaders, David Trimble and Mr Hume, respectively, having their arms raised together by Bono at the rock concert in the Waterfront Hall in Belfast, rather the scene of the two Republican leaders, Mr Adams and Martin McGuinness, raising their clenched fists to welcome the Balcombe Street gang to the special Sinn Féin Ard Fheis in Dublin on the Agreement.

True, too, the Civic Forum was introduced by the Agreement, largely through the efforts of the non-sectarian Women's Coalition. But it faced constant hostility from the DUP, which has no conception of the need for a separation of civil society from the state in a democratic polity (Keane, 1998, 88). And it faced incomprehension from the then First and Deputy First Ministers (designate), Mr Trimble and Séamus Mallon respectively, who burdened the Civic Forum with such a cumbersome structure when they designed it in 1999 that it was bound to fail after it was finally established the following year.

The 'Yes' campaign was wrong-footed by the revelation that the Northern Ireland Office (NIO) wanted to see a range of civic actors come out in support of an agreement if one was signed. And the agreement itself was pitched by the NIO as of interest to every citizen, as its cover text and image stressed (NIO, 1998). Yet Adrian Guelke (2003) is right to argue that the role of civil society in Northern Ireland declined, rather than increased, after the agreement referendum.

Not only has there been much suspicion among Northern Ireland's political (and paramilitary) élites towards civic-society initiatives – one adviser to the devolved government said there had been no sympathy for the Civic Forum around the executive table. More, in line with the consociationalist assumption that such élites represent the only significant actors, the agreement entrenched them in power. As the expert on 'constitutional engineering' Giovanni Sartori (1997, 190) argues, consociationalism thus risks an imbalance between state and civil society, with an invasive 'hypertrophy' of party politics.

This, however, only served to make successive 'crises in the peace process' more politically insoluble. As already indicated, the failure of the Brooke/Mayhew talks was offset by the Opsahl report offering a way forward. The violence following the Hume–Adams initiative was dampened by the trade-union demonstrations. The frail Protestant support for the Belfast Agreement was enlarged by the 'Yes' campaign. But the civic actors were powerless even to affect the bizarre construction of the Civic Forum – never mind to intervene as neutral brokers to break the decommissioning impasse in time, or to prevent the serial suspensions of the institutions once established.

## Conclusions

There have already been volumes of articles and books written on the Northern Ireland 'peace process'. Most have taken for granted the claims of participants, rather than subjecting these to close scrutiny, and most have ignored the wider dynamics of the society in which the conflict has taken place, and beyond. Most have therefore, by default rather than argument, attributed too much credence to the coherence and effectiveness of the former and too little to the latter.

An alternative hypothesis can be advanced. In as far as Northern Ireland is (thankfully) a less life-threatening place to live, it may be that this was more a product of secular, social trends than of 'high' – including high international – politics. As Rogers Brubaker (2002) argues, the state of ethnic 'groupness' that characterises divided societies is by no means natural or inevitable: it is sustained and reproduced by ethno-political entrepreneurs and may otherwise decay under the pressures of quotidian life upon the mass of the population not recruited by the protagonists.

It may be that lethal paramilitary violence could have been brought to a close rather earlier, had not some ill-conceived steps been taken by a range of actors, than as a result of the 'peace process'. It might be that a more proactive political approach by London and Dublin, allying themselves with civic actors to shoe-horn the political élites into an accommodation, could have seen power-sharing established earlier, and on a more stable footing, than the fragile political *bricolage* essayed in 1998. If so, the spirit of tolerance and intercultural dialogue that Northern Ireland so desperately needs if peace is to be accompanied by reconciliation might be rather more in evidence than the daily news diet of sectarianism and racism now suggests.

Instead, the acute 'crises in the peace process', which obsessed the political class, over time devolved into a chronic pathology. With the post-Agreement institutions in suspension for over four years, the situation acquired a perverse stability, by which most ordinary citizens felt increasingly unworried. Indeed, intriguingly, the incidence of violence, which had been on a rising graph from the 'ceasefires' of 1994, turned down following the 2002 political collapse (Wilford and Wilson, 2006, 20). Relatedly, perceptions of the state of community relations, which had been on a deteriorating trend over the same period – albeit with a blip at the time of the Belfast Agreement – turned up (Dowds, 2004). And the clichéd equation 'political vacuum' = upsurge of violence, even taking account of the outburst of violent Protestant sectarian rage in September 2005 in Belfast, clearly does not work now.

In particular, the Republican movement could no longer issue a credible threat – or even leave such a threat for others to glean from veiled language about another 'crisis in the peace process'. As late as October 2002 the Prime Minister, in his post-suspension speech in Belfast, confessed (for the first time) that Republicans had enjoyed political 'leverage' because of the capacity (as distinct from the intent) of the IRA to renew its campaign. But after an angry meeting between Tony Blair and Mr Adams at Downing Street in May 2004, when the Sinn Féin president emerged complaining, once again, of a 'deep crisis', the long-term IRA-watcher Ed Moloney concluded (*Irish Times*, 10 May 2004) that 'the passage of time' was rendering that implicit threat 'largely useless'.

Moreover, after the years of moral hazard associated with the 'peace process', which had disincentivised paramilitary disarmament moves, the Independent Monitoring Commission's reports from 2004 came like a blue sky of truth-telling to disperse the overcast atmosphere in which nothing could be said that any paramilitary might deem 'unhelpful' (and so source of another 'crisis in the peace process'). After decades of confusion as to whether paramilitaries should, first, be suppressed (by defeating 'the men of violence') or, alternately, appeased (by celebrating their 'commitment to peace'), the commission held out the clear middle way that the answer was to uphold without derogation the 'rule of law', a phrase that ran like a golden thread through its reports and was repeatedly adumbrated in an annex. This not only helped speed the placing 'beyond use' of IRA weapons, in a manner the hapless John de Chastelain of the decommissioning commission had failed otherwise to achieve, but it also placed the spotlight on the vast infrastructure of organised crime and the black economy on which all Northern Ireland paramilitaries had previously subsisted.

What is also intriguing, despite the political polarisation of the last decade, is the robust nature of support for the principle of power-sharing evident in the annual iterations of the Northern Ireland Life and Times Survey since the 2002 collapse of the associated institutions. Catholics are unsurprisingly more likely to agree 'strongly' with power-sharing than Protestants, but in both cases the majorities in favour are overwhelming. Moreover, despite the (again unsurprisingly) lukewarm attitude among respondents to the achievements of the political class under devolution, support for the idea of devolution as the best constitutional arrangement far outweighs that for the Union without devolution or a united Ireland. And some 35 per cent of the population each year refuse to be defined as 'unionist' or 'nationalist' – many more than those who adopt the latter category and within reach of those who embrace the former (data available at http://www.ark.ac.uk/nilt). Whether the two parties most committed to prosecuting the antagonism between the traditional ethno-national categories, at the time of writing dominating the restored devolued arrangements, can articulate that public mood remains to be seen.

## References

British Council Ireland. (2005) *Britain & Ireland: Lives Entwined*. Dublin: British Council.

Brubaker, R. (2002) 'Ethnicity Without Groups', *Archives Européenes de Sociologie*, 43:2, 163–89.

Democratic Unionist Party (2004) *Devolution Now*. Belfast: DUP.

Dowds, L. (2004) 'Public Attitudes', in Northern Ireland Devolution Monitoring Report. Available at: http://www.ucl.ac.uk/constitution-unit/monrep/ni/ni_august_2004.pdf [accessed 1 April 2007].

Foster, R.F. (2001) *The Irish Story: Telling Tales and Making it up in Ireland*. London: Allen Lane.

Guelke, A. (2003) 'Civil Society and the Northern Irish Peace Process', *Voluntas*, 14:1, 61–78.

Ignatieff, M. (1999) *The Warrior's Honor: Ethnic War and the Modern Conscience*. London: Vintage.

Independent Monitoring Commission. (2004) *First Report of the Independent Monitoring Commission*. London: The Stationery Office.

Jarman, N. (2004) *Demography, Development and Disorder: Changing Patterns in Interface Areas*. Belfast: Community Relations Council.

Keane, J. (1998) *Civil Society: Old Images, New Visions*. Cambridge: Polity Press.

Moloney, E. (2002) *A Secret History of the IRA*. London: Allen Lane.

Northern Ireland Office (1998) *The Agreement: Agreement Reached in the Multi-Party Negotiations*. Belfast and London: NIO.

Pollak, A. (1993) *A Citizens' Inquiry: The Opsahl Report on Northern Ireland*. 2nd edition. Dublin: Lilliput Press.

Purdie, B. (1990) *Politics in the Streets: The Origins of the Civil Rights Movement in Northern Ireland*. Belfast: Blackstaff Press.

Royal Ulster Constabulary (1995) *The Chief Constable's Annual Report*. Belfast: RUC.

Sartori, G. (1997 [1994]) *Comparative Constitutional Engineering: An Inquiry into Structures, Incentives and Outcomes*. Basingstoke: Palgrave Macmillan.

Whyte, J. (1990) *Interpreting Northern Ireland*. Oxford: Clarendon Press.

Wilford, R. and R. Wilson (2006) *The Trouble with Northern Ireland: The Belfast Agreement and Democratic Government*. Dublin: TASC at New Island.

# 10
## Power-Sharing and Civic Leadership in Lebanon and Northern Ireland

*David Russell*

Scholars and practitioners concerned with resolving ethnic conflicts have, in broadest terms, devoted a great deal of attention to the question of what political institutions might best advance peace and stability in divided societies. They have made recommendations as to the relative appropriateness of particular electoral systems, how legislatures and executives should be formed, and how decision-making procedures can best support power-sharing democracy. Yet when attempting to address the question of institutional choice in divided societies, it is also important to examine what sort of political attitudes and behaviours those institutions may foster and support over time. As power-sharing becomes embedded in the political culture of a divided society, the worry can arise that the measures put in place may themselves inhibit the development of a civic leadership that encourages elected representatives to make decisions that are for the benefit of everyone in society rather than simply for the benefit of their own ethnic group.

In this chapter I argue that, when it comes to the task of designing power-sharing arrangements for divided societies, there is a tendency to over-emphasise ethnicity as the principal unit for conducting politics and building sustainable democracy. As a result, the function of political representation is often reduced, even if wholly unintentionally, to a guardianship of mutually exclusive community interests. Indeed, the purpose of power-sharing itself may become little more than a platform for calculating tactical advantages over other ethnic groups, which, in turn, can act as a destabilising influence that threatens to collapse efforts at building peace and democracy. In order to support this argument, I consider the extent to which two contemporary peace agreements promote civic leadership.

The Ta'if Accord and Belfast Agreement represent endeavours to end violent conflict between Christians and Muslims in Lebanon and Irish Nationalists and British Unionists in Northern Ireland, respectively. Both have institutionalised ethnic identities within their political systems in the belief that such institutionalisation is a requisite for lasting, peaceful coexistence. And yet, despite numerous similarities, I argue that the two agreements have fared rather differently with respect to the task of promoting civic leadership. To this end, I begin, first, by analysing how the Ta'if Accord and Belfast Agreement have sought to address the vexed question of constitutional status. I argue that Lebanon is more successful than Northern Ireland in this regard because it has settled this question through an inter-ethnic consensus that opens up crucial space in which elected politicians are free to think beyond narrow sectarian agendas. Secondly, I consider whether power-sharing can encourage civic leadership in the making of everyday decisions. I argue, again, that the Ta'if Accord is more successful because it has reduced the political saliency of ethnic identities within the legislature and encouraged the formation of an executive premised upon collective government. In contrast, I show why the Belfast Agreement has not performed as well on this account. Thirdly, I examine how the two agreements have sought to widen democratic participation in order to reflect broader civil society interests, as opposed to purely ethnic readings of those interests, so as to further incentivise politicians to champion the goals and purposes of a longer-term social transformation. I conclude that there have been significant developments in each case seeking to foster a new political dispensation of this sort. In Northern Ireland, however, inter-ethnic competition coupled with the institutionalisation of ethnicity continues to predominate to the detriment of civil society interests. By contrast, in Lebanon, the tension between ethnic and civil society interests is not as pronounced, and hence elected politicians have more opportunity and freedom to act as civic leaders.

## Constitutional status

In both Lebanon and Northern Ireland, tensions between communities have been especially evident when it comes to deciding on the constitutional status. It is unsurprising that this should be the case. If people are indeed serious about living together, then they must also accept the need for a clear public statement defining the territory they are to share. This statement must be made in a way that the members of all ethnic groups can reasonably be expected to identify with, for otherwise there is a real danger that the state will lack legitimacy in their eyes. In a divided society, any decision on the constitutional status must also be settled in such a way that it enables civic leadership to emerge. What this means in practice is that the public statement defining the territory must help create a political context in which politicians are encouraged and feel at ease with thinking beyond their more particular ethnic affiliations. That context cannot be created, however, unless the decision-making process by which the constitutional status is settled is itself consistent with the principles of power-sharing. If the process is inconsistent with the principles of power-sharing, then the constitutional status will lack legitimacy and act as a politically destabilising force.

To be considered legitimate, the constitutional status in a divided society must be what Bhikhu Parekh refers to as 'a general consensus', by which he means an agreement which does not subject those involved to charges of divided loyalties (Parekh, 1999, 67). In order to avoid the charge of dividing loyalties, the constitutional status must be settled so as to facilitate the protection of ethnic interests and allow civic interests to emerge. The Ta'if Accord has aimed to balance civic and ethnic interests by declaring Lebanon a 'sovereign, free and independent country . . . Arab in its identity and in its association' (Ta'if Accord, 1991, Preamble, a. b. c. and j.). Lebanese Christians have in the past denied their Arab heritage because they were apprehensive that Arabism contained Islamic overtones and the possibility of a loss of sovereignty within a larger regional polity. The separation of Arabism and Islam added to the Ta'if Accord's affirmation of state independence is intended as a measure to allay this fear. Muslims have conceded that there can be no Islamisation of the state, that Lebanon is a sovereign power, and that Arabism must be rendered consistent with the principle of religious pluralism (Russell and Shehadi, 2005, 143). Having gained these assurances, Christians for their part have accepted that in all domains, and with no exceptions, foreign and domestic policies should be made on the basis of Lebanon's Arab identity (Maila, 1992b, 14).

The inter-ethnic consensus that lies, therefore, at the heart of the Ta'if Accord is dependent upon the accepted interdependency of a pluralist Arabism and state independence. This has been reaffirmed throughout the document. For example, the declaration that Lebanon is a member of the Arab League may be interpreted by some as an opportunity to stress their Arab identity. Others may choose to emphasise state sovereignty within the regional order. What is most important, however, is that the two interpretations are equally valid, have been recognised by the members of the main ethnic groups as such, and can be proclaimed openly without becoming a source of antagonism. The commitment to an independent Arab state balances the demands made by the constituent ethnic groups and successfully generates a public statement on the constitutional status which promotes a civic vision of a Lebanese society. No single community can hope to stamp its particular identity upon the civic character of the state to the exclusion of any other.

By comparison, all the parties to the Belfast Agreement have formally recognised the current constitutional status of Northern Ireland as part of the United Kingdom. Crucially, this recognition remains conditional, however, only until such a time as the majority of people decide otherwise (The Agreement, 1998, section 1, subsections (i)–(v), 2). Unlike the permanence of Lebanon's Arab character, the question of whether Northern Ireland should be identified as British or Irish in the long run remains open. The Agreement contains an acceptance by both Unionists and Nationalists that the constitutional status could change at some future point. Indeed, once there is a reasonable prospect of a majority in favour of seceding from the United Kingdom and becoming part of a united Ireland, the British Secretary of State for Northern Ireland is legally bound to call a referendum on the issue (The Agreement, 1998, annex A). In one respect, this approach is similar to Lebanon, since it has been drafted in such a way that it can claim to protect the interests of the constituent ethnic groups. In a second respect, however, an obvious distinction is that the situation in Northern Ireland seems unlikely to continue. The Belfast Agreement cannot be all things to all people *ad infinitum*. Sooner or later one side in the conflict may have to realise that their aspirations will not be met.

Defenders of the Agreement will doubtless be quick to reply at this point that, regardless of the constitutional status of Northern Ireland, there are significant guarantees of protection afforded to Nationalists and Unionists, both in the present and for the future. These guarantees are given precisely because the future is uncertain and the hope is that they will provide sufficient reassurance so as to allow civic interests to emerge in a way that helps soften the constitutional question in the minds of politicians and the ethnic groups they represent. No matter which government, Irish or British, has jurisdiction over the territory, a commitment has been made to promote 'rigorous impartiality on behalf of all the people in the diversity of their identities and traditions' (The Agreement, 1998, section 1, subsections (v), 2). Some commentators, such as Brendan O'Leary, have interpreted this commitment to mean that Nationalists are recognised and protected now on the same terms that will be given to Unionists 'should they ever become a minority in a united Ireland' (O'Leary, 1999, 1649). An objection to O'Leary's hypothesis, however, is that there is no explicit obligation contained within the Agreement requiring the Irish Government to comply with this interpretation following a change in sovereignty. The absence of clarity from the outset on critical issues in a divided society is conducive to creating a climate of suspicion and fear. Nationalists and Unionists do not know what a possible future united Ireland might involve in practical terms. This confusion reduces the Agreement's capacity to act as a source of political stability (MacGinty, 2003, 1–22).

Connected to the uncertainty of Northern Ireland's political future is the process by which the current settlement says that future is to be decided. When the Agreement was reached in 1998, its democratic credentials where evaluated on the basis that it was subject to popular referendums held simultaneously in Northern Ireland and the Republic of Ireland. At the time, there was a worry that the credibility of any decision endorsing the Agreement would depend on an overwhelming 'yes' vote. As it happened, the two results had a necessary sense of authority because 94 per cent in the Republic and 71 per cent in the North voted in favour the proposal (Wilford, 2001, 61). Yet this high level of support was a purely fortuitous outcome because, technically speaking, a simple majority of 50+ per cent in the two jurisdictions would have been enough for a democratic endorsement. The difficulty with this decision-making process is that simple majority rule is often unsuited to a divided society since it denies minority ethnic groups an equal say. Simple majority voting risks fixing outcomes in favour of the majority ethnic group and hence negates the uncertainty of outcomes that are a key element of democracy. Democratisation according to Adam Przeworski 'is a process of subjecting all interests to competition, of institutionalising uncertainty. It is thus the very devolution of power over outcomes which constitutes the decisive step towards democracy' (Przeworski, 1993, 62). The problem with a literal interpretation of the Belfast Agreement is that the possibility of a future change in constitutional status will be subject to simple majority rule. If demographic trends determine that nationalists will increase, and at some future point become greater in number than Unionists, then there will be nothing in principle to stop a united Ireland determined by exclusively Nationalist votes. This fixing of the constitutional question is not only undemocratic but has done little to foster a sense of confidence among Unionist politicians and their supporters.

Lebanon does not face the same difficulty as Northern Ireland because the accepted interdependency of a pluralist Arabism and state sovereignty contained within the Ta'if Accord represents an optimum inter-ethnic consensus. That is to say, it is a policy which reflects the most favourable of conditions where the antagonism between the constituent communities is reduced to a difference of opinion on the basic character of the state. If, on the other hand, the source of ethnic hostility in a divided society is grounded in a fundamental rejection that the entity should exist at all, as is argued by many Nationalists in Northern Ireland, then finding a solution to ethnic conflict becomes an altogether more difficult quest (see Porter, 2003). Despite the difference in favourable conditions, Lebanon does, however, have something important to say about how crucial decisions on Northern Ireland's constitutional future should be made. Moreover, the Ta'if Accord is arguably a better formula than the Belfast Agreement in this regard, not because the former is permanent and secure. But rather, because any decision in Lebanon that stands to affect the integrity of the state or its constitutional status must be made in keeping with the principles of power-sharing.

The Ta'if Accord may have settled the constitutional status of Lebanon with some degree of permanency unlike Northern Ireland, but this does not mean that cannot be changed in the future. While it is an admittedly unlikely scenario, the fact remains that there is no principled reason as to why a change in constitutional status could not happen in Lebanon. The only distinguishing features of the Belfast Agreement in this regard are the assumptions that a future debate will have taken place, that this underpins current politics, and that it should be confined to a choice between retaining a membership of the United Kingdom or creating a united Ireland. From a comparative perspective, it must be pointed out, however, that the constitutional status of all democratic societies ought, for reasons of flexibility and responsiveness to public demands, to contain rules that govern the possibility of making amendments and alterations. It is only to be expected therefore that in the interest of maintaining basic democratic credentials – rule by the people, for the people – that Lebanon's constitutional status remains open for both deliberation and reform (Preuss, 1993, 653). The Ta'if Accord is no different from the Belfast Agreement in this regard. At the request of at least ten of its members, the Lebanese parliament may recommend, by a weighted majority of two-thirds of its total membership, a revision of any article of the Ta'if Accord, including a revision of the constitutional status (Taif Accord, 1991, article 77).

The substantive difference between Northern Ireland and Lebanon is that any change to the constitutional status in the former case is to be determined by popular referendum, whilst in the latter it would be the product of a representative democratic process, with a vote taking place within the Lebanese parliament. What is more important in terms of the immediate discussion, however, is that in Lebanon the decision-making process is designed to ensure that any eventual decision would be in keeping with the inter-ethnic consensus that legitimises the current independent Arab state. In Lebanon, as explained above, democratic legitimacy on such a crucial issue is understood to require a two-thirds majority in parliament voting in favour. This figure has been set so as to guarantee that deliberation will take place between the political representatives of the Christian and Muslim communities. In accordance with the principles of power-sharing, any decision on the future of Lebanese Arabism or sovereignty would require that a significant proportion of political opinion from the main ethnic groups were in agreement. This is contrary to the situation in Northern Ireland, where Unionists and Nationalists are encouraged by the Agreement to hold out in the hope of achieving their maximalist aspirations at the expense of the other community. As Adrian Guelke suggests, the hope of ultimately winning the constitutional dispute through simple majority rule could well have been one of the reasons for the competing ethnic communities 'engaging with the Belfast Agreement in first place' (Guelke, 2000, 232). This does little to open up necessary space for the emergence of civic leadership.

## Legislature and executive

Addressing changes in the constitutional status is one thing. But in a divided society, everyday political decisions will also have to be made. Often these decisions will have implication for society as a whole and in this sense will call for civic leadership. However, it also happens that even the most general decisions in divided societies will sometimes be reduced to competing ethnic claims. In attempting to address the challenge of making everyday decisions, Lebanon and Northern Ireland have institutionalised power-sharing. While much has been written about the subject of power-sharing, perhaps the most salient consideration for this discussion is that both the Ta'if Accord and Belfast Agreement are, broadly-speaking, consociational. In keeping with the formula most readily associated with the name of Arend Lijphart, consociation is characterised by a grand governing coalition, group vetoes that guarantee political decisions will only be made with the consent of the main communities, proportionality rules applied throughout the government and public sectors, and segmental autonomy designed to ensure self-governance on issues relating to the protection and perpetuation of culture and ethnic identity (Lijphart, 1977).

Despite their basic underlying similarities, the Ta'if Accord and Belfast Agreement contain significantly different procedures for executive and legislative formation which in turn impact on the attitudes and behaviours of local politicians. In Lebanon seats in the legislature and executive are pre-determined. Hence, the communities which are to act as partners in power-sharing are named in advance and the number of seats to be held by them is rigidly fixed on a permanent basis (Lijphart, 1995). Political representation in the 128-member legislative Chamber of Deputies is divided equally between Muslims and Christians, with the 64 seats in each ethnic bloc allocated proportionally to the Sunni, Shia, Druze, and Alawite Muslims, the Maronite, Greek Catholic, Greek Orthodox, Armenian Orthodox, and a number of smaller named Christian denominations (Ta'if Accord, 1991, article 24).

When it comes to the task of executive formation, the distribution of the top three public offices, that of the President, Prime Minister, and Speaker of Parliament are reserved for the Maronite Christian, Sunni Muslim, and Shia Muslim communities respectively (Rieck, 1990, 300). Unlike a standard case of presidentialism, the incumbent Maronite Christian politician who acquires the office of president is not elected by the citizens, but must instead achieve support from a weighted majority of two-thirds of the legislature; in other words, 72 members of parliament (Taif Accord, 1991, article 49). The President is then responsible for nominating a Sunni candidate as Prime Minister. Before making the appointment, however, the President must consult with the legislature and win support from the Shia Speaker of Parliament, who is himself subject to parliamentary approval. Allocation of the remaining executive offices within the Council of Ministers requires the joint signatures of the President and Prime Minister. In addition, the executive as a collegial body must present its 'general statement of policy' to the legislature, and cannot exercise any functions before it 'gains the Chamber's confidence' by means of a parliamentary vote (Ta'if Accord, 1991, article 64, subsection 2). The net result of this complex set of checks and balances is that only those politicians who successfully present themselves as civic leaders, who appeal for support across party political lines and across the ethnic divide, stand a chance of being elected to the executive.

Turning to comparable institutions in Northern Ireland, the consociational features of the Belfast Agreement were altogether more flexible with respect to legislative and executive power-sharing. In this case, there was no pre-determination in either the 108-member Legislative Assembly, or in the formation of the Executive Committee (The Agreement, 1998, section 15, p. 7). Neither Unionists nor Nationalists are guaranteed a representative quota. Instead, returning politicians must designate a personal affiliation as a Unionist, Nationalist, or Other following their election and in order to take a seat in the legislature. Unlike Lebanon, there are no explicit assurances regarding the distribution of the top public offices. Both the First and Deputy First Ministers in Northern Ireland, neither of whom is subservient to the other, were jointly elected by the legislature on the basis of parallel consent. This was understood to mean a majority of those members of the Assembly present and voting, including a majority of designated Unionists and a majority of designated Nationalists (The Agreement, 1998, section 2, p. 5). The assumption was that the requirement of parallel consent would result in the selection of one Unionist and one Nationalist for the top two posts and the process of dual appointment will be able to claim democratic legitimacy having achieved an inter-ethnic consensus. This process has now been changed by the St Andrews' Agreement (see page 14).

While the substantial duties of the First Minister and Deputy First Minister include, *inter alia*, 'dealing with and co-ordinating the work of the Executive Committee and the response of the administration to external relationships', it is notable that they have no power to determine the allocation of ministerial offices (The Agreement, 1998, section 18, p. 7). Contrary to the situation in Lebanon, the appointment of the Northern Ireland Executive does not require approval from the legislature and the First Minister and Deputy First Minister have no responsibility for overseeing the appointments process. Executive positions are allocated to political parties in proportion to their strength in the legislature according to a mechanical algorithm known as the D'Hondt rule (Horowitz, 2002, 210). This guarantees any party that wins a significant share of seats in the legislature a reasonable chance of gaining access to the executive. It also allows political parties to choose, again in order of strength, their preferred ministerial portfolios. While individual ministers can be held accountable and removed from office if necessary by the Assembly, the party which held the relevant ministry remains free to appoint their successor from within its own ranks (The Agreement, 1998, section 25, 7–8). Taken together, these provisions mean that any political party will gain and retain representation in the legislature and executive if they win enough votes. In other words, there is in principle at least every chance that politicians will come to view themselves as having a genuine stake in the decision-making process and hence will have the confidence to move beyond their more particular ethnic reading of everyday decision-making towards a more civic minded outlook. The worry, however, is that unlike the Ta'if Accord, which mandates institutions that expressly aim to foster civic minded decisions, the Belfast Agreement relies on little more than dubious assumptions about the motivations of elected representatives.

The Ta'if Accord does not assume that politicians will be disposed of their own volition to engage in civic leadership, but instead explicitly requires them to 'represent the whole nation. No restriction or stipulation may be imposed upon their mandate by their electors' (Ta'if Accord, 1991, article 27). There is, in other words, a duty on elected representatives to consider the common good, and to make sure that their decisions reflect the collective interests of everyone in society, irrespective of the differences in ethnic identity. To further encourage civic leadership, the introduction of weighted majority voting ensures that major decisions by the executive require approval from two-thirds of the Ministers. With regard to some specified issues, such as amendments to the Ta'if Accord itself, two-thirds of the legislature must also give their approval (Ta'if Accord, 1991, article 77). Decisions made on issues that have not been specified require endorsement by a simple majority in Chamber of Deputies. In practice, this means that even if the politicians of an entire ethnic bloc, 64 Muslims or 64 Christians, voted in favour of a decision, they would still have to convince at least some parliamentarians from the other communities of the value to society as a whole (Ta'if Accord, 1991, article 34).

We might be tempted to think that the institutions of the Belfast Agreement yield the same consensual results as the Ta'if Accord. But closer examination reveals that this is not the case. There is an obligation on the Northern Ireland Executive to take collective responsibility for some specified policies, such as the programme for government, and to seek endorsement from the legislature (The Agreement, 1998, sections 19 and 20, p. 7). In addition, any decision can become one referred to in the text as 'a key decision'. Once a petition of concern is brought forward by 30 Assembly members, the subsequent decision is initially subject to a stringent test of parallel consent, which, as I have already indicated, requires a majority of those members present and voting to be in favour, including a majority from the two main communities. If this threshold cannot be achieved, then a second more conciliatory option, that of a weighted majority, requiring 60 per cent of the members present and voting to be in favour of a given proposal, including at least 40 per cent of each of the two communities, is considered enough of a democratic validation for the decision to pass (The Agreement, 1998, section 5, sub-section (d), (i) and(ii), 6). Yet despite these institutional measures what remains absent in Northern Ireland is any attempt to direct politicians on how they should view the decision-making process.

In Lebanon, the explicit requirement for civic leadership contained within the Ta'if Accord demands that politicians view decision-making procedures, such as weighted majority voting, as a method for promoting collective decisions for the good of everyone in society. For example, the fact that at least some Christians and some Muslims have to agree on the allocation of ministerial posts encourages a vision beyond insular community self-interest. This is further encouraged within the executive and legislature through a constant envisaging of an agreed future where the political saliency of ethnic identities will be substantially eroded. The Ta'if Accord anticipates the introduction of a bicameral political system, whereby during a period of phased elimination, ethnic interests will be guaranteed representation and protection within a senate. According to this plan, the Chamber of Deputies would be transformed into a secular legislative body, while the function of a newly formed Senate would be limited to what is referred to in the text as 'major national issues' (Hanf, 1993, 588). These issues are understood to be those which stand to affect the particular interests of ethnic groups, the character of the constitution, or the constitutional status.

Of course, one should not overplay the significance of civic leadership in Lebanon. Some commentators have been critical of the Ta'if Accord and have argued that it has failed to deliver. The former President Amin Gemayel points out that although the word citizen 'appears on political speeches, official and unofficial, in actuality the Lebanese citizen does not exist.' He maintains that civic leadership has not taken root in the political system and any attempt to do so is 'constantly challenged by the strength of community feeling' (Gemayel, 1992, 5). When it comes to executive and legislative formation, a further difficulty presented by the Accord is that the commitment to pre-determination places undue restrictions on candidates by determining who can stand for election and who cannot. As Amin Maalouf argues, it is surely unhealthy and does little to promote civic leadership among politicians when they are encouraged to think of positions of power as the property of one particular community, as opposed to an open competition wherein the purpose is to ensure that the best candidate gets the job (Maalouf, 2000, 120).

The criticisms made against the Ta'if Accord are valid, but so too is the commendation for promoting civic leadership. This should not be downplayed or overlooked. Because the Belfast Agreement provides no equivalent to the Ta'if Accord's explicit requirement that politicians behave as civic leaders, politicians in Northern Ireland are free to view power-sharing institutions in any way they wish. In principle, they could decide to view decision-making procedures, such as parallel consent and weighted majority voting, as a reflection of an overarching commitment to civic leadership. But they might just as easily view them as protections that afford Unionists and Nationalists the right to veto decisions that they disagree with. In this latter sense, what is seen in Lebanon as a positive form of political deliberation is, by contrast, often seen in Northern Ireland as a negative. The subtle move in Lebanon away from the vernacular of ethnic antagonism is, admittedly, perhaps little more than an elaborate charade, but its significance is nonetheless important. Not only does the positive attitude among Lebanese politicians tell us something about the relationship that people living there want to build with each other, but it differs sharply with what is at best little more than a vague aspiration in Northern Ireland. Whereas there is a sense that Lebanon seeks to build a future where the political saliency of Muslim and Christian identities are reduced, there is no sense that the Belfast Agreement is encouraging Northern Ireland's politicians to view themselves as having an equivalent responsibility. In fact, the opposite might just as easily be true (see Wilson and Wilford, 2003; Horowitz, 2002).

## Civil society interests

Even in a divided society, there will inevitably be times when the citizens feel motivated by considerations other than those driven by, or interpreted in terms of, ethnic identity. Political struggles relating to class, gender, or sexual orientation are sometimes of greater concern to individuals than political distinctions made on a basis of ethnicity (cf. O'Neill, 2003, 368). In addition, subjects such as transport, healthcare, housing, the economy, and the environment often transcend community divisions in the sense that decisions relating to those subjects typically impact on society as a whole. Interests that 'cannot be reduced to the interests of some particular ethnic group, but instead pertain to citizens in general' can according to Ian O'Flynn be referred to as 'civil society interests' (O'Flynn, 2006, 141). Crucially, making space for these interests is vitally important to building sustainable peace and supporting the transition to democracy because they afford the members of a divided society an opportunity to forge relationships that cut across community divisions, and hence provide a platform to build social and political networks that can advance the good of society as a whole. Accordingly, the question that this final section seeks to explore concerns the extent to which the institutions established under the terms of the Belfast Agreement and Ta'if Accords encourage politicians to think in terms of civil society interests rather than simply in terms of narrower ethnic interests. By extension, it considers the implications of this receptiveness for the development of a stronger sense of civic leadership.

In order to ensure that civil society interests are represented in political life, divided societies must aim to meet two key requirements. First, they must provide channels of access to the decision-making process for those who do not wish to, or cannot, voice their interests along ethnic lines. After all, democracy requires that everyone has an equal say. What is more, as pointed out by Robert Dahl, at the decisive stage of making collective decisions, democracy also requires that each citizen be 'ensured an equal opportunity to express a choice that will be counted as equal in weight to the choice expressed by any other citizen' (Dahl, 1989, 109). Secondly, they must ensure that power-sharing institutions are designed in ways that encourage elected representatives to refrain from reducing issues that are of a cross-community concern, such as healthcare, to narrow ethnic interests. Otherwise put, they must require them to act as civic leaders when it comes to making collectively binding, governmental decisions about matters of society-wide concern. Only when ethnic leaders begin to think of themselves as leaders of society as a whole, does a divided society begin to become just that bit less divided.

With regard to the first of these two requirements, one possible way of securing access to the decision-making process is through the creation and maintenance of public spaces within which a more consultative and inclusive political dispensation can be developed by enabling those who seek to represent civil society interests to take part in deliberation with, and inform the thinking of, elected representatives (Woods, 1999). In innovative and interesting ways, the Ta'if Accord and Belfast Agreement have aimed to provide just such a space through the creation of special dedicated public bodies. The Belfast Agreement provided for the establishment of a Civic Forum and the Ta'if Accord provides for the establishment of an Economic and Social Council. In terms of their institutional design, these two public bodies are very similar, with the same basic structure and dynamic, types of membership and envisaged roles.

More generally, the purpose of each is not to create an institution whose membership is a microcosm of society, but rather to ensure a means of participation in governance for a spectrum of interests from the public, private, community, and voluntary sectors whose voices might otherwise go unheard. The task of both the Civic Forum and the Economic and Social Council is to offer advice and suggestions to elected representatives in public policy formation, specifically in relation to issues of social, economic, and cultural life. In short, the primary aim of both bodies is to add a further, vital layer to democracy – one that sets in place a further mechanism designed to encourage politicians to look beyond sectional, ethnic interests towards the good of society as a whole, and hence to act increasingly as a civic leaders (The Agreement, 1998, section 34, 9; Ta'if Accord, 1991, 'Sections of the Ta'if Agreement not included in the Constitution', 164–5).

Of course, the creation of public bodies like the Civic Forum and the Economic and Social Council will not, of their own accord, engender civic leadership. For this to occur, politicians must also be encouraged to meet the second requirement outlined above, namely, to refrain from reducing issues of cross-community concern to narrow ethnic interests or inter-community competition. In Lebanon and Northern Ireland, the members of the Economic and Social Council and the Civic Forum are not elected and, unlike politicians, they cannot determine what decisions are made since they are not part of the elected legislatures *per se*. Moreover, when it comes to making political decisions in a divided society, ethnic interests will often take precedence over civil society interests. There need be nothing undemocratic about this state of affairs, since in a democracy, people are free to vote as they wish, and to combine their votes with others who see the world as they do in order to consolidate their collective power. These points are true of even the most progressive of societies and so the simple reality is often that numbers count (Raz, 1986, 209 and passim). However, the argument that I have tried to stress throughout this chapter is that in aiming to support the transition from violent conflict to democratic peace and stability, there is also a responsibility to incentivise elected representatives to make decisions that reflect as many of the interests in society as possible or, perhaps more importantly, to treat political questions from the perspective of society as a whole.

Although the Belfast Agreement and Ta'if Accord are alive to the necessity of encouraging politicians to take account of civil society interests, the worry remains that the two agreements contain institutional mechanisms that inhibit politicians from taking such interests seriously, if and when they emerge. Politics in Northern Ireland has been characterised to a great extent by pervasive intra-ethnic rivalry. This is a phenomenon which, in the comparative literature on divided societies and ethnic conflict, is often referred to as intra-ethnic outbidding. In short, divided societies are vulnerable to politicians who attempt to gain votes, normally at the expense of moderates from within their own ethnic group, by appealing to narrow, sectional interests. The basic strategy here is as follows. Divided societies are often characterised by fear and insecurity. Such feelings are especially prevalent in the aftermath of prolonged periods of internecine violence. But although peace and democracy depend on compromise, moderate politicians will know that the compromises they make may be denounced as a sell-out by members of their own group who seek to enhance their own political position. Denouncements of this sort can bring handsome electoral gains. But what is more, the danger of losing support may lead even the most moderate of politicians to frame their claims in increasingly exclusive terms (Barry, 1975, 502; Sisk, 1996, 574). Consequently, unless the structure of political incentives is organised in such a way that moderation is rewarded and outbidding punished, the implications for civic leadership may be dire.

Since the signing of the Belfast Agreement, electoral campaigns in Northern Ireland have been increasingly dominated by politicians appealing to exclusive, single-ethnic agendas. And such appeals have worked, because the electorate has consistently rewarded politicians on the extremes. In particular, both the hardline Democratic Unionist Party and hardline Sinn Féin have made substantial electoral gains, overtaking the moderate Ulster Unionist Party and moderate Social Democratic and Labour Party, who arguably made a negotiated settlement possible in the first place. In Lebanon, the situation is somewhat more ambiguous, since it seems that politicians are reasonably comfortable with representing civil society interests and ultimately acting as civic leaders. As indicated in the previous section, this behaviour is partly encouraged by the explicit requirement, contained within the Ta'if Accord, that elected politicians represent the people of Lebanon as a whole (Ta'if Accord, 1991, article 27). Arguably, however, what has done most to encourage Lebanese politicians to factor civil society interests into their decisions is the cumulative effect of the various power-sharing institutions under which they have to operate (including, but not reducible to, the Economic and Social Council). In sum, inter-ethnic consensus on the question of Lebanon's constitutional status combined with weighted majority voting procedures for everyday decision-making, the explicit requirement for collective government, and a constant visioning of an already agreed future where the political saliency of ethnic identities will be substantially eroded encourages Lebanese politicians to reflect upon their responsibilities as civic leaders in a way that is witnessed far less often in Northern Ireland. Recent deliberations over United Nations Security Resolution 1559, demanding the withdrawal of Syrian armed forces from Lebanon, are a case in point. These debates have taken place among elected representatives on non-ethnic grounds, with alliances forged between Christians and Muslims in pro- versus anti-Syrian camps (Blanford, 2004). The dynamic at play here clearly suggests that exclusive, ethnic interests in Lebanon can and do give way in some areas of public policy to ideologically motivated divisions determined by broader social concerns, international agendas and so forth (Russell and Shehadi, 2005, 147).

Arguably, then, the kind of ethnic group protections that the Ta'if Accord provides has given politicians the confidence and, crucially, the incentives to take account of civil society interests and the courage to present themselves as civic leaders. However, a word of caution is still necessary here. In Norman Porter's words, thinking about commonality 'becomes murky when we are constantly reminded of our differences. Here our points of separation often seem more engaging and readily acquires a disproportionate importance' (Porter, 2003, 151). Although I have argued that the form of power-sharing found in Lebanon is more favourable to civic leadership than that which is found in Northern Ireland, it is nevertheless important to acknowledge that the Lebanese emphasis on the pre-determination of ethnic representation in both the legislative Chamber of Deputies and executive Council of Ministers and the requirement for weighted majority voting, can be criticised. As Porter's words remind us, in a society where competition between the elected representatives of different ethnic groups is enshrined as the principal basis of political life, those representatives are all too often encouraged to see their own futures as being tied up with the perpetuation of the status quo. Under such conditions, challenging the primacy of ethnic identities may be viewed as a threat to individual power and prestige. Thus, the conundrum of power-sharing in Lebanon and Northern Ireland is that although ethnic groups require protection for peace and sustainable democracy to flourish, we must also acknowledge that if the structure of political incentives is such that it leads politicians to perpetuate the status quo, then those other interests in society above – namely, non-ethnic interests – will most likely continue to be overlooked.

## Conclusion

Nothing in this chapter challenges the need for power-sharing in divided societies. However, what the chapter does challenge, or at least seeks to highlight, is the failure on the part of some institutional designers to provide for the longer-term goal of promoting civic leadership. Civic leadership is important because it marks a crucial shift in the transition from conflict to democracy. The extent to which politicians see themselves as civic leaders will be a measure of the extent to which a divided society is no longer divided. Of course, conditions in many divided societies will be such that civic leadership will be no more than aspirational. However, it must also be remembered that much of what politicians do will depend on the structure of political incentives that confront them.

There is, of course, nothing new in the claim that politicians respond to incentives. However, this comparative exploration of the cases of Lebanon and Northern Ireland has demonstrated two key points that, in my view, have received insufficient attention in much of the current literature. First, it should not be assumed (as for example, many consociationalists seemingly assume) that the qualities of civic leadership will develop over time. True, the more ethnic leaders become invested in a political system, the more they will tend to do whatever it takes to make that system work. However, as I have argued, while this may be true of 'normal' democratic societies, the threat of intra-ethnic outbidding may thwart the development of such qualities in divided societies. In response, what the analysis of Lebanon and Northern Ireland shows is that institutional designers should provide for civic leadership from the outset through an appropriately structured system of rewards and penalties. Secondly, the comparison has demonstrated the need to ensure that the incentive to act as civic leaders is built into the system as a whole. Naturally, this will be easier in some aspects of an institutional design than in certain others. The inter-ethnic consensus that resolved Lebanon's constitutional status and the process of executive formation are, arguably, shining, positive examples of what is at issue here. By contrast, while ethnic identities are not enshrined within the terms of the Belfast Agreement, the institutional requirement of designation in Northern Ireland plays into the hands of unscrupulous politicians who are only too willing to engage in outbidding.

This exploration of the experience of power-sharing in, respectively, Lebanon and Northern Ireland has illustrated how negotiated peace agreements in divided societies can become so prescriptive that they risk restricting the capacity of elected politicians to act as civic leaders. By this I mean, a move beyond ethnicity to a complex multi-faceted conception of the role that elected representatives should be expected to play in a democracy. Political institutions that prioritise ethnicity as the principal medium through which political debate turns are one thing. But to allow this to run unchecked, however, is another prospect altogether. Civil society interests are fundamental to a democratic citizenship and as such must be balanced against and recognised as the interdependent partner of measures aimed at protecting communities. For this objective to be achieved, the particular types of power-sharing institutions in a divided society must be designed with consistency and be capable of engendering a cumulated effect on the attitudes and behaviours of elected representatives.

# Bibliography

Almond, G.A. and S. Verba (1963) *Civic Culture: Political Attitudes and Democracy in Five Nations*. Princeton, New Jersey: Princeton University Press.

Barry, B. (1975) 'Review Article: Political Accommodation and Consociational Democracy', *British Journal of Political Science*, 5, 477–505.

Blanford, N. (2004) 'Lebanese Voices Rise against Syria's Dominance', *Christian Science Monitor*, 4 October.

Collings, D. (ed.) (1994) *Peace for Lebanon? From War to Reconstruction*. Boulder, Colorado and London: Lynne Rienner.

Dagher, C.H. (2000) *Bring Down the Walls: Lebanon's Post-War Challenge*. New York: St Martin's Press.

Dahl, R.A. (1989) *Democracy and its Critics*. New Haven: Yale University Press.

Darby, J. and R. MacGinty (eds) (2003) *Contemporary Peacemaking: Conflict, Violence and Peace Processes*. Basingstoke: Palgrave Macmillan.

Gemayel, A. (1992) *Rebuilding Lebanon*. Maryland, Boston: University Press of America.

Guelke, A. (1994) *Northern Ireland: The International Perspective*. Dublin: St Martins Press; New York: Gill and Macmillan.

Guelke, A. (2000) ' "Comparatively peaceful": South Africa, the Middle East and Northern Ireland', in M. Cox, A. Guelke and F. Stephen (eds), *A Farewell to Arms? From 'Long War' to Long Peace in Northern Ireland*. Manchester and New York: Manchester University Press.

Hanf, T. (1993) *Coexistence in Wartime Lebanon*. London: The Centre for Lebanese Studies in association with I.B. Tauris and Co Ltd Publishers.

Horowitz, D. (1985) *Ethnic Groups in Conflict*. Berkeley, Los Angeles and London: University of California Press.

Horowitz, D. (2000) 'Constitutional Design: An Oxymoron?', *NOMOS, Designing Democratic Institutions*, 42, 253–84.

Horowitz, D. (2002) 'Explaining the Northern Ireland Agreement: The Sources of an Unlikely Constitutional Consensus', *British Journal of Political Science*, 32:2, 193–220.

Johnson, M. (2001) *All Honourable Men: The Social Origins of the War in Lebanon*. London and New York: I.B. Tauris & Co.

Jones, P. (1999) 'Group Rights and Group Oppressions', *The Journal of Political Philosophy*, 7:4, 353–77.

Kerr, M. (2006) *Imposing Power Sharing: Conflict and Coexistence in Northern Ireland and Lebanon*. Dublin, Portland Oregon: Irish Academic Press.

Lijphart, A. (1975) 'Review Article: the Northern Ireland Problem; Cases, Theories, and Solution', *British Journal of Political Science*, 5, 83–106.

Lijphart, A. (1977) *Democracy in Plural Societies: A Comparative Exploration*. New Haven and London: Yale University Press.

Lijphart, A. (1995) 'The Framework Document on Northern Ireland and the Theory of Power-Sharing', *Government and Opposition*, 31:3, 267–74.

Maalouf, A. (2000) *On Identity*. London: The Harvill Press.

MacGinty, R. (2003) 'Constitutional Referendums and Ethnonational Conflict: The Case of Northern Ireland', *Nationalism and Ethnic Politics*, 9:2, 1–22.

Maila, J. (1992a) *Prospects for Lebanon: The Document of National Understanding: A Commentary*. Oxford: The Centre for Lebanese Studies.

Maila, J. (1992b) *The Document of National Understanding: A Commentary*. Oxford: Centre for Lebanese Studies.

McGarry, J. (ed.) (2001) *Northern Ireland and the Divided World: Post-Agreement Northern Ireland in Comparative Perspective*. Oxford: Oxford University Press.

Oberschall, A. and K.L. Palmer (2005) 'The Failure of Moderate Politics: The Case of Northern Ireland', in I. O'Flynn, and D Russell (eds) *Power Sharing: New Challenges for Divided Societies*. London and New York: Pluto Press.

O'Flynn, I. (2006) *Deliberative Democracy and Divided Societies*. Edinburgh: Edinburgh University Press.

O'Leary, B. (1989) 'The Limits to Coercive Consociationalism in Northern Ireland', *Political Studies*, 37:4, 562–78.

O'Leary, B. (1999) 'The Nature of the Agreement', *Fordham International Law Journal*, 22:4, 1628–67.

O'Neill, S. (2003) 'Justice in Ethnically Diverse Societies: A Critique of Political Alienation', *Ethnicities*, 3:3, 369–92.

Parekh, B. (1999) 'Defining National Identity in a Multicultural Society', in, E. Mortimer and R. Fine (eds), *People, Nation and State: The Meaning of Ethnicity and Nationalism*. London and New York: I.B.Tauris.

Porter, N. (2003) *The Elusive Quest: Reconciliation in Northern Ireland*. Belfast: Blackstaff Press.

Preuss, U. (1993) 'Constitutional Powermaking for the New Polity: Some Deliberations on the Relations between Constituent Power and the Constitution', *Cardozo Law Review*, 14, 639–60.

Przeworski, A. (1993) 'Democracy as a Contingent Outcome of Conflicts', in J. Elster and R. Slagstad (eds), *Constitutionalism and Democracy*. Cambridge: Cambridge University Press.

Raz, J. (1986) *The Morality of Freedom*. Oxford: Clarendon Press.

Rieck, A. (1990) 'A peace plan for Lebanon? prospects after the Ta'if Agreement', *Aussenpolitik*, 41:3, 297–305.

Russell, D. and N. Shehadi (2005) 'Power Sharing and National Reconciliation: The Case of Lebanon', in I. O'Flynn and D Russell (eds), *Power Sharing: New Challenges for Divided Societies*. London and New York: Pluto Press.

Sisk, T.D. (1996) *Power Sharing and International Mediation in Ethnic Conflicts.* Washington, DC: USIP Press.

*The Agreement: Agreement Reached in the Multi-Party Negotiations* (1998) Belfast: The Stationary Office.

[The Ta'if Accord] 'The Constitution of Lebanon after the Amendments of August 21, 1990', (1991) *Beirut Review*, 1, 119–72.

Wilford, R. (2001) 'The Assembly', in R. Wilson (ed.), *A Guide to the Northern Ireland Assembly: Agreeing to Disagree?* Norwich: The Stationary Office. pp. 59–71.

Wilford, R. and R. Wilson (2001) *A Democratic Design? The Political Style of the Northern Ireland Assembly.* London: The Constitution Unit.

Wilson, R. and R. Wilford (2003) *Northern Ireland: A Route to Stability?* Economic and Social Research Council, Programme for Devolution and Constitutional Change.

Woods, J. (1999) *The Civic Forum and Negotiated Governance.* Belfast: Democratic Dialogue.

# Index